Health Economics of Japan

Health Economics of Japan

Patients, Doctors, and Hospitals
Under a Universal Health Insurance System

Aki Yoshikawa
Jayanta Bhattacharya
William B. Vogt

UNIVERSITY OF TOKYO PRESS

To our parents and spouses

Copyright © 1996 by University of Tokyo Press

ISBN 0-86008-518-X
ISBN 4-13-067105-7
Printed in Japan

99 98 97 96   6 5 4 3 2 1

Contents

Preface

Over the last few decades, health economics has emerged as a vibrant discipline in the United States and Europe. The increasing interest in health economics has been driven both by the rising importance of service industries in developed countries and also by the perceived need to control the spiraling costs of health care. The rise in popularity of health economics has fostered a variety of new and exciting interactions among government, industry, and academia, as governments, payers, and providers have drawn upon economists' thinking on such subjects as price theory, cost-benefit analysis, theories of moral hazard and adverse selection, and imperfections in insurance markets. These interactions have led to many substantive changes in policy and, even more importantly, in how policy debates are conducted.

This book represents the culmination of a research program begun in 1990 at the Asia/Pacific Research Center, with the founding of the Comparative Health Care Policy Research Project. In 1993, the Project produced a book entitled *Japan's Health System: Efficiency and Effectiveness in Universal Care* (Okimoto & Yoshikawa). This descriptive book covered a wide range of topics, including health insurance, geriatric health care, and use of medical equipment. After the two years it took to complete the earlier book, we were in a good position to conduct a more extensive study of the Japanese system.

With the publication of this book from University of Tokyo Press, we are hoping to promote an academic discipline—health economics—which is underdeveloped in Japan. We are hopeful that the benefits of active, robust, and rigorous economic inquiry will become inveterate and grow in Japan. Furthermore, we hope the development of health economics in Japan occurs in collaboration with colleagues from other countries. There are at least three reasons militating for this international interaction. First, many of the tools which have been honed elsewhere by health economists will be of great use to Japanese researchers as well. To derive the greatest benefit from these tools, interchange between Japanese and foreign health economists is critical. Second, to ensure the highest quality and most rigorous research in health economics, Japan should seek a wide and knowledgeable audience. Third, often the most interesting insights into the workings of a complex system such as health care arise from comparisons of disparate systems.

The absence of health economics research in Japan has been due principally to a lack of interest among economists in studying the health care field. This lack of interest has been largely caused by the unavailability of micro-level data in Japan.

We have been very fortunate to have a unique opportunity to analyze four different types of Japanese micro data. The two larger data sets, the Patient Survey (*Kanja Chosa*) and the Facility Survey (*Iryo Shisetsu Chosa*), are used in many of our studies. In addition to these two main sources, we also analyze patient-specific health insurance claims data from over 60,000 Japanese patients, and the patient records of all surgical inpatients at both a Japanese and an American teaching hospital. Use of these large sets of Japanese micro data allows us to conduct various empirical studies in broad areas of health economics. This book contains the outcomes of these studies.

There are two broad categories of questions which can be most effectively addressed by the use of micro data. The first of these is the behavior of patients. Economists are concerned with the interactions between institutional and individual characteristics in forming patients' incentives. Empirical studies using micro data shed light on how these incentives affect patients' choices and what effects these choices have on variables of interest to policy makers.

Providers are another important set of actors in the health care marketplace. Our understanding of their behavior is also greatly enhanced by access to data on individual providers. Providers affect outcomes of interest through many of their decisions. Virtually all decisions regarding how providers choose to provide care to their patients affect costs, use, and quality of health care.

We regard this book as only the initial volley of what we hope will be a long and fruitful intellectual interchange informed by economic theory and detailed data analysis. As with any undertaking of this size, the set of people making a significant contribution to the book far exceeds those on the author list. We are indebted to a large number of scholars for their discussions, comments, and ideas and to many others for their editorial and administrative support.

January 1996
Stanford, California

AKI YOSHIKAWA
JAYANTA BHATTACHARYA
WILLIAM B. VOGT

Acknowledgments

The Comparative Health Care Policy Research Project was established in 1990 when I moved to Stanford University from the University of California, Berkeley. This Project would not have been possible without the financial support and friendship we received from Nobuharu Okamitsu and Masataka Kohda. The Asia/Pacific Research Center at Stanford has provided our program a comfortable home for the last few years.

The process of writing this book was not an easy one. We have encountered various difficulties along the way, and I would like to acknowledge incredible support from many friends and to thank them upon the completion of this book. We began analyzing Japanese macro-level data as early as 1992, when the idea of writing a book was simply that. Our first finished product, an analysis of the copayment and income effects on the demand for medical care, a revised version of which is published in this book, was received warmly and encouraged us to continue our efforts. The authors of this first piece and the first generation of the Comparative Health Care Policy Research Project researchers were Scott Kupor, Yongchan Liu, and Jungwoo Lee. Of these three, Scott continues today as a researcher with the Project and as a contributing author to this book.

In 1994 we obtained various micro-level data, and the second-generation team, Jayanta Bhattacharya and William Vogt, began analyzing these data. We were lucky to obtain the micro data, but without the diligent work of Bill and Jay we could not have produced these studies. Our Japanese fellows at Stanford, Satoshi Nakanishi, Ken Aoki, and Noriyoshi Nakayama, also participated in several studies in this book, as did Scott Kupor.

Needless to say, we could not have conducted this research without having access to valuable data sources. We would like to thank

Toshitaka Nakahara, Shigekoto Kaihara, and Tsuruhiko Nanbu, who have also co-authored various previous studies with us. Their generosity in providing data to us as well as their participation in our studies has enabled us to complete many of these chapters.

Special thanks are due to Yumiko Mimi Nishimura, who single-handedly coordinated and managed this book project. She also managed the Health Care Project when I retreated to my self-imposed asylum to write this book, neglecting the Project at Stanford for a length of time. Without encouragement from Mimi and Professor Kaihara, this book would never have been dreamed of, let alone completed.

In addition to valuable advice from our collaborators, Kaihara, Nakahara and Nanbu, we also must acknowledge help from Alain Enthoven, Walter Falcon, Alan Garber, Jim Hahn, Ken'ichi Imai, Ted Keeler, Donald Kennedy, Mark McClellan, Shozo Nishimura, Takashi Takahashi, Shigeru Tanaka, and Harold Luft, as well as many anonymous referees and participants at the ASSA conference; at the industrial organization, economic applications, and health services research seminars at Stanford; at the health economics seminars at University of Kyoto and at the University of Tokyo Medical School. Of course, all errors remain our own.

When our research process faced the customary ups and downs, we were rescued by encouragement from our academic colleagues, including Michael Armacost, Michael Calhoun, Gary Saxonhouse, Takatoshi Ito, Lawrence Lau, Joan Lo, Etsuji Okamono, Akio Ono, and Brian Woodall.

Many colleagues in Tokyo and Stanford participated in our joint study with the University of Tokyo. To this end, we would like to acknowledge: Diane Christ, Hong-Lin Du, David Hopkins, Koichi Ishikawa, Hiroyoshi Kobayashi, Scott Kupor, Blackford Middleton, Hideaki Saito, Linda Slezak, Annie Woo, and Yoshitsugu Yamada.

We also acknowledge the editorial support of Annie Woo, Scott Kupor, and Sylvia Stein Wright, and thank Etsuko Hamao and Susan Schmidt of the University of Tokyo Press for their commitment to publishing this book. Thanks also to the publishers of previous versions of several chapters. Zera Murphy, Dan and Nancy Okimoto, and James Raphael put up with the idiosyncrasies of the Project's members.

I would also like to thank Nassos Daphnis, the artist of the cover painting, for granting us permission to use his work. Special thanks are also in order to his agent Evangelos Stamatopoulos.

Finally, I would like to acknowledge my wife, Nancy, and our two children, Alex and Minna, for their patience and support over the past six years. As many of my colleagues well understand, I look forward to the opportunity to spend more time with my family now that this book is published.

We have been assisted by various grants and fellowships. Jay and Bill have been supported by AHCPR predoctoral fellowships. I acknowledge support from the Abe Fellowship Program of the Social Science Research Council and the American Council of Learned Societies with funds provided by the Japan Foundation Center for Global Partnership. Research funds were also provided by the Zengin Foundation. This work has been supported by an endowment established by the Council for Better Corporate Citizenship, Tokyo, Japan, and also by the Global Health Institute, Menlo Park, Ca.

AKI YOSHIKAWA

Health Economics of Japan

1

Overview of Japan's Health Care System

Japan's universal health insurance system, which covers the country's 122 million residents, is segmented according to workplace. The type of company one works for determines the insurance society to which one belongs and the financial contributions one must make. Although thousands of independent societies therefore exist, they are all interwoven by the uniform framework mandated by the national government; the Japanese health financing system for all societies is based upon fee-for-service reimbursement under a uniform national price schedule. Nearly all services covered by the various insurance societies are reimbursed according to this schedule, independent of the insured person's society and of the actual arena of health care delivery.

Because the universal insurance system is portable, Japanese residents can walk into any medical facility and pay only a modest copayment at the point of service. The copayments, coupled with fee-for-service reimbursement and insurance portability, create interesting incentives for providers and patients. In addition, the structure of competition among hospitals in a fixed-price environment provides fertile ground for economic analysis. These issues and others, such as the rapidly growing elderly population and the proliferation of expensive medical technologies, are the subjects of this book.

The Japanese Universal Health Insurance System and Its Financing Mechanism

The extensive safety net of universal health insurance, a social insurance system known as *Kai Hoken*, provides Japan's 122 million residents with freedom to choose medical care services and delivery locale. "Universal" means that anyone who is insured—virtually every Japanese citizen—can walk into any hospital or clinic in the country and receive care. As is common to all systems that provide universal access, coverage is compulsory; citizens enroll through their employers or local societies, depending upon their age and employment status.

The Japanese system is also characterized by equity in the provision of medical care. All patients, rich or poor, are assured equal access to all medical services due in large part to a uniform fee schedule for reimbursement. Because all patients have health insurance, there are few financial incentives for doctors to withhold services or to differentiate among persons seeking care. Even though copayments vary among insurance societies, the minimum scope of covered services is mandated by the national government. Insurance societies are free to tinker with additional services (e.g., childbirth allowances), but each plan covers the same mandated basic services. The upshot of this standardization is that medical providers do not care which insurance society their patients belong to.[1] Consistent with the overall emphasis on equity, the extent of supplemental private health insurance policies in Japan is very limited, covering only peripheral services of limited scope.

Premiums collected from subscribers provide the financial backbone of Japan's system. Premium contributions are based not on health status, but on income level, a deliberate decision by the national government to maintain equity within the system. Subscribers are also responsible for a copayment at the point of service. Government subsidization assists insurance societies that cover the financially disadvantaged or large numbers of elderly. This is an intricate system of cross-subsidization, in essence redistributing wealth from the younger, healthier insurance societies to those burdened with more demand-intensive subscribers.

The Structure of Japan's Universal Health Insurance System

The Japanese *Kai Hoken* is a complex system with various plans categorized into three basic groups: (1) employees' health insurance for employees of firms and other public sector organizations and their dependents; (2) national health insurance, or *Kokuho* (abbreviation of *Kokumin Kenko Hoken*) for the self-employed, retirees, and their dependents; and (3) the *Roken* system, a special pooling fund for the elderly. Table 1-1 outlines the entire health insurance

Table 1-1
Outline of the Japanese Health Insurance System

Insurance Provider	Insured Person	Insurer (March 1990)	No. of Subscribers (in 10,000s) (March 1991)	1-Copayment Rate
Seikan Government-managed Health Insurance	Salaried workers at small corporations	State	3,682 (1,809 insured) (1,873 dependents)	Insured: 90% Dependent: Inpatient: 80% Outpatient: 70%
Kumiai Society-managed Health Insurance	Salaried workers at large corporations	Health insurance societies (1,822)	3,201 (1,467 insured) (1,734 dependents)	Insured: 90% Dependent: Inpatient: 80% Outpatient: 70%
Sen-in Seamen's Insurance	Seamen	State	41 (14 insured) (27 dependents)	Insured: 90% Dependent: Inpatient: 80% Outpatient: 70%
Kyosai Mutual Aid Associations	National and local public employees	Mutual aid associations (82)	1,195 (504 insured) (692 dependents)	Insured: 90% Dependent: Inpatient: 80% Outpatient: 70%
Kokuho National Health Insurance	Farmers, self-employed, etc.	Municipalities (3,258) Associations (166)	4,307	70%
	Retirees formerly under employees' insurance	Municipalities (3,258)	1,033	Insured: 80% Dependent: Inpatient: 80% Outpatient: 70%
Roken Health Services for the Aged	Persons age 70 and over, persons age 65 and over who are bedridden, etc.	(Implementing bodies) Head of municipalities	995 (tentative)	Copayment: Jan. 1992 Outpatient: ¥1000 per month Inpatient: ¥700 per day

Source: Insurance Bureau, Ministry of Health and Welfare.

structure. Different health insurance plans provide comparable medical and other benefits though they have different copayment rates. The scope of services offered, which the government determines, is generous. It includes medical and dental care delivered in both inpatient and outpatient settings, hospitalization, nursing, pharmaceuticals, and transportation. The menu is continuously expanded to include innovations and new medical and pharmaceutical technologies.[2]

EMPLOYEES' HEALTH INSURANCE
Employees' health insurance is a system for employees and their dependents. As shown in Table 1-1, this type of insurance is broken down into four categories, depending upon the type of employer. These categories are: (1) government-managed health insurance, or *Seikan*, (2) society-managed health insurance, or *Kumiai*, (3) seamen's insurance, or *Sen-in Hoken*, and (4) mutual aid associations, or *Kyosai*.

Seikan: Government-managed health insurance covers the employees of small and medium sized companies (with more than 4 and fewer than 300 employees) and their dependents.
Kumiai: Society-managed health insurance covers those employed by larger firms and their dependents. Companies such as Toshiba and Nomura maintain their own *Kumiai* societies.
Sen-in: This insurance covers seamen (on designated vessels) and their dependents.
Kyosai: Public employees, both national and local, as well as private school teachers and staff, are covered under this system. Dependents are also covered.

Under each of the plans, insured employees pay a 10% copayment for all medical services. Their dependents are responsible for a 20% copayment for inpatient medical services and 30% for outpatient services.

Employers deduct employees' insurance premiums directly from their paychecks and remit this collection to the appropriate insurer. Employees' premiums are calculated as a percentage of the insured person's standard monthly wages and may also be deducted from the customary semiannual bonuses. In principle, premium contributions for employees' health insurance are shared equally by employer and employee. For *Kumiai*, however, many companies choose to contribute more than half of their workers' premium costs. In

1990, the premium rate for *Seikan* was 8.4% of the employee's monthly standard salary, 4.2% of which was paid by the employer.

NATIONAL HEALTH INSURANCE
National health insurance (*Kokuho*), which provides health care coverage to the self-employed, unemployed, and workers at firms with fewer than five employees, is administered by local municipalities. The *Kokuho* system is further divided into three subsystems. Two of the subsystems, run by municipal governments and insurance associations (*Kokuho kumiai*), cater to self-employed workers such as farmers, carpenters, medical doctors, lawyers, and the owners and employees of small businesses. As of 1990, there were 166 insurance associations and 3,258 municipal insurers, with a combined membership of 43.1 million people. The third subsystem, *taishoku-sha iryo seido* (retiree's health insurance), was established in 1984 to incorporate a separate system for retirees, many of whom were insured previously by employees' insurance.

Copayment obligations are greater for *Kokuho* members than for those insured under employees' insurance. Under *Kokuho*, both principal subscribers and their dependents pay 30% of the costs of medical care. Retirees pay 20% for all services, and their dependents shoulder a 20% copayment for inpatient care and 30% for outpatient care.

Unlike company employees, the majority of the self-employed declare their earnings and pay taxes and insurance premiums on their own. *Kokuho* premiums are collected mostly in the form of a local tax, the *Kokuho* tax. The amount to be taxed is calculated for each household based on income, other fixed assets, and other wealth. The procedures used in this calculation are determined by the respective insurers, the municipal governments. Thus, as with employees' health insurance plans, *Kokuho* premium rates differ among insurers, though the annual contribution per household is subject to a ceiling (¥440,000 in 1991). The premium is reduced for low-income households.

POOLING FUND FOR THE ELDERLY
In 1973, Japan changed the system of financing care for the elderly, making medical care free for patients over 70. These elderly were still covered by their local *Kokuho* societies and as such paid the same income-based premiums. All copayments were eliminated, however. The 1974 oil shock coupled with the unexpectedly large use of medical services stemming from the elimination of any personal financial responsibility for the costs of medical care created a

financial problem for the national government. Hence in 1983, the government reinstituted minimal cost sharing by elderly patients. Elderly outpatients now pay ¥1,000 per month if they use medical services, and elderly inpatients pay ¥700 per day.

The health and medical services system for the elderly (*Roken* system) is a pooling fund through which the national government has attempted to distribute across all Japanese the burden of paying for geriatric care. Established in 1983 following the passage of the 1982 Health and Medical Services Law for the Elderly, the pooling fund covers all those over 70 years and bedridden people over 65. The fund pools contributions from all insurance schemes, as well as tax revenues from the national government, prefectures, cities, towns, and villages.[3] The *Roken* system may thus be viewed as a systematic mechanism to redistribute premiums from the *Kumiai* societies to the poorer societies. The creation of the pooling fund not only removed the elderly from the local *Kokuho* societies and shifted their affiliation to the *Roken* system, but also lessened the financial burdens previously facing *Kokuho* by increasing those of the employer-based societies.

In 1990, employee health insurance systems (*Seikan, Kumiai,* and others) contributed ¥2.6 trillion, or 43.6% of total *Roken* funding. *Kumiai* alone contributed ¥1.0 trillion, of which ¥568.9 billion was paid directly by employers. This cost-sharing mechanism was created when the employer-based societies were fiscally strong and when the elderly population was small enough to be supported by an ample sized working population. As the proportion of elderly persons seeking assistance from *Roken* grows relative to the number of workers paying into the employer-based societies, the ability of the Japanese government to sustain this financing system may be impaired.

CATASTROPHIC COVERAGE

The High-Cost Medical Care Benefits Law of 1973 was amended in 1984 to introduce a cap on the monthly copayment. The measure established a ceiling on household out-of-pocket copayments, most recently set at ¥63,000 per month for families of middle to high income and ¥33,600 per month for low-income families.[4] With the ceiling, the actual daily copayment rate for an inpatient suffering from a major, catastrophic illness approaches zero over time. Hence, although copayments are already merely incidental, reduction of the average copayment over time further decreases patient cost sharing. This feature of the Japanese system has important implications for government efforts to affect the demand for medical services and may help explain the dramatically longer stays for Japanese elderly inpatients.

Comparison of Japan's Systems

Although differentiated by place of employment, Japan's various health insurance schemes effectively provide universal health insurance coverage. Japanese workers in large companies might change insurance plans three times during their lives, from *Kumiai* to *Seikan*, to *Kokuho* (retirees' health insurance system), and finally be covered by the *Roken* system. Workers who started out working for smaller companies may change health insurance plans only twice: from *Seikan* to *Kokuho* and then to *Roken*. Farmers or other self-employed entrepreneurs are covered by the community-based *Kokuho* scheme throughout their lives, until entering the *Roken* system. This segmentation creates distinct characteristics in terms of income, age structure, and utilization of medical services among the three systems. In terms of age structure, *Kumiai* is the youngest scheme, and *Kokuho*, with the retirees' subsystem, is the oldest, as shown in Table 1-2.

On average, *Kumiai* enrollees have the highest incomes, followed by *Seikan* and *Kokuho* subscribers, respectively. This is due to higher salaries in larger (*Kumiai*) versus smaller companies (*Seikan*) and to the high number of unemployed and other low-income people in *Kokuho*. In 1990, 23.7% of the *Kokuho*-insured households received "breaks" on premiums for reasons of indigency. The

Table 1-2
Age Structure of Various Insurance Plans (1990)

Age	Total	*Kumiai*	*Seikan*	*Kokuho*	Others
(1,000 persons)					
0–14	22,486	6,853	6,954	5,894	2,786
15–59	79,159	23,406	25,527	23,067	7,158
60–	21,640	1,963	4,093	14,441	1,141
Total	123,611	32,221	36,574	43,401	11,415
(Percent)					
0–14	18.19	21.27	91.01	13.58	24.41
15–59	64.04	72.64	69.80	53.15	62.71
60–	17.51	6.09	11.19	33.27	10.00
Total	100.00	100.00	100.00	100.00	100.00

Source: Health and Welfare Statistics Association (1992), *Hoken to Nenkin no Doko.*

average per household monthly income for *Seikan* and *Kumiai* enrollees respectively was ¥245,711 and ¥308,384 in 1990. By contrast, in the same year, the average household monthly income under *Kokuho* was ¥200,417 (Kenko Hoken Kumiai Rengokai, 1990).

In fiscal year 1990, annual household premiums for *Seikan*, *Kumiai*, and *Kokuho* were ¥125,294, ¥126,156, and ¥150,352, respectively. Thus, even though *Kokuho* members have the lowest average incomes, the *Kokuho* premium was the highest of the three, though the poorest households do not pay the full amount. The household premium rates for *Seikan*, *Kumiai*, and *Kokuho* were 4.2%, 3.4%, and 6.6% of income, respectively. Hence, as a percentage of household income, *Kokuho* rates are twice as high as *Kumiai* rates.

As mentioned, the copayment rate differs between *Kokuho* and employees' health insurance such as *Seikan* and *Kumiai*. *Kokuho* covers only 70% of medical care expenses. *Seikan* and *Kumiai* cover 90% of expenses for the insured and 80% of dependents' hospitalization costs. Insured persons in employees' plans (*Kumiai* and *Seikan*) enjoyed 100% coverage until the Health Insurance Law was amended in 1984, introducing a 10% copayment.

One important economic question is whether these differences in price (copayment) and income affect the demand for medical services for patients who belong to different insurance schemes. If the demand curve is downward sloping, there are important implications for the national government's efforts to contain the costs of medical care. Increasing the marginal price of medical care (i.e., raising copayments) should lower the total quantity demanded.

A second important policy question that has been a centerpiece of the Japanese system is the extent to which equity in the delivery and availability of medical care is achieved. If demand is price-sensitive, then subscribers to the *Roken* and *Kokuho* societies face greater disincentives to seek treatment than do the wealthier *Kumiai* and *Seikan* members. In effect, some of the progressivity of the cross-subsidization program is undermined by the regressive nature of copayments in a demand-elastic environment. We investigate these issues in greater depth in Chapters 2 and 3.

The "Fee-for-Service" System Based on the Uniform Fee Schedule

Under the Japanese universal health insurance system, all medical facilities (clinics and hospitals) are reimbursed for medical services according to the official fee schedule (*shinryo hoshu*). There is a separate reimbursement schedule for pharmaceuticals. Patients are responsible only for the copayment at the point of service, and hospitals and clinics send the bills to intermediary clearing organizations for reimbursement.[5] All costs incurred by medical facilities are reimbursed on a fee-for-service basis. Figure 1-1 outlines the flow of medical fees.

Over 900 million claims are submitted annually. The review process may seem rather primitive because the system is not computerized. The average time spent reviewing each bill is less than ten seconds.[6] The medical providers' bills itemize each procedure, including the dispensing of drugs, for which a predetermined number of points is assigned according to the fee schedule. Currently, each point is worth ¥10.

There are two different stages of fee schedule revision: (1) setting total medical expenditures and determining the distribution of funds to different groups (physicians, dentists, pharmacists, pharmaceutical companies, etc.) and (2) after determining the share for each of the players, modifying the fees for the 3,000 procedures. The first stage in determining the size of total health care expenditures takes place in December through budget negotiations for the following year.[7] After the national government sets total spending, responsibility for specific changes shifts to the Central Social Insurance Medical Council, the central fee-setting committee (*Chuikyo*). *Chuikyo*, an independent advisory board, is responsible for all facets of reimbursement. It is composed of 20 members, 8 representing providers (5 physicians, 2 dentists, and one pharmacist), 8 representing payers (4 insurers, 2 employees, and 2 employers), and 4 representing public interest groups. In principle, *Chuikyo* takes the leading role in fee schedule revision. Some have suggested that the fee schedule setting process is dominated by political rather than economic cost-benefit considerations.[8]

The fee schedule lists the amount of reimbursement medical facilities will receive for individual procedures and pharmaceuticals. Medical procedures in the fee schedule are categorized by physicians, dentists, and pharmacists. The fee schedule is a very detailed form of pricing control, listing more than 3,000 medical procedures for physicians alone. For example, according to the 1990 fee schedule, an initial physician's consultation is worth 210 points (210 × ¥10 = ¥2,100). Table 1-3 shows the points for several other procedures according to the 1990 fee schedule.

In essence, the Japanese health care financing system is a global

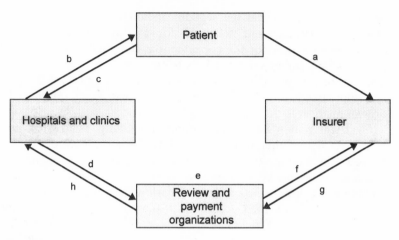

Figure 1-1
A Flow Chart of Reimbursement
a. To be covered by health insurance, the insured must pay a premium to the insurers.
b. When sick or injured, the insured visit medical facilities to receive services.
c. Patients pay a copayment at the time they receive medical services from hospitals and clinics.
d. At the end of each month, medical facilities send bills for all patients calculated.
e. Review and payment organizations review and check bills.
f. They then send bills to the insurer under which the patient is covered.
g. The total amount of reimbursement is sent from insurers to review and payment organizations.
h. These organizations pay each medical facility.
* This process takes approximately two months.
Source: Ministry of Health and Welfare, Japan.

budget system with a very tight bureaucratic pricing control. *Ko-seisho* officials maintain that each fee covers the actual costs of providing the service. However, the current process, which first determines the size of the whole pie, then rations pieces to each player, and finally sets each fee, is unlikely to effectively account for the cost structures of particular providers.

Indeed, two features of the Japanese system suggest that the reimbursement schedule consistently understates the true costs. One is *Yakka saeki*, the so-called "doctor's margin" (Iglehart, 1988): the difference between the reimbursement rates for pharmaceuticals and the prices the drug companies charge physicians. It is common knowledge that doctors augment their earnings from regulated medical services by freely prescribing drugs and keeping the doc-

Table 1-3
1990 Fee Schedule for Reimbursement

Procedure	Points (each worth ¥10)
Initial consultation	210
Second and subsequent consultation at hospital	71
Second and subsequent consultation at clinic	81
Hospitalization: Room (per day)	127
Standard nursing (per day)	282
Meals (per day)	137
At-home consultation (Travel allowances can be added)	400
Examination: Urine test	25
Blood test	30
Imaging: CT scan (body)	1,150
MRI scan	2,100
Surgery: C-section	5,900
Emergency C-section	8,000
Appendectomy	4,800

Source: Ministry of Health and Welfare (1990), *Shinryo Kijun Hayamihyo.*

tor's margin. Whether this practice results in drug costs appearing higher than they might otherwise be is arguable; the Japanese government's tolerance of a system that encourages overprescribing may reflect its understanding of the need to supplement physicians' incomes because of the fee schedule's meager reimbursements.

A second practice is the blurred distinction between the billing of peripheral and core medical services. Although providers are prohibited from charging more than the legal copayment rates for core medical services, they may charge for peripheral, uncovered services. In practice, distinguishing between the two is difficult and leads to abuse; informal out-of-pocket payments often accompany the provision of core medical services.[9]

This fee schedule, based on the so-called point system, has proven a useful resource for the nation's health care policymakers because it gives them the power to influence and alter the behavior of health care providers and facilities. Manipulation of the fee schedule serves as one of the primary mechanisms by which *Koseisho* regulates the supply of medical services, utilization rates, and aggregate health care expenditures. Lower health care expenditures have not been realized accidentally; systemic manipulation of the fee schedule has been a cost containment tool.

PHARMACEUTICAL PRICE CONTROL

The price schedule for pharmaceuticals lists more than 13,000 drugs by brand name, and the schedule for medical equipment (e.g., artificial pacemakers and X-ray film) also categorizes by brand name. Such detail is necessary because if a product has been approved for sale but has not been listed on the fee schedule, doctors and hospitals will not use it. That such a product's use will not be reimbursed through the universal health insurance system illustrates the power of *Koseisho* to affect the practice of medical care through the fee schedule.

Because Japan's health care expenditure is relatively low compared to other industrial nations, it is often presumed that drug prices in Japan are lower than those in other nations (Kimura et al., 1993). However, an empirical survey conducted by a physicians' group in Osaka questions the validity of this presumption. Hama (1994) and his colleagues at *Osaka Hoken-i Kyokai* find that new drug prices tend to be higher in Japan than in other nations, including the U.S., though prices of older drugs are lower because the government cuts their prices in each subsequent fee schedule revision.

With the existence of *Yakka saeki* (or doctor's margin), predictably, Japanese physicians often opt to sell higher-priced drugs, because the more expensive a drug is the bigger the margin. During the 1993 fiscal year, the Universal Health Insurance insurers paid a total of ¥6.46 trillion to medical facilities for pharmaceuticals, but the medical facilities' buying costs were only ¥5.26 trillion, leaving ¥1.2 trillion, or 18.6%, for the dispenser to pocket as profit.

National Medical Expenditures

Many problems arise when attempting to compare medical care expenditures across different countries. Not only do practice patterns and input prices differ among nations, but often the definitions of health care services as well as cultural and political considerations mask the true disparities in health care costs. In Japan, the government estimates that medical care costs consume roughly 5% of total GNP. The Organization for Economic Cooperation and Development (OECD) researchers report the figure at 6.8% for 1991 (Schieber et al., 1993).

One reason that the Japanese government's estimate is lower than the OECD's is the more stringent definition of national medical care expenditures employed in Japan. The official national medical care expenditures published by *Koseisho* include the estimated costs of treating diseases or injuries (including medical and dental expenses for treatment in hospitals, clinics, and *Roken* facilities) for a particular fiscal year. Nursing fees and patient transportation costs which are covered by health insurance are also included in the official accounting. Finally, national medical care expenditures include disbursements for medical insurance, workers' compensation insurance, public assistance (for persons with special diseases such as tuberculosis), and personal expenses (copayments and/or full payment).

Hence, the majority of the direct costs of medical care are accounted for in Japan. What is often excluded, however, are many of the more indirect expenses to support medical institutions and infrastructures. Specifically, uncomplicated birth costs, direct medical education subsidies and research grants, subsidies to government hospitals, and preventive and health promotion interventions are excluded from Japanese medical expenditure accounts. In addition, expenses for nontreatment procedures (i.e., medical examinations and immunizations) and nonillness conditions (i.e., normal childbirth and puerperium) are not included.

When Japanese health care expenditures are compared to those of other OECD countries, four items excluded from the official Japanese data become particularly important: (1) various costs associated with government hospitals, including construction costs and financial subsidies; (2) research and development funding for medical research; (3) welfare-related expenses, such as nursing home costs; and (4) medical expenses not covered by the universal health insurance system, such as fees for amenities, care givers, over-the-counter drugs, and so forth.

Japanese government hospitals receive large public subsidies; these exceeded ¥550 billion in 1991. Because national medical schools and university hospitals fall under the jurisdiction of the Ministry of Education instead of *Koseisho*, their budgets are also excluded from national medical expenditures. Finally, subsidies for capital development are also covered by the Ministry of Education and hence are absent from the health care expenditure data.

The magnitude of the effect of excluding nursing home costs is likely small. Because many Japanese hospitals function as surrogates for long-term elderly care facilities, total expenditures for nursing homes are rather limited. Hence, the amount by which total health care costs are underestimated as a result of the nursing home accounting exclusion is fairly insignificant.

Informal out-of-pocket expenses do, however, contribute to some of the differences between the Japanese and OECD estimates of expenditures. In theory, Japanese patients pay only the legal co-payment rate at the point of service (in the range of 10–30%). In practice, though, many hospitals charge patients additional informal fees.[10]

HEALTH EXPENDITURE TRENDS

Spending for Japanese health care reached ¥20,607 billion in 1990, an increase of 4.5% over 1989 spending. The 1990 per capita medical expenditure of ¥166,700 was nearly 1.5 times the figure for 1980. From 1961 to 1990, health expenditures grew at a rate of 14.2% per annum, far greater than the 11.6% annual growth rate of gross domestic product (GDP) in the same period. As a result, health care expenditures as a percentage of GDP nearly doubled between 1961 and 1990. Despite high growth rates in the 1960s and 1970s (averaging 19.9% and 17.2%, respectively), the 1980s ushered in an era of relative slowdown. From 1981 to 1990, health expenditures grew at roughly 8.6% per annum, a rate that dwarfed the growth rate of GDP for the years 1987–1990 (Figure 1-2).

Figure 1-3 provides a snapshot of health care spending for 1990 by source of payment (e.g., premiums, out-of-pocket expenditure), by health care facility (e.g., clinics and hospitals), and for 1991 by factor of production (e.g., wages and drugs).[11]

By Payment Route—The Japanese health care financing system moved toward greater reliance on government funding until the early 1980s. In 1960, 80.4% of total health expenditures was financed by private payers; by 1990, that number fell to 68.4%. The share of out-of-pocket payments decreased dramatically from 1960 to 1982, but it has since risen. The share of health insurance premiums also increased gradually during the same time period. The Japanese government's financial share grew rapidly from 19.6% in 1960 to 36.4% in 1983, at which time the share began to fall.

As the Japanese government's share of expenditures increased, the government adopted various mechanisms by which to reduce its burden. First, premiums were increased beginning in the mid-1970s. Second, out-of-pocket payments for members of the employee health insurance societies were introduced in 1984. Third, the Japanese government created the *Roken* pooling fund in 1983 to transform the source of funding for elderly care from one of direct public subsidy to one relying primarily on cross-subsidization by the other insurance societies.[12]

As a result, private spending as a percentage of total health

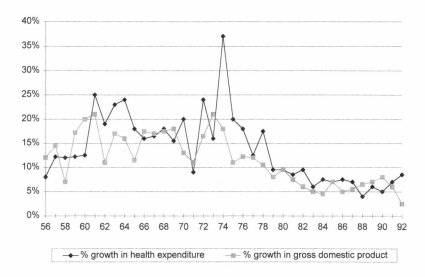

Figure 1-2
Percent Growth in Health Expenditures and GDP in Japan for Fiscal Years
1956–1992

expenditures in Japan increased from 63.4% in 1983 to 68.4% in
1990. More than 80% of the increase in private spending is accounted for by premium increases; out-of-pocket payments make
up the rest. At the same time, the share of public money has fallen
from 36.4% in 1983 to 31.4% in 1990.

By Health Care Facility—In 1990, Japanese hospitals received
¥12,632.4 billion for medical services provided on an inpatient and
outpatient basis, the largest single category of health care spending.
From 1962 to 1990, spending for hospital services increased at an
annual rate of 14.6%, slightly higher than the growth rate of 13.6%
for total health expenditures. As a result, spending for hospital services as a percentage of total health expenditures increased from
48.0% in 1962 to 61.3% in 1990. Until 1985, the share of outpatient
expenditures had been declining, but since then, it has begun to
consume an increasing percentage of hospital expenditures.

Spending for medical care provided in clinics increased at a rate
of 12.4% per annum from 1962 to 1990 to reach ¥5,939.5 billion in
1990. However, the share of total expenditures devoted to clinic
services fell from 39.6% in 1962 to 28.9% in 1990. The percentage
of clinic budgets devoted to inpatient care has increased to 8.6%
while the share of outpatient care has declined dramatically.

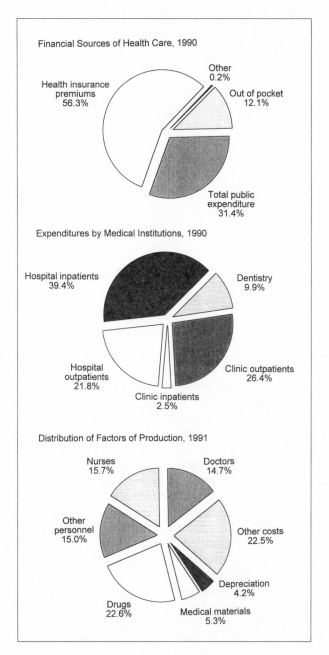

Figure 1-3
Flow of Health Expenditures in Japan

In 1990, dental services accounted for 9.9% of total health expenditures, down from 12.4% in 1962. With a total tab in 1990 of ¥2,035.4 billion, the share of dental services as a percentage of total health expenditures has remained the most stable in the health care industry.

By Factor of Production—In 1991, Japanese medical institutions spent 22.6% of total expenditures on drugs, an increase of 0.9% since 1982.[13] This increase in the share of money devoted to pharmaceuticals is interesting given that the real reimbursement rates for drugs in Japan have fallen since the early 1980s. The share of total costs devoted to medical materials and drugs increased from 27.4% in 1982 to 27.9% in 1991. Expenditure for capital depreciation costs as a share of total health industry costs increased from 3.7% in 1982 to 4.2% in 1991.

Health services labor costs have remained relatively constant over the past decade. The percentage of health expenditures devoted to labor in 1991 (45.4%) represents a 3.4% decrease from the 1982 figure. Of the 45.4%, 14.7% was attributed to physician salaries and wages, 15.7% to wages for nurses, and the remaining 15.0% for other personnel.

By Age Group—In 1990, 41.5% of the total health care expenditures went to people over age 65. As the proportion of elderly in the population has been rising, so too has the per capita medical care expenditures for this group. The 1990 per capita medical care expense for persons aged 65 and over reached ¥499,600. This figure was 3.44 times greater than the average expense and 5.2 times greater than the per capita expense for those under age 65.

Among Japanese aged 65 and over, the most expensive diseases were those of the circulatory system, accounting for 39.9% of total medical care expenses for this group in 1989. Of circulatory diseases, the three most prominent as measured by health care expenditures were cerebrovascular diseases (43.1%), hypertensive diseases (29.9%), and ischemic heart diseases (12.2%).

FACTORS AFFECTING HEALTH CARE EXPENDITURES

Four major factors contribute to the growth in health expenditures in Japan: (1) demographic changes; (2) economywide price inflation; (3) medical price inflation in excess of the general inflation rate; and (4) other factors, including increases in the per capita use and intensity of medical services.[14] Because the first two factors are generally beyond the control of health care policymakers,[15] we focus on the latter two. Medical price inflation may be controlled through supply-side interventions, such as the uniform fee schedule. At the same time, the use of health services may be affected through demand-side interventions that determine copayment and premium rates. Indeed, during the 1980s, the Japanese government adopted a cost containment strategy aimed at limiting reimbursement rates while increasing copayment rates.

For the period 1980–1990, Japanese health expenditures grew at an annual rate of 5.6%. According to our estimates, inflation accounted for 56.2% of that growth, the bulk of it (43.7%) attributable to economywide price inflation. The remaining 12.5% may be attributed to medical price inflation in excess of the general inflation rate. Demographic changes were responsible for roughly one-fourth (26.8%) of the growth. Other factors contributed 17.0%.

Using data from *Kokumin Iryo-hi* (National Medical Expenditure Estimates), we conduct a more in-depth times series analysis of the major components of the increases in Japanese health care costs between 1977 and 1990. Table 1-4 presents the results. We employ several definitions in our calculations. Real health expenditures$_{(1)}$ are nominal expenditures divided by a GDP deflator (base year =1977). Real health expenditures$_{(2)}$ are nominal expenditures divided by a national health expenditures (NHE) deflator (base year = 1977). Health expenditures are then adjusted by population as follows. We calculate real health expenditures$_{(2)}$ for each age structure and standardize those health expenditures by the 1977 age structure and sum, such that:

$$ME_t = \sum_{i=1}^{4} Q_t^i N_0^i, \tag{1-1}$$

where ME_t is the t-th year health expenditures adjusted by population, Q_t^i is real health expenditures for t-th year and i-th age cohort, and N_0^i is 1977 population of the i-th age structure. In effect, this formula adjusts real health expenditures$_{(2)}$ by population, based upon the 1977 population structure.

We define the factors affecting health expenditures as follows. (1) Economywide inflation is the difference between nominal health expenditures and real health expenditures$_{(1)}$. (2) Excess medical inflation is the difference between real health expenditures$_{(1)}$ and real health expenditures$_{(2)}$. (3) Demographic change is the difference between health expenditures adjusted by population and real health expenditures$_{(2)}$. (4) Other factors$_{(t)}$ is health expenditures$_{(t)}$ − health

Table 1-4
A Decomposition of Health Expenditure Trends

	1977	1978	1979	1980	1981	1982	1983	1984	1985	1986	1987	1988	1989	1990
Health expenditures	85,685	100,042	109,511	119,805	128,709	138,659	145,437	150,933	160,159	170,690	180,758	187,555	197,290	206,074
Real health expenditures adjusted by population	85,685	87,891	92,349	98,017	101,722	105,080	108,338	108,395	104,496	107,448	108,254	110,215	111,930	113,261
Factors in the increase of NHE in Japan, 1977														
Excess medical inflation	0	5,901	5,964	3,162	1,251	2,452	1,058	979	8,488	9,132	13,808	14,254	14,510	14,093
Economywide inflation	0	4,775	8,013	13,578	18,741	22,063	24,919	28,654	32,352	36,888	39,064	41,108	46,053	51,518
Demographic change	0	1,475	3,184	5,048	6,995	9,064	11,123	12,905	14,823	17,223	19,633	21,979	24,796	27,201
Other factors	0	2,206	6,664	12,332	16,037	19,395	22,653	22,710	18,811	21,763	22,569	24,530	26,245	27,576

Source: Ministry of Health and Welfare, 1990. Kokumin Iryo-hi (National Medical Expenditure Estimates).

expenditures$_{(t-1)}$ – (economywide inflation$_{(t)}$) – (excess medical inflation$_{(t)}$) – (demographic change$_{(t)}$).

In sum, economywide price inflation was the major factor affecting the increase in health care expenditures from 1980 to 1990. Demographic changes comprised the second major factor, with medical price inflation in excess of the general inflation rate having a smaller effect. The volume and intensity of services were significant contributors, notwithstanding the diligence with which the Japanese government has increased copayment rates to limit use of medical services.

Patients, Doctors, and Hospitals in Japan

Patients

The national Patient Survey (*Kanja Chosa*) is a data set collected by *Koseisho* for the purpose of providing objective medical information on Japanese patients and disease incidence. The Patient Survey was conducted during three days in September 1990 from a one-third random sample of all hospitals and clinics in Japan that provided either inpatient or outpatient services. Data were collected from each hospital during only one of the three days of the survey and reported to *Koseisho*; a third of the hospitals were surveyed on each day. Because all medical care facilities are compelled to participate, there is no response bias.

When the survey was taken in 1990, hospitals and clinics across Japan treated 1,500,900 inpatients and 6,865,400 outpatients (Ministry of Health and Welfare, 1990, *Kanja Chosa*). There were also 1,244,400 dental patients. Almost all (93.7%) of the inpatients monitored in the survey were treated in a hospital; few inpatients were in clinics. Clinics, however, do play a leading role in outpatient care. Japanese clinics treated 71.2% of the nation's outpatients in 1990, whereas hospitals treated only 28.8%. However, for both inpatients and outpatients, there is an increasing preference for care in large tertiary care hospitals.

The greatest strength of Japan's health care system, aside from its low cost, is guaranteed access to comprehensive medical care provided for virtually every member of the population. In surveys of Japanese who have chosen not to seek medical care at one time or another, an overwhelming majority of the respondents cited reasons other than problems of access and cost. A 1985 national survey by *Koseisho* showed that only 0.2% of the respondents cited problems of access and 0.4% cited economic problems (Ministry of Health

Table 1-5
One-Day Utilization of Medical Care by Age Group (per 100,000 population) in 1990

Age Group	Inpatient			Outpatient		
	Total 1,214	Male 1,199	Female 1,229	Total 5,554	Male 4,864	Female 6,220
0	1,397	1,436	1,356	5,505	5,721	5,278
1–4	213	242	183	5,945	6,102	5,781
5–9	165	194	134	4,375	4,572	4,168
10–14	154	170	137	2,442	2,492	2,390
15–19	244	286	200	2,183	1,982	2,395
20–24	410	421	398	2,867	2,194	3,563
25–34	593	539	647	3,409	2,623	4,212
35–44	738	878	597	3,721	3,212	4,235
45–54	1,140	1,365	918	5,480	4,667	6,282
55–64	1,761	2,149	1,394	8,435	7,754	9,076
65+	4,652	4,415	4,812	13,568	13,127	13,866

Source: Ministry of Health and Welfare (1990), Kanja Chosa.

and Welfare, National Health Survey, 1986). Using the Patient Survey we investigate the factors influencing Japanese patients' demand for medical care in Chapters 2, 3, and 4.

The utilization rate is defined as the number of patients in a given day per 100,000 population. In 1990, the inpatient utilization rate in Japan was 1,214, and the outpatient utilization rate was 5,554.[16] Utilization of medical care, both inpatient and outpatient, is higher for females than for males. Inpatient utilization is lowest for ages 10–14 (154) and increases thereafter with age. Outpatient utilization is lowest for the age group 15–19 (2,183) and again increases with age (Table 1-5).

When utilization of medical services by age group is examined over time, several interesting trends appear. Table 1-6 shows that between 1955 and 1965, utilization rates increased dramatically, probably in large part due to the establishment of universal health insurance in 1961. For all Japanese younger than 55, utilization of medical services has been decreasing ever since. Even the utilization rate for infants has declined roughly in proportion to other age groups. This is at least partially explained by general improvements in health status in Japan. For the elderly, however, utilization of medical services increased slightly between 1975 and 1990 (Table 1-6).

Table 1-6

Trend of One-Day Utilization of Medical Care by Age Group (per 100,000 population)

Age Group	1955	1965	1975	1984	1990
Total	3,301	5,910	7,049	6,403	6,768
Male	3,503	5,997	6,586	5,902	6,063
Female	3,107	5,827	7,498	6,888	7,449
0	3,662	7,512	7,733	7,281	6,902
1–4	2,749	5,733	7,222	5,495	6,158
5–9			6,944	4,404	4,540
10–14	1,844	4,259	3,865	2,614	2,596
15–19			2,993	2,598	2,427
20–24	3,582	4,904	4,428	3,660	3,277
25–34	4,686	5,997	5,187	4,204	4,001
35–44	4,057	6,470	6,334	4,705	4,459
45–54	3,696	7,016	8,143	7,010	6,620
55–64	3,402	7,958	10,336	9,824	10,196
65–69	NA	NA	13,383	13,455	13,755
70+	NA	NA	18,750	19,936	20,546

Source: Ministry of Health and Welfare Kanja Chosa (1955, 1965, 1975, 1984, 1990).

Another interesting observation about Japanese patients is that, relative to other nations, the per capita number of physician visits is quite high; yet the inpatient admission rate is by far the lowest in the industrialized world. The rate of surgical procedures per capita has been estimated at under one-quarter that of the U.S. Estimates of annual surgical rates per 1,000 population are 27 for Japan and 91 for the U.S. (American Hospital Association, 1986; Ministry of Health and Welfare, Kanja Chosa). Surgical utilization is analyzed more completely in Part VI.

Table 1-7 shows that the average length of stay (ALOS) for Japanese hospitals is far longer than that found elsewhere. According to the 1990 Kanja Chosa, the average length of hospitalization was 44.9 days (hospitals, 47.4 days; clinics, 28.2 days).

ALOS is especially high for the elderly. For patients of 65 years and above, the ALOS is 79.3 days. The fact that there are very few Japanese facilities classified officially as nursing homes is partially responsible for this trend. Many Japanese believe hospitals serve a dual purpose: providing in- and outpatient care for the sick and acting as rest homes for the elderly. However, even the use of hospitals as geriatric nursing facilities cannot fully explain Japan's long ALOS. If we look at individual disease categories, such as

Table 1-7
International Comparison of Patient Contact and Inpatient Admissions
(1990)

Country	Patient Contact[1]	Patient Care Admission Rates[2]	Average Length of Inpatient Care[3]
Japan	12.9 (1988)	8.3	50.5
U.S.A.	5.3	13.7	9.1
U.K.	5.7	15.9 (1988)	14.5
W. Germany	11.5 (1987)	20.9	16.5
France	7.2	23.3	12.3
Sweden	2.8	19.5	18.0
Canada	6.8	14.1	13.9

[1] Consultations and visits per capita; these data are from 1989.
[2] Percent of population.
[3] Patient days per admission.
Source: Organization for Economic Cooperation and Development, 1993.

pregnancy complications, which are not affected by geriatric factors, the length of stay is still considerably greater in Japan, as shown in Table 1-8.

Doctors

After the aggressive establishment of new medical schools in Japan during the 1970s, the number of doctors increased dramatically from 103,131 in 1960 to 211,797 in 1990, roughly 171 per 100,000 population (Ministry of Health and Welfare, 1990, *Ishi, Shika, Ishi Yakuzaishi Chosa*). There are five categories of doctors in Japan according to their place of service: doctors who own clinics, doctors who are employed at clinics, doctors who own hospitals, doctors who are employed at hospitals, and others. In 1990, there were 58,213 clinic owners, 2,936 hospital owners, 16,819 doctors employed by clinics, 125,829 doctors employed by hospitals, and 8,000 "others" (Ministry of Health and Welfare, 1990, *Ishi, Shika, Ishi Yakuzaishi Chosa*).

Doctors who own clinics or hospitals are called *kaigyo-i*; the overwhelming majority (95.2%) of *kaigyo-i* are clinic owners. Doctors who are not self-employed are called *kinmu-i*; 88.2% of such doctors are hospital-based. If we separate doctors into two groups, clinic-based doctors and hospital-based doctors, the former group is essentially composed of *kaigyo-i*, and the latter is composed of *kinmu-i*. Thus, the words "clinic doctors" and "*kaigyo-i*," and "hospital doctors" and "*kinmu-i*" are often used interchangeably.

Table 1-8
Mean Length of Stay in Days for Disease Categories by Country (1990)

Disease Category	Japan	U.K.[1]	U.S.A.[2]	Canada[2]	W. Germany[1]
All categories	44.9	20.0	6.5	11.4	15.2
Infectious and parasitic diseases	36.7	7.3	7.7	9.3	15.4
Neoplasms	46.0	9.5	8.3	14.4	14.3
Endocrine and metabolic diseases	46.6	13.4	6.8	13.4	17.4
Diseases of the blood	39.9	8.9	6.0	9.5	14.8
Mental disorders	325.5	216.7	12.7	31.3	35.0
Nervous system diseases	40.1	11.8	5.5	21.0	13.2
Circulatory system diseases	80.9	17.5	7.6	18.8	18.9
Respiratory system diseases	29.5	9.8	6.7	8.1	11.2
Digestive system diseases	30.4	7.5	6.3	7.3	13.4
Genito-urinary system diseases	30.6	5.0	5.2	6.5	11.0
Complications of pregnancy and childbirth	8.3	3.5	2.8	4.1	6.4
Skin and subcutaneous tissue diseases	27.7	10.5	8.0	9.6	15.9
Congenital anomalies	30.6	9.9	5.9	9.5	12.3

[1] 1988 data.
[2] 1989 data.
Source: Organization for Economic Cooperation and Development, 1993.

Though once dominating the medical field, *kaigyo-i* are becoming less prominent, especially among younger doctors (Table 1-9). Traditionally, the majority of doctors set up their own clinics and became *kaigyo-i*; recently the overwhelming majority of young doctors have chosen to become *kinmu-i*. The average age of the *kaigyo-i* reached 60.2 years in 1992, and their political power appears to be waning along with their numbers (Ministry of Health and Welfare, 1992, *Ishi, Shika, Ishi Yakuzaishi Chosa*).

In the past two decades, the physician population has undergone a dramatic change in both size and makeup. Not only did the number of doctors increase nearly 125% from 1960 to 1990, but the prominence of *kaigyo-i* also declined dramatically from 47.3% to 28.9% of all doctors. At the same time, *kinmu-i* became the dominant force, increasing from 44.0% to 67.4% of the physician population. A changing of the guard from the older small clinic owners to the younger hospital-based *kinmu-i* appears to be at hand.

Four factors are responsible for this change. First, as the original

Table 1-9
Number of Doctors by Type of Employment

Type of Employment	1960	Share	1990	Share
Kaigyo-i				
Hospital owners	2,302	2.4%	2,936	1.4%
Clinic owners	42,340	44.8%	58,213	27.5%
Kinmu-i				
Those working at hospitals, clinics,				
university hospitals	41,702	44.1%	142,648	67.4%
Others (physicians at local health centers)	8,319	8.7%	8,000	3.8%
Total	94,563	100%	211,797	100%

Source: Ministry of Health and Welfare (1990), *Ishi, Shika, Ishi Yakuzaishi Chosa.*

kaigyo-i have grown older, they have not been replaced by younger physicians interested in clinic-based medicine. Second, the escalation of land prices in Japan has made the creation of clinics by young doctors financially prohibitive. Unless one inherits a clinic, an option available to only a few of the young physicians leaving their residency periods, working in hospitals remains the most viable option. Third, young doctors are attracted to larger hospitals that are complete with sophisticated medical equipment. Finally, advances in technology have begun attracting increasing numbers of outpatients to large hospitals, making it difficult for the less-well-equipped *kaigyo-i* to compete. Many *kaigyo-i*, however, have recently shown an increasing tendency toward greater technological specialization.

Table 1-10 compares the supply of Japanese medical practitioners to that of other major industrialized countries. Although Japan has more physicians and nurses per capita than the U.K., it has far fewer doctors per capita than the U.S. and many European nations. The U.S. has nearly one million more nurses than Japan and a nurse staffing ratio (number of nurses per occupied bed) almost five times that of Japan.

SPECIALIZATION OF PHYSICIANS
Specialty board certification does not exist in Japan, so physicians may represent themselves as practitioners of any specialty they choose. Nearly all clinic doctors specialize in internal medicine (Kaihara, 1991), although this effectively means that they are generalists and spend most of their time providing primary care.

U.S. primary care physicians typically earn less than specialists,

Table 1-10
International Comparison of Physicians and Nurses, 1990

Country	Practicing Physician Total	Per 1,000 Population	Nurse Total[1]	Nurse Staffing Ratio[2]
Japan	203,797	1.6	745,301	0.42
U.S.A.	601,010	2.3	1,666,200[5]	2.02[3]
U.K.	80,991	1.4	243,854[4]	0.72
W. Germany	195,254	3.1	320,637[5]	0.45[4]
France	152,096	2.7	304,480[5]	0.38[5]
Sweden	24,600	2.9	84,000	N/A
Canada	59,409	2.2	223,965	0.94[4]

[1] Persons with at least two years of professional training.
[2] Number of nurses per available bed.
[3] 1987 data.
[4] 1988 data.
[5] 1989 data.
Source: Organization for Economic Cooperation and Development, 1993.

but Japanese clinic owners/general practitioners (kaigyo-i) earn significantly more on average than hospital-based "specialists." In 1989, the average net monthly revenue for kaigyo-i was ¥2,979,317, whereas the average net monthly salary for a physician employed in an ordinary hospital was ¥812,170.[17] These hospital-based physicians, however (especially those employed in large, well-respected hospitals), enjoy a higher status among medical professionals than do the kaigyo-i. Hence, as is customary among many professional positions in Japan, physician incomes are inversely proportional to their level of social prestige.

THE GEOGRAPHICAL DISTRIBUTION OF PHYSICIANS
The geographical distribution of doctors in Japan is uncovered by calculating the coefficient of variation[18] of the number of doctors per 100,000 people in each of the 47 prefectures,[19] for every year between 1956 and 1990.[20]

According to Figure 1-4, the variance in the per capita number of hospital-based physicians by prefecture has declined dramatically since the late 1970s. The 1973 governmental initiative to establish a medical school in each prefecture probably played an important role in lowering regional inequality. In contrast, the coefficient of variation of clinic doctors declined from 1956 to 1970 and has re-

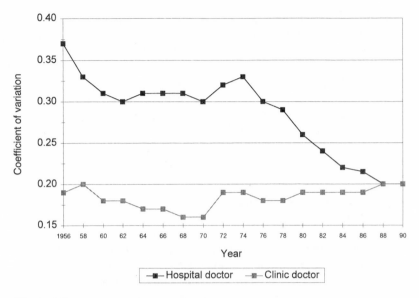

Figure 1-4
Transition of Coefficient of Variation

mained almost constant after a small jump in 1972.[21] In Chapter 11, we analyze the labor market for physicians in Japan.

Hospitals

The national Facility Survey (*Iryo Shisetsu Chosa*) is a comprehensive data set of medical facilities in Japan collected by *Koseisho*. Similar to the American Hospital Association Annual Survey, it contains data describing each hospital in Japan. It is collected in September of each year by *Koseisho*. Because it is mandatory, the survey contains full information for each of the 10,096 hospitals in Japan including size, ownership, number of inpatients and out-patients, measures of staffing, complexity of services, and utilization of services.

In Japan, the definition of a hospital is a medical facility with 20 or more beds. Facilities with fewer than 20 beds are classified as clinics. In comparison with other industrialized countries, the number of hospitals and beds in Japan is high. For example, whereas the U.S. had 6,343 hospitals with 1,188,168 beds in 1990, Japan had 10,096 hospitals with 1,676,803 beds. This difference is even greater when one considers that Japan's population is half that of the U.S.

Among OECD nations, Japan has the second highest number of inpatient beds per thousand population (15.8), while the U.S. has 4.7, France has 9.7, Germany has 10.3, and the United Kingdom has 5.9.

Some of the disparity between these countries may be attributable to differences in the definitions of hospitals and hospital beds among different countries. For example, some of Japan's hospital beds are used as substitutes for long-term geriatric care, making an accurate comparison difficult. Japanese hospitals, known as *byoin*, may function slightly differently than hospitals in other nations.

HOSPITAL CATEGORIES
General Hospitals (*Sogo Byoin*)—Some larger Japanese hospitals are called *sogo byoin*, or general hospitals. Hospitals are classified as *sogo byoin* if they have at least 100 beds and all of the following departments: internal medicine, surgery, obstetrics, gynecology, ophthalmology, and otolaryngology. *Sogo byoin* must be certified by the governor of the prefecture. General hospitals are much larger than average Japanese hospitals. The average number of beds for all hospitals was 166 in 1990, but the average number of beds in general hospitals was 426. The smallest general hospital had 100 beds, and the largest had 1,673. There are 1,130 hospitals classified as general hospitals, 582 of which are private and 548 of which are public.

Geriatric Hospitals (*Rojin Byoin*)—With the 1982 Health and Medical Services Law for the Elderly, *Koseisho* created the category of "geriatric hospitals" (*Tokurei kyoka rojin byoin*).[22] As of October 1990, there were 1,165 such approved geriatric hospitals with a total of 148,863 beds (Ministry of Health and Welfare, 1990, *Iryo Shisetsu Chosa*). All these geriatric hospitals are long-term hospitals, with 72.5% of their patients staying more than six months in 1988 (Niki, 1990). These geriatric care hospitals are also subject to a different fee schedule than are other hospitals.[23] Furthermore, these hospitals have a lower nursing staff : beds ratio than ordinary hospitals. The elderly care facilities in Japan have been undergoing some changes as a result of recent *Koseisho* efforts to reshape the care structure.

HOSPITAL OWNERSHIP ARRANGEMENTS
The 10,096 hospitals in Japan can be classified according to ownership and scope of services provided. Although there are several different types of ownership, the hospitals in this study are classified into only two ownership groups, the private and public sectors. Pri-

Table 1-11
Number of Hospitals and Beds Classified According to Ownership in Japan
(1990)

Type of Ownership	All Hospitals	*Beds	General Hospitals	Beds
Public				
National government	399	158,746	154	79,434
Regional government	1,079	248,892	394	155,386
Insurance association	136	39,080	85	30,342
Other public	292	99,334	173	78,058
Private				
Iryo-Hojin	4,245	656,348	118	38,607
Individual	3,081	263,304	7	1,905
Other private	864	211,099	199	98,250
Total	10,096	1,676,803	1,130	481,982

* General hospitals are included in the All Hospitals category.

vate ownership dominates the Japanese hospital system. In 1990, private hospitals occupied 80% of the hospital market and 70% of total hospital beds. Table 1-11 presents some descriptive statistics of Japanese hospitals, classified according to ownership.

Among public hospitals, there are three major subdivisions: national government facilities, local government facilities, and other public facilities. In each of these subdivisions, ownership may rest with one of various government agencies. *Koseisho* operates a number of national hospitals, which are mostly specialist centers focusing on research and treatment of a particular disease or group of diseases. Teaching hospitals affiliated with state university medical schools are under the jurisdiction of the Ministry of Education. Local government hospitals may be run by the prefecture or the municipality. In some instances, a hospital is owned by the local government but is managed by a private contractor. Apart from the hospitals operated by governments, a variety of public, nonprofit organizations own a large proportion of the public hospitals. Philanthropic hospitals (Red Cross and *Saiseikai*) and 136 hospitals owned by insurance associations (*Kokuho*) compose the public not-for-profit (NFP) hospitals.

Private sector hospitals may be classified into four groups: those owned by insurance associations, *iryo-hojin* hospitals, individual (physician)-owned hospitals, and others. The so-called *iryo-hojin* hospital, a form of private hospital, is the most prevalent in Japan. *Iryo-hojin* is a special legal status for nonprofit foundations in the medical care sector. It is *de jure* illegal to operate health care facilities on a for-profit basis in Japan. An *iryo-hojin* is prohibited from distributing profits to anyone outside the hospital (e.g., shareholders). This prohibition on distributing profits may make Japanese *iryo-hojin* private hospitals superficially seem to resemble American NFP hospitals.

Although dividends or profits are prohibited, an *iryo-hojin* hospital is essentially a private entity, an entrepreneurial business owned by a doctor (or doctors) operating under more or less the same financial incentives as for-profit enterprises. Japanese law merely prohibits the distribution of profits to noninsider shareholders. Hence, although they may not distribute profits, *iryo-hojin* hospitals are most analogous to American for-profit hospitals. A more accurate characterization would be to name them "not-necessarily-for-profit" hospitals, locating them somewhere on the continuum between NFP and for-profit hospitals.

There are 4,245 *iryo-hojin* hospitals with 656,348 beds. Private hospitals owned by individual physicians are the second most prevalent form in Japan with 3,081 hospitals with 263,304 beds. There are 864 hospitals under the category of "other private" hospitals. They include those owned by corporations, such as Toyota and Toshiba, and those owned by private universities. On average, public hospitals are larger than private ones. The average public hospital has 286 beds; the average private hospital has 141 beds.

OPEN AND CLOSED SYSTEMS

It is important to understand the difference between U.S. and Japanese hospitals and their relationship with community physicians. Traditionally, doctors in the U.S. have privileges at community hospitals while maintaining private offices where they provide primary care. This is known as an open system. Essentially, in an open system, doctors and hospitals are firms contracting with one another, usually without direct cash payment from one to the other. In Japan, there are virtually no open hospitals (Yoshikawa, 1993). Japanese clinic-based doctors do not have visiting privileges at hospitals. In Japan's closed system, the doctors are employees of the hospital.

MARKET FOR HOSPITALS: MEDICAL ZONE

Despite resistance from many in the medical profession, *Koseisho* amended the Medical Service Law in 1985, forcing prefectures to prepare *Chiiki Iryo Keikaku* (Regional Health Care Plans), to control increases in hospital beds in a market. *Koseisho*, as a definition of the markets, introduced the administrative area of *dai-niji iryo-ken* (medical zones). For each of 345 medical zones, the government introduced a strict limit on the total number of beds permitted. Today it is virtually impossible to increase the number of hospital beds in a medical zone and to establish new hospitals in urban areas.

HOSPITALS' FINANCIAL PERFORMANCE

According to the Japanese hospital association, in 1992, 73.1% of all hospitals reported year-end losses on their medical service operating margins.[24] By ownership, 86.2% of public hospitals (owned by local governments) and 55.4% of private hospitals were suffering from net operating revenue losses in 1992. Local government-owned hospitals can be characterized by their heavy financial losses annually. Two theories have been posited to explain these losses. One maintains that public hospitals owned by local governments provide more "intensive and expensive, high-quality" medical care (i.e., more tertiary and acute care). The second theory maintains that local government-owned public hospitals are losing money because of their inefficiency, rather than their alleged high quality. *Koseisho* seems to subscribe to the "high price = quality" hypothesis, as evidenced by its continued support of subsidies to hospitals that would otherwise become insolvent. In 1991, the subsidy to government hospitals totaled ¥558.3 billion, a figure equivalent to ¥2,413,000 per bed annually, much larger than the annual loss per bed.

The impact of the subsidies is not limited to the government hospitals. The large losses of government medicine and the high subsidies have also affected private sector medicine. Private hospitals, lacking substantial financial subsidies, are required to finance capital expansion and wage increases by either increasing revenues or reducing delivery and facility costs. Traditionally, both government and private hospitals have depended upon the "doctor's margin" for such capital development; without the luxury of a financial subsidy, the ongoing efforts by *Koseisho* to eliminate the doctor's margin will affect private sector hospitals disproportionately. More than 50% of private hospitals faced operating losses in 1992, indicating that the subsidy treatment favoring public hospitals has already taken its toll on the private sector. If revenues continue to shrink, private hospitals will be forced to cut expenses, leaving the quality of care hanging in the balance.

Hospitals owned in the private and government sectors may behave differently for two basic reasons. First, they may have different objectives. Government hospitals and government-owned organizations in general seem unlikely to be pursuing profit as their primary objective. Such things as budget maximization or output maximization have been posited as more plausible objectives. By contrast, private institutions likely hold profitability (and thus efficiency) as a primary goal. Second, private and government hospitals may face different constraints. If government and private hospitals receive different levels of compensation, treat dissimilar case mixes of patients, face varying regulatory requirements, or have differing input costs, then their behavior may not be alike.

COMPETITION AMONG HOSPITALS IN JAPAN

Under Japanese fee-for-service medicine with the uniform fee schedule, there is little incentive among medical facilities to refer patients to other hospitals. Patients are free to utilize any medical facilities, regardless of their size, teaching status, and so forth. The lack of a systematic division of labor or functional differentiation is a major problem in Japanese hospitals.

In Great Britain, GPs provide routine primary care to their patients. Any patient wishing to see a specialist in the National Health Service (NHS) must go through a GP. Hence, British GPs act as gatekeepers, ensuring that specialists see only those patients who need the benefit of their advanced training. Such systemic organization is absent (though slowly developing) in Japan.[25] Japanese *kaigyo-i* often provide not only primary care, but also more specialized care, thus diffusing highly sophisticated medical technology to small clinics and hospitals.

Similarly, there is no clear systematic division between primary and secondary care, resulting in much competition between clinics and hospital outpatient departments for patients.[26] For example, university hospitals in theory are supposed to provide tertiary care and frontier medical research. However, they have also begun accepting many outpatients with primary care needs, often competing with private hospitals and clinics. Efforts to restructure Japan's medical delivery system by defining the functions of each medical facility are receiving high priority from *Koseisho* officials.

Hospitals cannot engage in price competition because medical fees are set uniformly by the government. Under such market conditions, hospitals tend to engage in nonprice competition in order to attract patients. With legal restrictions on advertisement, a hospital's options are quite limited. Hence, many hospitals may be purchasing high-tech medical equipment to signal a level of medical sophistication that will attract more patients. There is an interesting relationship between the level of competition among hospitals in a market and incentives to acquire high-tech medical equipment. Hospitals also appear to be employing more nurses, another proxy for a signal of higher quality, in order to attract more inpatients. Thus, there may be a strategic linkage between market competition and the decision to hire more nurses. One major purpose of this book is to explore the mechanisms of competition among Japanese hospitals and their effect on health care delivery.

Notes

[1] This situation stands in stark contrast to that in the United States, where hospitals receive different reimbursement rates for the same procedures, depending upon the insured's insurance coverage.

[2] Exceptions to these otherwise liberal benefits are preventive care and uncomplicated childbirths, both of which fall outside the "medical treatment" category (as defined by the *Koseisho*). However, for these "nonmedical" needs and other potentially costly events, the Japanese system offers cash benefits. For example, though the costs of normal childbirth are not reimbursed, compensation for childbirth is provided in the form of a one-time bonus. The Japanese system also provides compensation for funeral expenses.

[3] Prior to the creation of the *Roken* system in 1983, each insurer supported its own elderly members, and variations in the number of elderly covered by each scheme caused disparities in the financial burden across insurers. The high enrollment of elderly in *Kokuho* is a serious threat to the financial stability of the *Kokuho* system.

[4] To qualify for the benefits provided under the current High-Cost Medical Care Benefits Law reflecting the 1984 amendment, each household member has to spend at least ¥30,000. In other words, only expenditure exceeding ¥30,000 by a household member is counted toward the calculation for high-cost medical care benefits. If three members of a household spend ¥28,000 each in a month, that household would not qualify for any benefit even though the household as a whole pays ¥84,000.

[5] These clearing organizations are the Social Insurance Medical Care Fee Payment Fund for the employees' insurance and the Federation of National Insurance Association in each prefecture for the insurance for the self-employed and retirees.

[6] The review process has a number of weaknesses. The auditing database is not computerized, and data for a given patient cannot be readily linked across time. This makes it difficult to identify many abuses—for example multiple charges over time for a single test or procedure (Araki, 1993).

[7] The main players in this stage of negotiation are *Koseisho*, Ministry of Finance, Japanese Medical Association (JMA), representatives of payers, and politicians.

[8] One prominent critic of the Ministry of Health and Welfare (*Koseisho*) policies, Niki (1993), has called *Chuikyo* a de facto "fig leaf," mechanically following *Koseisho* policy.

[9] The government reports that informal charges in geriatric hospitals average ¥22,500 per patient month, but some independent researchers believe the value of such payments to be much higher (Niki, 1992).

[10] *Koseisho* estimates that the amount averages ¥22,500 per patient month, although Niki (1992) claims that the amount is two to three times higher than the reported rate.

[11] The following analysis follows Nakanishi et al. (1993).

[12] In effect, the shift in funding may have been nothing more than an accounting convention designed to conceal attempts to determine the level of government contributions to the system.

[13] The 1982 distribution of health services costs was estimated by Kikuchi (1985). We used the same method to estimate 1989 costs.

[14] Because "other factors" is a residual term, any errors in the measurements of the other three variables are incorporated into this variable.

[15] We recognize the ability of macroeconomic policies to affect inflation rates.

[16] Ministry of Health and Welfare (1990 *Kanja Chosa*). This one-day survey was conducted at each medical facility on one of three days: October 16, 17, or 18.

[17] Chuo Shakai Hoken Iryo Kyogikai (1990). The net monthly revenue of *kaigyo-i* does not include wages for nonpaid labor (i.e., a doctor's spouse or other family member), so the figure may overestimate true income.

[18] The coefficient of variation is calculated by the formula:

$$CV = \frac{s}{\overline{X}}$$

where $\overline{X}$ is the mean and s is the standard deviation.

[19] Until 1970, we exclude Okinawa Prefecture. Since 1972, we include Okinawa Prefecture.

[20] Using aggregated data, Urushi (1986) calculated the coefficient of variation. His study excluded Okinawa Prefecture. He calculated the coefficient of variation for five different categories of doctors: (1) all doctors, (2) *kaigyo-i* (clinic owners and hospital owners) and *kinmu-i* (those employed either at a hospital or a clinic), (3) *kaigyo-i*, (4) *kinmu-i*, and (5) doctors working in teaching hospitals. Even though it was not conclusive whether the degree of inequality had increased or decreased for all doctors, for *kaigyo-i* the degree of inequality declined steadily until 1972 and has since been almost constant. For *kinmu-i* (doctors working in clinics or hospitals), Urushi found the degree of inequality increased during the period. His conclusion is probably due to the fact that he excluded *kinmu-i* working at teaching hospitals.

[21] In 1972, the United States returned Okinawa Prefecture to Japan, and this may explain the small increase in coefficient variation in 1972.

[22] Geriatric hospitals without "formal approval," those with a large percentage (60%) of elderly patients, also exist. In 1989, there were 99 such hospitals. Because these hospitals are subject to a lower fee schedule than are those "with approval," the thrust of government policy seems to be to force geriatric hospitals without approval to choose between becoming a geriatric hospital "with approval" or a general hospital that has fewer elderly patients. At present, the former is more financially advantageous.

[23] Geriatric hospitals are reimbursed at a progressively lower rate for hospitalizations (i.e., fees go down as length of patient stay increases). Some argue that this geriatric fee is lower than those for nongeriatric general hospitals. See, for example, Niki (1990).

[24] Shakai Hoken Kenkyujo (Social Development Research Center) (1993). "Byoin keiei no do ko" (Trends in hospital management), *Shakai Hoken Junpo*, no. 1791, p. 39.

[25] For example, in 1991, the Medical Service Law was amended to allow tertiary care hospitals, such as university teaching hospitals, to see only those outpatients referred from smaller hospitals and clinics. Such hospitals, *tokutei kino byoin*, will be allowed to charge a differential (i.e., higher) rate for complicated procedures. In the future, the Japanese system may move toward the type of referral system seen, for instance, in Great Britain (i.e., the gatekeeper system).

[26] In order to provide a financial incentive to doctors to refer their patients, *Koseisho* introduced a special fee for referral service, *shinryo joho teikyoryo* (medical information providers' fee), in 1985.

Part I

Patient Behavior

People thinking about the demand for health care for the first time often believe that health care as a good is fundamentally different from other goods. In many ways, this intuition is correct: health care has features that distinguish it from the demand for other economic goods and services. For example, patients often have difficulty evaluating the technical quality of the services they have purchased. Also, patients generally cannot predict their future medical needs. This uncertainty can have important economic consequences because doctors know more about their patients' health than the patients do. Financing arrangements introduce nonlinearities into the pricing of medical care. For example, deductibles, which are a common part of many health insurance plans, may be viewed as a fixed cost to the patient.

Despite these considerations, health care demand is subject to economic forces and thus is accessible to economic analysis. In fact, the previously mentioned considerations, which purportedly make the demand for health care unique, are also characteristics of other goods or services that are undeniably amenable to economic analysis. Take, for instance, automobile maintenance. Most consumers cannot evaluate authoritatively the technical quality of the services rendered. The informational asymmetry between the mechanic and the vehicle owner is similar to that between the doctor and the patient. Forecasting expected future demand for maintenance services often can be problematic for owners. And, finally, warranties insuring against manufacturing and material flaws often result in nonlinear prices. Despite these analogous considerations, some authors have subjected to rigorous economic analysis the demand for automobile maintenance.

Another argument commonly raised against applying economics to health care demand is that because patients seek health care in order to improve their health status, and in some cases to avoid death, monetary considerations are not a factor in their decisions. Life is the most precious of all possessions, some argue, so it is unrealistic to believe that people are influenced by such petty considerations as the price they must pay to live. In other words, people display a lexicographic preference for life over other economic commodities; to place a price on life is a meaningless activity.

The largest contribution that an economic analysis of the demand for health care can bring to the evaluation of the preceding argument is that empirical and statistical tests can be constructed to examine its truth. If the preceding argument is true, then estimates of the effect of price on the demand for medical care should be zero. But if people are responsive to price in constructing their demand for health care, the lexicographic ordering previously suggested must be rejected. The following chapters further investigate this empirical issue.

Estimating Demand Curves

Estimating demand curves is conceptually easy: one simply varies prices and observes how people respond. The main object of the measurement is to learn the price elasticity of demand, which indicates the slope of the demand curve. Under most circumstances, however, one cannot conduct a proper scientific experiment with a control group, experimental groups, and subjects who are randomized into one of the categories. Instead, one generally has a data set consisting of observations at some level of aggregation on prices and quantities demanded at those prices, as well as ancillary characteristics of the unit of observation. With historical data of this type, one must combine economic theory with the appropriate econometric method to measure the price elasticity.

There are a number of important issues to consider in the econometric estimation of demand curves. For example, the appropriate technique to estimate demand curves with aggregate data is different from that required for consumer-level data. Another critical issue has to do with the fact that there may be unobserved quality differences distinguishing two goods in consumers' eyes that the analyst does not observe. The good or service may be available only to a select portion of the population, but the demand curve for the whole population may be the object of interest. Finally, the source of the price variation that allows a demand curve in the first place must be considered. For example, if it arises from differences in product quality, the implications for the estimation are quite different from those when it arises from some other exogenous reason. There are econometric methods that are sometimes appropriate to deal with all of these issues.

Data Limitations

Analysts often have access only to aggregated data, such as sample means, and very little information on the joint distributions of the random variables that are critical to estimating parameters of interest, such as the price elasticity of demand. Such data restrictions often arise because government agencies are reluctant to release individual-level demand information due to concern over violation of privacy rights.

Though such limitations often seem to impede accurate estimation of demand elasticities, policymakers need to have some idea about these parameter values. It is often noted, only partially in jest, that assumptions serve as an effective substitute for data in the social sciences. In this case, some rather stringent assumptions about the shape of individual-level demand functions allow measurement of the desired elasticities.

Suppose that individuals $i = 1 \ldots n$ have demand functions, q_i, for a good that depends on prices, p_i, income, y_i, and socioeconomic demand "shifters," x_i. Thus, $q_i = f(p_i, y_i, x_i)$ for $i = 1 \ldots n$. Heterogeneity among individuals is introduced through variation in the arguments. Suppose further that these individuals make up the entire market for this particular good. Then the market demand is given by

$$q = \sum_{i=1}^{n} f(p_i, y_i, x_i). \tag{I-1}$$

Notice that knowledge of the market demand depends upon the whole distribution of x, y, and p and not just on their mean values. Stronger assumptions are required to make the demand function estimable with the aggregate data on hand. One possibility is to assume that f is linear with no cross-effects: $f(p_i, y_i, x_i) = a_1 p_i + a_2 y_i + x_i' a_3$, where a_1, a_2, and a_3 are parameters to be estimated. Another possibility is to assume that these cross-terms exist, but that there is no heterogeneity in one of the variables across individuals. For example, if $p_i = p \ \forall i = 1 \ldots n$, then the following specification, $f(p, y_i, x_i) = a_1(p) + a_2(p)y_i + x_i' a_3(p)$, yields a market demand function that depends only on the mean values of x

and y while allowing for cross-terms with price.[1] Finally, if one assumes both that $p_i = p \; \forall i$ and that there are no cross-terms, then consumers can have different elasticities of demand: $f(p, y_i, x_i) = a_{1i}p + a_2 y_i + x'_i a_3$. In this case, one can measure the average elasticity with aggregate data. In all cases, elasticities are identified by price variation across markets, rather than variation across individuals. Which assumption is most appropriate depends on the particular situation at hand.

Equipped with these additional assumptions, one can measure the desired microlevel effect from aggregate data. The most commonly used econometric technique when estimating demand elasticities is some variation of ordinary least squares. When disaggregated data are unavailable and information on such parameters is necessary for informed policy-making, such assumptions and methods are appropriate. Furthermore, these estimates can often serve as a check on the estimates derived using more disaggregated data and different statistical techniques.

Identifying Price Effects

If all consumers faced the same price in each time period, one could not estimate the effect of a price change on the demand for a good. Such an exercise would be analogous to a physicist attempting to measure the impact of velocity on the position of a body if all observable bodies were stationary. Although it is conceivable in principle that velocity changes might affect the relative positions of the bodies in the system, one could never measure the magnitude of this effect without observing a change in the relative positions of the bodies in response to a velocity change that under the hypothesis never occurs.

In economics the two most common sources of price variation used to measure price elasticities correspond to the two most common types of data structures: cross-sectional and time series variation. Panel data sets display both types of variation by following the same set of individuals over time. In this book mostly cross-section data sets are used, though time series variation will be briefly discussed.

Time series variation is appropriate where the price of the commodity under consideration changes for exogenous reasons relative only to other commodities in the economy. For example, if price variation arises due to cost increases in the relative price of the good in question, then price can most likely be considered exogenous. However, if the price shifts over time are correlated with shifts in unobserved variables that influence demand, then price is endogenous, and ordinary least squares estimates will yield biased estimates of the price elasticity. In this case, the appropriate estimation technique is instrumental variables, but an appropriate instrument must be found. Invariably this will be an observed random variable that enters the supply equation but does not enter the demand equation.[2]

Cross-sectional variation in prices may arise for a variety of reasons, but the same condition applies to the use of this variability to identify price elasticity: The variation must arise exogenously (i.e., price must be uncorrelated with unobserved determinants of demand). One example of exogenous cross-sectional variation used in two of the chapters in this section is geographical price variation. In determining whether using this to identify price effects is valid, one must ask the question: Does the geographical price variation arise for exogenous reasons, or does it come from factors correlated with unobserved determinants of the demand for medical care? If the price paid for doctor visits varies by region because of practice style variations, for example, the exogeneity of price can be maintained. But if it arises from unobserved geographical variations in illness prevalence, then the price variable is likely to be endogenous, because the presence of illness clearly belongs in a demand function for medical care.

Structural Econometric Modeling

A great advantage of using microlevel data in estimating demand relationships is that the econometrician can consider more complex and realistic data generation processes than those postulated when only aggregate data are available. In the latter case variations on the linear model are the only possible models that are theoretically consistent with demand functions generated at an individual level. With microlevel data, some of the stringent assumptions required to obtain linear demand curves from the utility maximization problem can be relaxed, more nonlinear data generation processes can be considered. The aggregation problem can be sidestepped altogether. Microlevel data allow more realistic interpretations of parameter estimates, in addition to allowing for accurate estimation. Chapters 3 and 4 in this section provide good examples of the types of models that are possible when disaggregated data are available.

An important difficulty in estimating the demand for medical care is identifying exactly what is being consumed. Product differentiation is an important feature of medical markets, as it is of other

service industries. One possible measure of the demand for outpatient medical care is number of visits in a fixed period. One may
argue that such a measurement ignores product differentiation
issues: Is a visit to the doctor for a cold the same as a visit for a
sports injury? Is a visit to a small clinic the same product as a visit
to a large hospital? In the following chapters, we try at least implicitly to accommodate the analysis to these issues. For example, in
Chapter 3, we estimate separate demand curves for outpatient care
for patients in different disease categories. In Chapter 4 we directly
test the degree of product differentiation among small, large, and
teaching hospitals.

However, one can carry this effort to disaggregate commodities
too far. Efforts at specifically describing the characteristics of differentiated products within a particular category should respect the
availability to consumers of product information. For example,
treating a visit to a hospital with magnetic resonance imaging (MRI)
facilities as different from a visit to an otherwise similar hospital
without MRI facilities may or may not make sense in light of
consumer information constraints. Fortunately, this designation of
product differentiation does not have to be an arbitrary one. It is
possible to measure statistically whether consumers respond to certain product characteristics, as we do in Chapter 4.

In Chapter 2, we present an aggregate-level study of the demand
for outpatient care in Japan. This study uses ordinary least squares
to estimate the price elasticity of demand for medical care while
controlling for income and other socioeconomic and health variables. The unit of analysis is the prefecture, and the identification of
the price effect is based on prefecture-level variation in the average
copayment level. The main outcome of this study is that the demand
for outpatient care is downward-sloping with an elasticity of -0.133.
This result challenges the view that patients have a lexicographic
preference for health.

Chapter 3 examines the same question using a different methodology and individual rather than aggregate data. Using the time
between outpatient visits as a measure of the demand for health
care, we fit a hazard model to the data to estimate the price elasticity of demand. We obtain separate estimates of this figure for
different diagnostic categories and determine the influence of heterogenous insurance plan membership on it. The estimate of the
price elasticity of demand given in this chapter, ranging from -0.12
to -0.54 for different diagnostic groups, is remarkably close to the
one obtained in Chapter 2.

Chapter 4 focuses on the demand for inpatient care in Japan. As explained in the chapter, due to financing arrangements peculiar to the Japanese universal health care system, inpatients pay virtually nothing per day for hospital visits. Hence, we argue that patients select different types of hospitals based on quality considerations. Using a nested logit model of demand, we estimate the degree of substitutability among small, medium, and large hospitals and teaching hospitals. The result that product differentiation is not an important factor in estimating inpatient medical demand makes the assumption implicit in Chapters 2 and 3—that it is not a feature of outpatient demand—more plausible. Finally, we measure what dimensions of hospital quality are important to patients seeking care. We conclude that patients value staffing ratios biased toward skilled practitioners more highly than high-technology medical equipment.

Notes

[1] See Deaton and Muellbauer (1980, p. 150). This source also contains a more thorough discussion of the aggregation problem than can be presented here.

[2] See Greene (1993) for a discussion of the formal conditions required for identifying such models.

2

Aggregate Demand for Medical Care

This chapter analyzes the impact of income and insurance copayments on utilization of medical care under Japan's national health insurance system (*Kokumin Kenkohoken*, or *Kokuho*). We wish to determine whether universal coverage in Japan has eliminated the income effect on the demand for medical care. Our multivariate regression analysis of annual utilization of health care for *Kokuho* subscribers measures the impact of copayment rates, per capita income levels, and other demand-side variables on utilization. Under a truly egalitarian medical care delivery system, income should not be a significant predictor of the annual utilization of medical services, holding the health effect on the demand for medical care constant.

Other studies of the income effect on medical care under universal health insurance systems have analyzed health outcomes rather than service utilization. For example, despite rising real incomes, Great Britain has a differential in mortality rate between social classes, which has increased consistently since the 1930s despite the introduction of universal coverage in 1945 (Wilkinson, 1986). In Scandinavia (Anderson, 1991) and Sweden (Callthorp, 1989), age-standardized mortality measures differ significantly among employment groups.

Disentangling inequities in health outcomes caused by income constraints from those caused by people's preferences for medical care or by personal habits that may affect health outcomes is dif-

This chapter is based on: Kupor, S., Liu, Y.C., Lee, J., and Yoshikawa, A. 1995. "The Effect of Copayments and Income on the Utilization of Medical Care by Subscribers to Japan's National Health Insurance System," *International Journal of Health Services* 25(2). This revised version is published with the permission of the Baywood Publishing Company.

ficult. Health outcomes may be more strongly influenced by the level of technology, industrial development, and nonmedical considerations (e.g., diet) than by medical care utilization. In addition, differentials in microlevel health outcomes (excluding crude, aggregate measures such as age-specific mortality) attributable to income in developed countries are generally considered insignificant (Fuchs, 1986; Wilkinson, 1992), confirming the intuition that the level of economic development is a better predictor of health outcomes than is income per se. Thus, in an industrialized society such as Japan, we expect that aggregate measures of health outcomes will not vary significantly, even among prefectures with lower per capita incomes. But because medical care utilization often involves a direct out-of-pocket expenditure, per capita income and copayments may predict utilization rates. For these reasons, we analyze utilization of medical services, rather than health outcomes.

As is discussed more fully in Chapter 3, few controlled studies on the effect of copayments and income levels on medical service utilization have been reported. A series of studies conducted by Cherkin, Grothaus, and Wagner (1990) on utilization rates for subscribers to the Washington State health maintenance organization reveals differential impacts of increases in copayment rates across different populations and medical services. For employed persons, a $5 office visit copayment has an insignificant impact on utilization of preventive care services, but the number of primary care visits and specialty care physician visits declines significantly (Cherkin, Grothaus, and Wagner, 1989). Another study finds that the magnitude of the copayment effect on primary care visits does not vary between high- and low-income individuals (Cherkin, Grothaus, and Wagner, 1992).

Background

Enrolling over one-third (35.29%) of Japanese residents in 1990, *Kokuho* is the largest of the Japanese health insurance societies. *Kokuho* is further subdivided into three systems. Two are run by municipal authorities and insurance associations that cater to the self-employed (i.e., farmers, doctors, lawyers, and carpenters). The third group, designed for retirees, is covered under its own system. Under *Kokuho*, both principal subscribers and their dependents must pay 30% of the cost of all medical services. Retirees face a 20% copayment for inpatient and outpatient medical services, whereas their dependents shoulder a 20% copayment for inpatient services and a 30% copayment for outpatient services (see Table 3-1).

We analyze the impact of copayment rates and prefectural per capita income levels on the utilization of medical services under Japan's national health insurance system. Using data collected from *Kokuho* enrollees, we measure demand in terms of the utilization rate—the number of health insurance claims per 100 insured *Kokuho* members. Among *Kokuho* members, the overall utilization rate has tripled in the past 30 years, though rates vary greatly among Japan's 47 prefectures. In addition to analyzing the income and copayment effects on medical care utilization, we introduce several other variables, including age, number of medical and dental clinics, number of hospital beds, number of doctors and dentists, and population density. We include such variables in our model to help explain additional variations in medical utilization across different periods of time and different prefectures. We run multiple regressions for 1984 and 1989 to encompass various changes in the copayments instituted by the Japanese government. Subsequent regressions analyze the model with the prefectures grouped by per capita income levels and by the proportion of elderly over age 65.

Medical Utilization Among Kokuho Members
Increasing from 257.9 claims per 100 in 1961 to 770.2 claims per 100 in 1989, the combined utilization rate for inpatient, outpatient, and dental services for *Kokuho* members has more than tripled since the advent of the national insurance system (Ministry of Health and Welfare, 1961–1989, *Kokumin Kenkohoken Jigyonenpo*). The rapid increase in utilization is not attributable solely to the introduction of universal health insurance in 1961. It began prior to the enactment of universal insurance as various regional governments began to offer extended medical coverage.

The copayments required of *Kokuho* members have also changed over time. At the inception of the universal insurance system, *Kokuho* members paid a 50% copayment. In 1968, the copayment was reduced to 30%. As a result of financial assistance programs and the 1973 copayment ceilings, the real copayment has decreased for some groups over the past 30 years.

Model, Data, and Variables

Model
Several Japanese researchers have investigated the predictors of medical care utilization among subscribers to the Japanese insurance system. Senoo's (1985) cross-section study of 1980–1981 *Kokuho* utilization closely parallels our approach. In light of the

major policy changes enacted by the Japanese government since 1980 (i.e., the 1982 Health and Medical Service Law and the establishment of a retirees' insurance system within *Kokuho*, among others), we intend our work to serve as a complement to Senoo's.

Using the utilization rate as the dependent variable, Senoo finds a negative, statistically significant relation between copayment and inpatient utilization for both 1980 and 1981.[1] Outpatient and dental care utilization rates are not significantly affected by the copayment. As might be expected under the Japanese universal health insurance system, Senoo finds no significant effect of income on medical care utilization.[2] Senoo also analyzes the copayment and income effects using time series data for the years 1955 to 1979. The model yields a significant and negative relation between the copayment rate and medical care utilization. Income is found to be a positive, significant predictor of medical care utilization.[3]

We employ a series of multiple regression models designed to measure the influence of real per capita income, copayment, and other demand- and supply-side variables on the utilization rate of medical care services in the *Kokuho* system for two years. We estimate equations for the overall utilization, inpatient services, dental care, and outpatient services for 1984 and 1989. By examining differences across prefectures at a single point in time, we can, in effect, hold other factors (e.g., medical technology) fairly constant.

The first set of regression equations includes all *Kokuho* members in 1984 and 1989. We stratify the data according to real per capita income, allowing us to group the 47 prefectures into three different income classifications: lowest, middle, and highest per capita incomes. We run regressions on each of the three groups to isolate the effect of copayments on various income level groupings. We then generate a separate grouping according to the proportion of *Kokuho* members over age 65 and run regressions for each of the three ordered groupings. In each equation, utilization of medical services (total, inpatient, dental, or outpatient) per 100 members is the dependent variable. We obtain heteroskedasticity-consistent estimates of the standard errors.

There are some advantages to our approach. First, by grouping the prefectures into three categories according to relative per capita incomes, we can delineate more clearly the impact of copayments on utilization with fewer statistical assumptions than Senoo's study. In the aggregate, the wealthier prefectures may mask the utilization differentials introduced by changes in the copayments in the less wealthy prefectures. However, isolating the poorer areas may make such differences discernible. Second, by grouping the prefectures according to the proportion of *Kokuho* members over age 65, we can also isolate the age effect on the utilization of medical care, again with fewer assumptions. This stratification of the data enables us to disaggregate further the utilization of medical care into its financially induced and health status-induced components.

Data

The data used in this study are aggregated data gleaned from various surveys conducted by the Japanese government in 1984 and 1989. The utilization rate, income, and age variables for *Kokuho* members are from three surveys specifically designed to study *Kokuho* subscribers. *Kokumin Kenkohoken Jigyonenpo* is an annual reporting of the financial performance of *Kokuho*. *Kokumin Kenkohoken Jittai Chosa* surveys *Kokuho* members' income, occupation, and so forth, by randomly selecting 1 out of every 500 *Kokuho* households. The survey is conducted each May, and a total of 33,265 households were included in 1989. *Kokumin Kenkohoken Iryokyufu Jittai Chosa* details medical care provided *Kokuho* members each May. The survey randomly selects 1 out of every 50 inpatient cases, 1 out of every 500 outpatient cases, and 1 out of every 500 dental cases. We obtain data not specific to *Kokuho* members from *Iryo Shisetsu Chosa*, a triannual survey of Japanese medical facilities, and from *Nippon Tokei Nenkan*, the Japanese annual statistical abstract.

Variables

DEPENDENT VARIABLE: UTILIZATION RATE

The utilization rate (UR) is defined as the number of health insurance claims per 100 *Kokuho* members in a given year. Aside from an individual's health status, equilibrium UR may be affected by personal preferences for medical care, physician behavior, seasonal trends in illness incidence, and access to medical care (due to both proximity and financial constraints). All other things being equal, we predict that UR will decrease with an improvement in health status, an increase in the number of physician holidays, a decrease in proximity to health care facilities, and an increase in financial barriers to care.

There are problems associated with this definition of utilization. Because insurance claims are submitted once a month, a patient hospitalized for two months with the same illness will be entered as two claims. If a patient moves from an outpatient to an inpatient setting in a single month, two claims will be submitted. If a patient visits two different hospitals for the same illness in one month, two claims will be submitted. Such multiple consultations were alleged to be quite common among the elderly, particularly between 1973 and 1982 when all medical services were free for them.

Data collection may also create certain problems. Claims are aggregated according to the location of the facility which provided the service. However, the data on numbers of *Kokuho* members are categorized by the municipality of patient residence. For example, a patient who lives in Osaka Prefecture and seeks care in Hokkaido Prefecture will depress the utilization ratio in Osaka and augment the utilization ratio in Hokkaido. Thus, care received outside the patient's area of residence may bias the results by creating situations in which the denominator and numerator in the UR calculation do not match for a particular prefecture.

COPAYMENT

The copayment rate (CP%) has changed several times since 1961. *Kokuho* members originally paid a 50% copayment, but the rate was lowered in 1968 to 30%. Retirees originally paid 80% for all care, whereas their dependents contributed 70% for outpatient and dental care and 80% for inpatient care. The 1973 High Cost Medical Care Benefits Law instituted a maximum monthly copayment for *Kokuho* members of ¥63,000 ($583), or ¥33,600 ($311) for low-income households. To qualify under the law as amended in 1984, each member of a household must spend at least ¥33,600 on medical services. Only monthly expenditures in excess of ¥33,600 per member are counted toward the benefits.

With such a ceiling on copayments, the actual copayment rate (ACP%) today is less than 30%. As a patient receives expensive inpatient care that exceeds ¥63,000 in copayments, ACP% will approach zero. In 1989, the average ACP% for all *Kokuho* members for all services combined was 20.3%.

In our analyses, we use the amount of copayment per patient day (CP_i), in each prefecture i as an independent variable. We also attempt to analyze outpatient, dental, and inpatient care separately. However, separate data for daily inpatient ($^{in}ACP\%_i$), dental ($^{dental}ACP\%_i$), and outpatient ($^{out}ACP\%_i$) actual copayments in prefecture i are unavailable. Only aggregate $ACP\%_i$ data for prefecture i are available. Thus, we estimate CP_i for inpatient, dental, and outpatient care by assuming that the actual copayments for each type of medical services are equal. The copayment per patient day is thus calculated by multiplying $ACP\%_i$ by the total cost of medical care per patient day (CD_i).

Under this assumption, our estimates for CP_i may be downwardly biased for inpatient care and upwardly biased for outpatient and dental care. For example, our method estimates the 1989 $^{in}CP_i$ for Tokyo as ¥57,000, or 15% of the average cost per inpatient case. However, $ACP\%_i$ for Tokyo in 1989 was 17%, slightly higher than our estimate. Similar comparisons for dental and outpatient care reveal our estimates to be slightly higher than the true average copayments.

OTHER INDEPENDENT VARIABLES

The regression equations also include for each prefecture the percentage of *Kokuho* members over age 65, per capita income, population density, number of beds and clinics per 1,000 persons, and number of doctors and dentists per 1,000 persons. We include the number of physicians, dentists, beds, and clinics because increases in such variables may decrease travel costs and waiting. Population density is also believed to influence utilization rates (Senoo, 1985). Table 2-1 provides a complete glossary of all regression variables.

Results

Regression on Combined Data

The results for all *Kokuho* members for both 1984 and 1989 reveal a significant ($p < 0.05$), negative effect of copayment on all medical services utilization (see Tables 2-2 and 2-3). The copayment coefficients are smallest for inpatient service utilization and greatest for outpatient services. Positive and significant income effects are noted for dental care utilization only. Finally, the number of beds per 1,000 *Kokuho* members is the only consistently significant supply-side variable, positively predicting the utilization of inpatient care only.

Regression on Stratified Income Groups

We subsequently group individual prefectures into the bottom, middle, and upper third according to levels of real per capita income. In the bottom third, copayments exhibit a negative and significant effect on the utilization of inpatient medical care only.

Table 2-1
Glossary of Regression Variables

$^{Total}UR_j$	Total utilization[1]
$^{In}UR_j$	Inpatient utilization
$^{Out}UR_j$	Outpatient utilization
$^{Dental}UR_j$	Dental utilization
$^{Total}CP_j$	Total copayment[2]
$^{In}CP_j$	Inpatient copayment
$^{Out}CP_j$	Outpatient copayment
$^{Dental}CP_j$	Dental copayment
Income	Adjusted per capita income
Bed	Beds/1000 members
NHB	Nursing home beds/1000 members (1989 only)
Doctor	Doctors/1000 members
Clinic	Clinics/1000 members
Dentist	Dentists/1000 members
Dental Clinic	Dental clinics/1000 members
Density	Population density/1000 members
Age 65	Percentage of members age 65 and over

Note: Suffix $_j$ denotes the year (1984 or 1989).
[1] Utilization is defined as the number of health insurance claims submitted per 100 members of the national health insurance system.
[2] Copayment is figure on a per patient day basis.

As with the combined data, the number of beds per 1,000 *Kokuho* members is a positive and significant predictor of inpatient service utilization only. The middle income classification displays small and significant negative copayment effects on the utilization of inpatient medical services. Number of beds continues to show a significant impact on the utilization of inpatient medical care. The upper third income group yields results similar to the other two. Copayment exhibits a significant negative effect on utilization of inpatient services. The number of beds also displays a significant positive effect on inpatient utilization. Although we run the full model for the income stratifications, we report only results for consistently significant variables (Table 2-4).

The differences in the copayment effects among the three income groups are small. Inpatient utilization in the lowest income group shows the greatest sensitivity to copayment, and it is least affected in the highest income group. This result is consistent with the identification of an income effect on dental care utilization in the lowest income classification.

Table 2-2
Regression Results: Combined Data (1984)

Total	Coefficient	Inpatient	Coefficient
$^{Total}CP_{84}$	$-0.19^{\dagger}$	$^{In}CP_{84}$	$-0.01^{\dagger}$
Income	$0.22^{\dagger}$	Income	0.003
Bed	0.17	Bed	$1.24^{\dagger}$
Doctor	19.48	Doctor	-2.45^*
Dentist	51.90	Density	-0.00005
Dental Clinic	-3.23^{**}	Age 65	14.73^*
Clinic	$3.01^{\dagger}$		
Density	$-0.02^{\dagger}$		
Age 65	-84.11		

Outpatient	Coefficient	Dental	Coefficient
$^{Out}CP_{84}$	$-0.19^{\dagger}$	$^{Dental}CP_{84}$	$-0.04^{\dagger}$
Income	$0.17^{\dagger}$	Income	$0.05^{\dagger}$
Clinic	$2.42^{\dagger}$	Dental Clinic	0.38
Doctor	2.79	Dentist	18.23
Density	$-0.02^{\dagger}$	Density	-0.003^{**}
Age 65	-68.96	Age 65	-16.32

Significance based upon robust t-stats.
* denotes significance at the 10% level.
** denotes significance at the 5% level.
† denotes significance at the 1% level.

Stratified Regression

As with income, we order the prefectures into three groups sorted by proportions of *Kokuho* members age 65 and over in each prefecture. In the lowest third, we note significant copayment and income effects for dental service utilization only. The middle third also reveals significant income effects on dental care. Copayment has a negative impact on the utilization rate, whereas income positively impacts utilization. Significant and negative copayment effects on inpatient utilization are also displayed for the middle third. The grouping with the greatest proportion of elderly members reveals a similar income effect on dental care utilization, and significant copayment effects negatively affect inpatient and outpatient utilization rates. The number of beds is the only consistently significant supply-side variable and positively affects only inpatient utilization for the eldest grouping. As with the income stratification, we run the full model, but report results only for consistently significant variables.

Table 2-3
Regression Results: Combined Data (1989)

Total	Coefficient	Inpatient	Coefficient
$^{Total}CP_{89}$	$-0.18^{†}$	$^{In}CP_{89}$	$-0.009^{†}$
Income	0.02	Income	0.003
Bed	-1.33	Bed	$1.77^{†}$
NHB	-3.71	NHB	0.36
Doctor	-24.04	Doctor	$-3.71**$
Dentist	$299.68^{†}$	Density	0.17
Dental Clinic	0.56	Age 65	$38.14^{†}$
Clinic	0.12		
Density	2.81		
Age 65	$1061.95^{†}$		

Outpatient	Coefficient	Dental	Coefficient
$^{Out}CP_{89}$	$-0.12^{†}$	$^{Dental}CP_{89}$	$-0.05^{†}$
Income	0.01	Income	$0.04^{†}$
Clinic	$0.95*$	Dental Clinic	$0.38**$
NHB	-3.59	Dentist	$45.06*$
Doctor	$-51.53*$	Density	-2.20
Density	7.12	Age 65	11.53
Age 65	$992.50^{†}$		

Significance based upon robust t-stats.
* denotes significance at the 10% level.
** denotes significance at the 5% level.
† denotes significance at the 1% level.

Differences Between 1984 and 1989

The combined regression data reveal more consistently negative copayment coefficients in outpatient utilization in 1984 than in 1989. Significant positive income effects on outpatient utilization are seen only in 1984. When the data in the relative income groupings are analyzed, the 1984 copayment effect for inpatient utilization for the middle income group is more negative than that in 1989. For outpatient care, this situation is reversed. In the highest income group, significant negative copayment coefficients for outpatient care and significant positive income coefficients for dental utilization are realized only in 1984. In the elderly population stratification, the 1984 copayment and income effects are uniformly greater in absolute value than those in 1989. Significant positive income effects on outpatient utilization in the lowest and oldest population groupings

Table 2-4
Regression Coefficients for Income Grouping

Variable	Bottom 1/3	Middle 1/3	Upper 1/3
Copayment			
$^{Total}CP_{89}$	$-0.015^{\dagger}$	$-0.01^{\dagger}$	$-0.008^{\dagger}$
$^{In}CP_{84}$	$-0.009^{\dagger}$	$-0.02^{\dagger}$	$-0.01^{\dagger}$
$^{Out}CP_{89}$	-0.12^{**}	$-0.28^{\dagger}$	-0.14^{*}
Income			
$^{Dental}Income_{89}$	$0.08^{\dagger}$	$0.07^{\dagger}$	0.03^{**}
Beds			
$^{In}Bed_{89}$	$1.40^{\dagger}$	$1.81^{\dagger}$	$2.48^{\dagger}$
$^{In}Bed_{84}$	$1.00^{\dagger}$	$1.33^{\dagger}$	$1.98^{\dagger}$

Significance based upon robust t-stats.
* denotes significance at the 10% level.
** denotes significance at the 5% level.
† denotes significance at the 1% level.

are seen only in 1984, whereas the income effect on dental utilization in the middle group is greater in 1984 than in 1989. The middle group also displays a significant negative copayment effect on inpatient utilization for 1984 only.

Discussion and Conclusions

The results of our cross-sectional regression analysis indicate that for 1984 and 1989, the copayments exhibit a significantly negative effect on the utilization of inpatient, dental, and outpatient medical care. As measured by the absolute value of the copayment coefficients, utilization of outpatient medical care is most sensitive to copayment. The magnitude of the copayment effects on inpatient, dental, and outpatient care is consistent with our expectations. Assuming that the decision to undergo inpatient treatment may be more influenced by the physician, whereas the decision to seek outpatient or dental care may be more influenced by the individual, one would expect the copayment effect on inpatient care to be the lowest. That is, a physician's recommendation to receive inpatient care, whether supply- or health-induced, is likely to mollify the importance of financial concerns. The income effect on dental care utilization follows from this reasoning. Dental care most closely re-

Table 2-5
Regession for Age >65 Grouping*

	Bottom 1/3	Middle 1/3	Upper 1/3
Copayment			
$^{Dental}CP_{89}$	−0.10†	−0.03†	−0.02
$^{Dental}CP_{84}$	−0.09†	−0.03	−0.01
$^{In}CP_{89}$	−0.007**	−0.01†	−0.01†
$^{In}CP_{84}$	−0.003	−0.01†	0.01†
$^{Out}CP_{89}$	−0.13	−0.09	−0.24†
$^{Out}CP_{84}$	−0.05	−0.08	−0.25†
Income			
$^{Dental}Income_{89}$	0.04†	0.02†	0.06†
$^{Dental}Income_{89}$	0.02†	0.06†	0.05†
Bed			
$^{In}Bed_{89}$	1.23†	2.20†	1.44†
$^{In}Bed_{84}$	1.69†	1.59†	1.69†

Significance based upon robust t-stats.
* denotes significance at the 10% level.
** denotes significance at the 5% level.
† denotes significance at the 1% level.

sembles a preventive intervention, so one might expect individuals with higher incomes to utilize greater amounts of dental care.

Our results are consistent with those reported in the Rand studies (Manning et al., 1987). The Rand researchers described the copayment effect across income groups as a shallow U-shaped response curve; that is, utilization of combined inpatient and outpatient services was high for the lowest and highest income groups and low for the middle income group. When the copayment effect across different income groups was disaggregated into inpatient and outpatient care, the effect was positive for outpatient care and negative for inpatient care. Although we noted negative copayment coefficients for both inpatient and outpatient services, the influence of the copayments on utilization was similar to those found in the Rand studies: Inpatient care is less sensitive than outpatient care to copayment rates.

When we control for income stratification across prefectures, only inpatient utilization is consistently affected by the copayment rates. As might be expected, the lowest income group displays the greatest copayment coefficient, whereas the group with the highest income is least affected by the inpatient copayment rate. This result highlights the connection between income levels and copayment effects that was clouded in the first set of regression equations: Groups with lower incomes are more sensitive to higher copayment rates for inpatient care. Our finding of an income effect on dental utilization in the lowest income group reinforces our findings in the first set of regressions. Once again, utilization of a typically nonemergency medical procedure seems to be depressed in lower income groups.

These findings underscore the potential limits of both the Cherkin, Grothaus, and Wagner (1992) and the Rand (Manning et al., 1987) studies. Although both studies report that the copayment effect does not vary across income groups, the assignment of individuals to different income groupings may cause the lack of differentiation of copayment effects. In particular, Cherkin, Grothaus, and Wagner (1992) use individuals in families that qualified for full employer-based health insurance, meaning that there were no bona fide low-income persons. Similarly, in the Rand study, the upper limit of each family's annual out-of-pocket expenses was related to the family's income. As Cherkin, Grothaus, and Wagner (1992) note in their review of the Rand experiment, one cannot conclude that, had the copayment amounts been assigned without regard to household income, differential impacts on utilization would not have been realized.

The regression results stratified by age support popular notions about the use of hospital services by the elderly in Japan. The group with the highest proportion of enrollees age 65 and over was the only one to have significant outpatient and inpatient copayment coefficients and dental income effects. As a result of the very modest copayments for geriatric care, elderly Japanese have been noted to use hospitals as surrogates for the social environment of elder care facilities (Yoshikawa, Shirouzu, and Holt, 1991). The long average lengths of stay in hospitals may confirm this substitution effect. The significant copayment effect in the oldest population grouping leads one to posit that factors other than the individual's health affect the utilization of inpatient and outpatient medical care. Although our study design does not allow us to identify specifically this third factor, this finding supports speculation on the presence of substitution away from elder care facilities.

Although the separate examinations of the 1984 and 1989 copayment effects on utilization rates suggest that the short-run effects of the 1982 Health and Medical Service Law for the Elderly are greater in the elderly population strata than in 1989, our use of cross-sectional data limits the conviction of these findings. Changes in the size of the elderly population, per capita incomes, supply of medical services, and personal preferences for treatment may all be confounding the apparent short- and long-run effects. A rigorous analysis of time series data adjusted for these variables would merit such a conclusion.

As discussed in the "Data" section of this chapter, several characteristics of both the utilization and copayment values must be considered when weighing the impact of our findings. The imperfections in gathering utilization data and our estimation of the separate inpatient, dental, and outpatient copayment rates merit special attention. Similarly, the use of aggregate data is less desirable than the use of microlevel hospital- or patient-specific data. In Chapter 3, we present a study utilizing such patient-level microdata.

Notes

[1] The independent variables Senoo introduces include daily copayment, average income, population density, and various supply-side variables, including numbers of beds, hospitals, and doctors (all weighted by the individual prefecture's population).

[2] As a measure of ease of access to care, population density was found to be significant and negatively correlated with utilization of all types of medical care. Among the supply-side variables, only the number of beds weighted for population yielded positive and significant effects on inpatient care utilization.

[3] The supply-side variables of number of beds per person and number of medical facilities per person were also found to be significant and positive predictors of inpatient care utilization.

3

Outpatient Medical Demand

"In today's affluent Japan, with the Universal Health Insurance system's modest copayment for medical services, income and copayment play a relatively minor role for the population at large when they decide to receive medical services" (Utsunomiya and Yoshikawa, 1993).

Many argue that the demand for medical care, unlike other goods, does not depend on its price. Once sick, the argument goes, people will pay whatever they can afford in order to get well. Within the Japanese universal health insurance system, the question of price sensitivity is rarely raised. The conventional wisdom is that the modest copayment levels render moot cost considerations in patients' choices. The truth of this argument in the Japanese context has never been tested in a large-scale, patient-level study.

The aim of this chapter is to estimate the elasticity of demand for outpatient services with respect to its price. We use patient-level information collected by the Ministry of Health and Welfare (*Koseisho*) in the 1990 Patient Survey (*Kanja Chosa*), a sample of nearly 440,000 outpatients, to obtain our estimates. Because the Patient Survey is a randomized and nationally representative picture of medical service utilization for all Japan, the model has broad implications for both Japanese and U.S. policymakers in designing cost-containment mechanisms in an environment of spiraling health care costs.

A significant goal of most universal health care systems is to guarantee equitable access to high-quality medical services while controlling excessive costs. The price elasticity of demand for med-

This chapter is based upon: Bhattacharya, J., Vogt, W.B., Yoshikawa, A., and Nakahara, T. 1996. "The Utilization of Outpatient Medical Services in Japan," *Journal of Human Resources* 31(2). This revised version is published with the permission of the University of Wisconsin Press.

63

ical care on an individual level has consequences for both equity and efficiency in the allocation of health care resources. For example, if the elasticity is zero, then copayments on each outpatient visit are not necessary to prevent moral hazard arising from the provision of health insurance. Additionally, forecasting utilization rates and costs hinges critically on an accurate estimate of this elasticity.

This chapter demonstrates that patients who expect to pay a high price tend to have a longer interval between outpatient visits with respect to others in the same diagnostic and demographic categories. This result challenges the conventional wisdom that there is a zero price elasticity of demand for outpatient care in Japan. Price matters, even in a fixed-reimbursement, universal insurance coverage setting.

Background

The Japanese government guarantees health insurance to virtually all its citizens and legal foreign residents. This guarantee is maintained by enrolling everyone in one of several health insurance societies, administered by either the government or corporations. What benefits individuals receive depend on their employment status and age. Japanese law requires employers to provide health insurance to all employees and their dependents, including a minimum package of benefits specified by the government.

Larger corporations often manage their own health insurance societies. Smaller companies group together to form societies that the government manages. Those who are unemployed, self-employed, or retired and their dependents are covered by the National Health Insurance Plan. The elderly receive health care insurance from a system consisting of a special pooling fund from the other health insurance societies (Utsonomiya and Yoshikawa, 1993). Cross-subsidization guarantees the financial viability of all the societies.

Reimbursement to providers is calculated on a "points" system in Japan. At the beginning of the year, the Central Fee-Setting Committee (*Chuikyo*), following recommendations from *Koseisho*, sets the number of points for each diagnosis and procedure. For each point of service it renders, a medical facility is reimbursed ¥10 by the appropriate health insurance society. The points system applies throughout Japan, so for any given diagnosis or procedure performed, the same price is charged everywhere in the country. Facilities may not turn away patients who require care more costly than the point-based compensation. Patients pay a percentage of the costs via a copayment rate set by their health insurance society.

Despite the national medical fee schedule, patients still face price variation with respect to their out-of-pocket expenditures for medical services. This is true for several reasons. First, the copayment rate varies with health insurance society and dependency status. Employees of corporations typically pay a lower coinsurance rate than the self-employed, and heads of families pay less than their dependents. Second, there are regional variations in the expected price of a physician visit, perhaps due to practice variations or systematic movement of patients across medical zones. Third, patients who go to the doctor for an outpatient visit with different symptoms expect to pay different prices. Fundamentally, the price variation arises because people purchase outpatient visits, rather than particular procedures. Though the price of the components is fixed by the fee schedule, neither the composition of the whole package nor its price is.

In 1990, there was a ¥54,000 (approximately $420) cap on individual monthly out-of-pocket expenditures for outpatient services (Powell and Anesaki, 1990). The cap has risen since then to ¥63,000 (approximately $505) (Utsonomiya and Yoshikawa, 1993), which was and is significantly more than the average copayment level for an outpatient visit under most insurance plans.

Previous Studies

Several studies from the 1970s estimate the price elasticity of demand for medical services in the United States (Newhouse and Phelps, 1976).[1] Unfortunately, the elasticity estimates found by these studies vary considerably. Generally, those studies which consider the type of insurance plan to be exogenous find a relatively inelastic, negatively sloping demand curve, while those studies which attempt to account for the endogeneity problem find a slope close to zero (Manning et al., 1988). A recent series of studies (Cherkin, Grothaus, and Wagner, 1989, 1990) examine the impact of copayment rates on utilization of preventive care services at health maintenance organizations in the state of Washington. They conclude that a $5 office visit copayment had an insignificant impact on utilization.

The Rand health insurance experiment is the most comprehensive study on this topic and the only one to use a randomized control trial methodology (Keeler et al., 1988; Manning et al., 1988). Between 1974 and 1976, the 3,000 families that participated in the study, coming from six diverse U.S. cities, were randomly assigned to various insurance plans. Families stayed with the same plan for either three or five years, depending on random placement. Plans stipulated varying copayment rates, including a free plan, 25%, 50%, and 95% copayment rates. All plans had a ceiling on annual out-of-pocket expenditures for outpatient services.

The following are some of the main results of the Rand experiment:

1. Annual demand for outpatient services decreases with increases in copayment.
2. The elasticity of demand for outpatient care at copayment rates between 0% and 25% is −0.16 for acute patients and −0.20 for chronic patients (Manning et al., 1988).
3. Although the probability of using outpatient services at any point varies negatively with the coinsurance rate, the intensity of an encounter, measured in cost to the provider, given that it occurs, does not change with the copayment rate.

Several macro-level studies show a negative relationship between copayment and utilization of services in Japan. Kupor et al. (1995) examine prefecture-level cross-section data from the government-sponsored National Health Insurance Society (*Kokuho*) and find that the number of claims per 100 plan members decreases with average copayment for inpatients, outpatients, and dental patients. Their estimate of the price impact on utilization for outpatients implies a price elasticity of demand of −0.133.[2]

Senoo (1985), using prefectural data on patients in the same insurance plan as Kupor et al. (1995), shows that inpatient length of stay varies negatively with copayments, but finds no price sensitivity for outpatients and dental patients. However, in the same paper, using a 1955–1979 time series data set from the same insurance society, Senoo finds a negative relationship between daily number of outpatient cases per capita and expected price. He estimates a price elasticity of demand for outpatient care between −0.178 and −0.187. Unfortunately, the presence of significant structural change in the Japanese health care system during this period makes this result suspect. For example, both universal coverage and free care for the elderly were instituted during this period.

Finally, Nishimura (1987), using aggregate data, finds that average cost per case is negatively associated with percent copayment rate. His study asks how the intensity of treatment, rather than the frequency of visits, varies with copayment and thus is not directly comparable with this chapter.

A difficulty with the macrolevel studies on Japanese health care is that they pool patients from many different diagnostic categories in order to obtain their elasticity estimates. A priori, one would expect different elasticities for these different groups because the desirability of a doctor visit most likely varies with disease type.[3] In addition, none of the studies use a nationally representative survey to obtain estimates; all data are from only one of the five major insurance societies in Japan. Finally, they all have a small sample size; the largest is a prefecture-level cross-sectional study with 47 observations and eight parameters.

Data

Most of the data used in this chapter come from the 1990 Japanese Patient Survey (*Kanja Chosa*). The survey was conducted during three days in September 1990 from a one-third random sample of all hospitals and clinics in Japan that provide either inpatient or outpatient services. Data were collected from each hospital during only one of the three days of the survey and reported to *Koseisho*; a third of the hospitals were surveyed on each day. We include information on all outpatients in the data set. Because all medical care facilities were compelled to participate in the survey, there is no selection effect with respect to which type of institution responded. All medical care in Japan is available almost exclusively from clinics and hospitals, so the survey is a representative sample of all outpatient visits in Japan.

The information in the outpatient part of the data set includes the patient's age, gender, prefecture of residence, main diagnosis, and insurance plan. There are five main insurance schemes in Japan; we call them A, B, C, D, and E.[4] Each individual in our final data set is enrolled in one of these five plans. Table 3-1 provides some characteristics of these plans. Patients are generally assigned to a plan based on their place of employment. Plan A is for the employees of small and medium-sized companies and is managed by the government. Plan B is for the employees of large firms and is managed by the firms themselves. Plan C is the national health insurance plan, and anyone who does not otherwise qualify for insurance is covered under it. Plan D is for employees of the government. Plan E is for people 70+ years of age and bedridden patients

Table 3-1
Selected Characteristics of Insurance Plans

Plan	Copayment			Description	Total Enrollees (1,000s)	Age		
	Head of Family	Dependent Inpatient	Dependent Outpatient			0–14	15–59	60+
Plan A	10%	20%	30%	Government managed; covers small company employees	36,574	19%	70%	11%
Plan B	10%	20%	30%	Society managed; covers large company employees	33,221	21%	73%	6%
Plan C	30% (general) 20% (retiree)	30% (general) 20% (retiree)	30%	Self-employed, retirees, etc.	43,401	14%	53%	33%
Plan D	10%	20%	30%	Covers public employees and teachers		N/A	N/A	N/A
Plan E	All enrollees face the same copayment	¥700 per day inpatient	¥1000 per month outpatient	Covers elderly (70+ years) and bedridden (65+ years)	Fewer than 11,415	0%	0%	100%

Source: Hoken to Nenkin no Doko (Trends in Health Insurance and Pensions) (Health and Welfare Statistics Association, 1991).

over 65. Retired persons under the age of 70 are generally covered under plan C.

Other patient-specific data include whether the visit was to a hospital or clinic, the prefecture where the service took place, whether the patient is the head of family or a dependent, and the length of time since the patient's last visit to a doctor. Diagnosis data are coded by a system based on the ICD-9 CM code book, with rarer diseases grouped together in categories. For the purposes of this study, only information on major ICD-9 code categories is used, though we examine the effect of using both more and less detailed diagnostic information. A glossary of major ICD-9 code categories is included in Appendix 3-1.

The time interval between outpatient visits (utilization interval), measured in weeks, is available only for patients who had previously visited the facility where they were sampled (approximately 85% of the whole sample) and was cut off after 13 weeks in the data set. Because utilization interval is the main measure of demand for outpatient services used in this study, we exclude from analysis the 15% of patients who were first-time visitors to a medical facility.

Some cautions regarding the utilization interval variable should be mentioned here. First, it is properly measured only for those patients who are likely to maintain a steady relationship with their doctor.[5] However, this is not as significant a limitation as it may first appear. Sociologists of the Japanese health care system characterize the physician-patient relationship in Japan as stable (Powell and Anesaki, 1990). Given that this is the case, our conclusions likely apply to most Japanese citizens because a large majority have some lasting physician-patient relationship. They are therefore likely to visit the same facility repeatedly for outpatient care.

Second, we do not observe exactly who determines the utilization interval. One possibility is that patients make their own choices when to visit doctors' offices. But the physician's recommendation might play a decisive role in the length of the patient's wait. Or, finally, the variable may be jointly determined by both these agents.[6] In all these cases, the measurement of demand sensitivity to price is still valid and interesting.

The appropriate price variable to use in a study of consumer demand for outpatient medical care is the expected out-of-pocket expenditure to the patient for a doctor visit, given available information. We construct for each patient this expected price from aggregate data on the cost of an outpatient visit given the facility's prefecture,[7] insurance plan of membership, disease category, and dependency and retirement status multiplied by the appropriate copayment rate paid by the patient.[8] We obtain these aggregate data from various governmental sources.

Data on the average charge by a facility for an outpatient visit to the patient's health insurance society per day by prefecture and insurance plan in 1990 are obtained from Regional Health Care Costs (*Chiiki Iryohi Soran*) (Shakai Hoken Kenkyujo, 1991). We obtain data on average charge by major ICD-9 code from the 1990 Japanese Patient Survey and the National Medical Health Expenditure Estimates (*Kokumin Iryo-hi*) (Ministry of Health and Welfare, 1992). With the latter data, we construct an index of charges by ICD-9 code by dividing them by the average charge for the median ICD-9 code, mental disorders (ICD-9 code V). We construct the expected charge of an outpatient visit by multiplying this index by the average charge by insurance category and prefecture of services. We use the average charge for the median ICD-9 code as an approximation of the weighted average charge for an outpatient visit, which is not available from this data source.

Patients on plan E are imputed an expected price of ¥0 because they have a monthly cap on out-of-pocket expenditures of ¥1,000, and the average cost of visiting the doctor exceeds the cap for all combinations of covariates. Their payment may be viewed effectively as a small deductible for the first visit in a month. The zero price is appropriate because it is the marginal price of any outpatient visit after the first for patients in plan E. The results change little if the average price per visit, ¥500, is imputed instead to these patients.

More formally, let a_i be the average cost of an outpatient visit for diagnosis i (where i ranges over the major ICD-9 codes), and let $a_{\text{med}} = \text{median}\{a_\text{I} \ldots a_\text{XVI}\}$. Let $b_{j,k}$ be the average cost of a visit by a patient with insurance plan j and receiving services in prefecture k. And let $c_{j,l}$ be the percent copayment stipulated for outpatient visits by insurance plan j for an individual with dependency/retirement status l. The expected out-of-pocket expenditure, $E[p_{i,j,k,l}]$, of the visit imputed to each patient with diagnosis i, insurance plan j, and dependency status l receiving services in prefecture k is given by:

$$E[P_{i,j,k,l}] = \frac{a_i}{a_{\text{med}}} b_{j,k} c_{j,l}. \tag{3-1}$$

Table 3-2 shows the average cost of an outpatient visit for insurance plans A, B, C, and D.

Table 3-2
Average Price of an Outpatient Visit by Insurance Plan

Insurance Plan	Average Price of an Outpatient Visit
Plan A	
Enrollee	¥5,111
Dependent	¥4,304
Plan B	
Enrollee	¥5,096
Dependent	¥4,253
Plan C	
Nonretiree	¥4,650
Retiree	¥5,120
Plan D	
Enrollee	¥4,934
Dependent	¥4,248

Source: Regional Health Care Costs (*Chiiki Iryohi Soran*) (Shakai Hoken Kenkyujo, 1991).

We obtain average yearly income by prefecture from the Report on the Status of Municipality Taxation (*Shichouson-zei Kazei Jyokyo-tou no Shirabe*) (Ministry of Home Affairs, 1991) and population density and the percentage of population living in large urban centers by prefecture from the 1990 Population Census of Japan. These figures are imputed to each patient depending on their prefecture of origin.[9]

In addition to excluding patients who were visiting an institution for the first time, patients who present with complications of pregnancy or childbirth (ICD-9 code XI), congenital anomalies (XIV), diseases in the perinatal period (XV), and injuries and poisonings (XVII) are also omitted from the analysis. We do not analyze some of these diagnostic categories because most insurance plans do not cover the expenses of childbirth and the extent of supplemental insurance is unknown. Therefore, expected out-of-pocket expenditures cannot be computed for those diagnoses. Additionally, the sample sizes for some of the groups are too small to obtain accurate estimates. See Table 3-3 for mean values of the patients who meet the inclusion criteria.[10]

Methods

We use the Cox proportional hazards model to analyze the patient's decision regarding length of time between visits. This model has

Table 3-3-A
Mean Values of Patient Data (Part 1)

ICD-9 Category	I	II	III	IV	V	VI	VII
Time (weeks)[a]	2.80	3.33	3.32	2.97	3.30	3.29	2.75
(% censored)	(3.5%)	(4.5%)	(2.6%)	(2.9%)	(2.1%)	(3.4%)	(1.5%)
Hospital[b]	50%	89%	65%	56%	78%	47%	46%
Age (years)	43.4	59.0	58.9	45.2	48.7	53.0	67.2
In prefecture[c]	97%	95%	97%	97%	94%	97%	99%
Dependent	53%	41%	42%	56%	61%	46%	30%
Plan A	30%	21%	23%	31%	22%	22%	15%
Plan B	18%	14%	12%	18%	14%	12%	7%
Plan C	28%	30%	32%	25%	42%	27%	26%
Plan D	9%	6%	6%	9%	7%	6%	3%
Male	43%	46%	44%	20%	44%	38%	41%
ln (pop dens)[d] (people/km^2)	5.99	6.10	6.05	5.93	6.07	5.91	5.86
% Urban[e]	53%	56%	55%	52%	55%	53%	51%
ln (income) (¥10,000)	19.5	19.6	19.6	19.5	19.6	19.5	19.4
E [Price] (points = ¥10)	275	968	481	365	291	278	351
Index of average charge by ICD-9 code	1.063	3.051	1.717	1.334	1.000	0.903	1.474
Number of patients in subsample	11767	15389	23890	3340	11697	46212	104144

Notes: [a] Time elapsed since the last doctor visit.
[b] Visit was to a hospital (more than 20 beds) rather than a clinic.
[c] Service took place at an institution within the patient's prefecture.
[d] Natural log of prefectural population density measure in people per square kilometer.
[e] Percent of population in the prefecture living in urbanized areas.

Table 3-3-B
Mean Values of Patient Data (Part 2)

ICD-9 Category	VIII	IX	X	XII	XIII	XVI	Whole Sample
Time (weeks)	2.39	2.69	2.75	3.02	1.96	3.02	2.41
(% censored)	(3.6%)	(2.5%)	(3.1%)	(4.0%)	(2.1%)	(3.4%)	(2.6%)
Hospital	39%	58%	68%	42%	47%	71%	52%
Age (years)	32.2	55.1	47.4	41.1	63.3	50.1	55.0
In prefecture	98%	97%	96%	97%	98%	96%	98%
Dependent	66%	39%	54%	54%	32%	48%	43%
Plan A	31%	27%	28%	30%	20%	26%	23%
Plan B	20%	14%	18%	19%	8%	16%	12%
Plan C	26%	31%	29%	28%	25%	30%	28%
Plan D	11%	7%	8%	9%	4%	8%	6%
Male	50%	53%	36%	46%	35%	42%	43%
ln (pop dens) (people/km^2)	5.94	5.99	6.05	5.99	5.92	6.12	5.95
% Urban	52%	53%	54%	53%	52%	55%	53%
ln (income) (¥10,000)	19.5	19.5	19.6	19.5	19.4	19.6	19.5
E [Price] (points = ¥10)	210	67	820	231	103	202	285
Index of average charge by ICD-9 code	0.784	0.523	2.937	0.920	0.841	0.872	N/A
Number of patients in sample	53,031	49,603	21,344	16,702	70,273	5629	437,901

become standard in the modelling of duration data because of its ease of implementation, its ability to estimate the effects of covariates without parametric restrictions on the underlying baseline hazard function, and its ability to deal easily with censoring. Although the Cox model is not strictly appropriate in this case because the dependent variable—utilization interval—is discrete valued, the predicted hazard function for every patient in the sample is contained in the unit interval. Because the effect of price probably varies with disease type, we estimate separately the model for data subsets consisting of patients from the same major ICD-9 code category.

The Cox proportional hazard model allows us to obtain consistent estimates of covariate impacts, as well as the hazard rate function, despite the problem of censored data. In this case, let $\lambda_i(t)$, the hazard rate in week t for person i, be the probability of going to a doctor in week t given no visit in the preceding $t - 1$ weeks. This modelling technique makes no assumption about whether the patient or the doctor decides the utilization interval. Because the Cox model is a semiparametric method, we obtain estimates of the hazard rates without specifying the form of the baseline hazard function, the portion of the hazard rate that is common to all individuals. Formally, the hazard rate in the Cox model is given by

$$\lambda_i(t) = \lambda(t) \exp(X_i'\beta) \tag{3-2}$$

where $\lambda(t)$ is the baseline hazard rate on day t, X_i is a vector of patient i's characteristics, and β is a vector of parameters.

Let A be the set of censored observations, and let B be the set of uncensored observations. The likelihood contribution for an individual $i \in$ A is given by

$$L_i^A = \prod_{t=1}^{13}(1 - \lambda_i(t)) \tag{3-3}$$

because 13 weeks is the censoring point. For an individual $i \in$ B, who has a utilization interval of T_i, the likelihood contribution is given by

$$L_i^B = \lambda_i(T_i) \prod_{t=1}^{T_i-1} (1 - \lambda_i(t)). \tag{3-4}$$

The likelihood function, hereafter LF, is given by

$$LF = \prod_{i \in A} L_i^A \prod_{i \in B} L_i^B. \tag{3-5}$$

We obtain our estimates of β by using the Cox partial maximum likelihood estimation procedure[11] to obtain consistent starting values for β and then maximizing the full LF with respect to $\lambda(t)$ and β.[12] Because the sample size is quite large, we estimate all models using a random 90% of the appropriate data set, hereafter the estimation sample. We reserve the remaining 10% of the data, hereafter the validation sample, to evaluate the performance of the model.[13]

One potential source of bias in our results is an artifact of the sampling methodology used by *Koseisho*. If the patients in our sample who visit the physician after only a short length of time are also habitual frequent users of outpatient services, then these patients are oversampled in a single-day snapshot survey, as was used to collect the data. Because we cannot know with certainty the strength or direction of this bias solely from information in this data set, we must rely on theoretical presumptions to tell us the extent of the problem.

Suppose there are two groups of people in the population, one containing patients who are quite ill and thus have a low price elasticity, the other with less seriously ill people with a higher price elasticity (e.g., patients seeking preventive care). If the former group tends to have shorter times between doctor visits, as one would expect, then estimates of price elasticity are biased toward zero because patients in the second group are systematically missed by the sampling methodology. If patients in the first group visit the doctor less frequently, the bias holds in the opposite direction. The most likely scenario seems to be an elasticity estimate biased toward zero. Therefore, this selection problem is not likely to explain away the result of the downward sloping demand obtained in this study.

Another related potential problem is that the data set does not include healthy patients who never visit the doctor, even at zero price. Of course, to the extent that these people do not contribute to the market demand curve for outpatient care, their elasticities at actually observed prices are not of policy interest. If these people do not visit physicians at zero price, then they will never visit in any interesting policy experiment. Alternatively, if such patients do very infrequently visit the doctor, they will be included in the data set, though underrepresented, and they will bias the estimates in the direction indicated in the previous paragraph.[14] Finally, a bias toward zero in the elasticity estimate may be introduced by the fact that frequent visitors may exceed the cap on out-of-pocket expenditures.[15]

In order to get a better idea about the impact of price on demand for outpatient visits, we conduct simulations using the conditional probability estimates from the Cox model. In each trial of the simulation, we draw a random patient i, with equal weight on every patient in the estimation sample, and calculate the estimated utilization interval hazard function, $\lambda_i(t|X_i, \beta)$ for $t = 1 \ldots 13$, using Equation 3-2. We subsequently simulate the number of times patient i sees a doctor in a year as follows: Starting on week zero of the simulated year, we draw $Y_t \sim U[0,1]$ for $t = 1 \ldots 13$, where t denotes the number of weeks as before. Let $C = \{t|\lambda_i(t) > Y_t\}$. Note that because $\lambda_i(t)$ is the probability of visiting the doctor in week t for person i given no visit in week $1 \ldots t - 1$, if $t \in C$ the patient would see the doctor on week t if he had not gone in the previous weeks. Therefore, the simulated utilization interval for a single spell is given by $T = \min C$.[16] We add T to the number of weeks that have elapsed since the beginning of the year and subsequently repeat the procedure of picking Y_t for the same patient until a visit falls past week 52. Counting the number of repetitions yields the simulated number of yearly visits by patient i.

We repeat this procedure 100,000 times by picking a new random patient each time. Averaging the simulated number of yearly patient visits over these trials yields an estimate of the unconditional mean number of visits per year. The sample standard deviation is an estimate of its standard error. If censoring were not a problem, this simulation would yield a consistent estimate of the unconditional mean number of outpatient visits per year for patients for the sample used in estimating the Cox model. In addition to the mean number of yearly visits, we obtain as additional output from the simulation an estimate of the unconditional mean utilization interval, its sample standard error, and the median utilization interval, though simulation is not necessary to calculate these quantities. Because the realized percentage of censored spells is much smaller than 50% in all the simulations, the median is never subject to bias due to censoring in any of the results we report; the median is never in the unobserved tail of the utilization interval distribution.

We run the simulation three times for each ICD-9 code category, using one-half, two, and three times the expected price imputed to each individual while respecting the cap on out-of-pocket expenditures. These simulations can be interpreted as experiments of halving, doubling, and tripling the copayment rates for all individuals and examining the impact on annual utilization. From these simulations, we calculate the price elasticity of demand at various prices for each ICD-9 code category. We use the estimate of unconditional mean number of yearly visits from adjacent price categories to find the elasticity evaluated at the midpoint of the two prices. For example, in order to estimate the price elasticity at 1.5*E[Price], we use the following formula:

$$e_{1.5} = \frac{Q_2 - Q_1}{P_2 - P_1} * \frac{P_2 + P_1}{Q_2 + Q_1} \tag{3-6}$$

where P_a is E[Price]*a $(a = 1, 2)$, Q_a is the number of outpatient visits per year at P_a, and $e_{1.5}$ is the price elasticity at 1.5*E[Price].

Finally, we perform two more policy simulations giving everyone a 10% copayment rate and then a 30% copayment rate. We report the same statistics from these experiments as we do for the other simulations.

Results

Table 3-4 presents the 95% confidence interval for the hazard ratio estimates associated with the covariates. The interpretation of the hazard ratios is given by the following:

$$Haz.\ Ratio = \frac{\lambda(t)\ e^{(\beta_1 X_1 + ... + \beta_i(X_i + 1) + ... + \beta_n X_n)}}{\lambda(t)\ e^{(\beta_1 X_1 + ... + \beta_n X_n)}} = e^{\beta_i} \tag{3-7}$$

where the subscripts now index the covariates, not the patients, and n is the number of covariates.

For variables measured in levels, such as age, the hazard ratio is the proportionality constant of the change in the hazard rate, for any value of t, when that variable is increased by one unit. For variables measured in log units, such as price, the same interpretation holds, except if the natural log of the covariate is increased by one, the covariate itself is multiplied by e. Whatever the unit of measurement, a hazard ratio of less than one means that increasing the variable decreases the probability of seeing the doctor in week t (given no visit in the previous $t - 1$ weeks) for every t. Of course, a hazard ratio of greater than one means an increase in the same probability. For binary variables, such as sex, which partition the sample into two subgroups, the hazard ratio is the hazard rate for one subgroup divided by the hazard rate for the other subgroup.

The point estimates of the hazard ratio for log of expected price in all ICD-9 categories are less than 1 except for genitourinary disease (ICD-9 code X), and in that case, one cannot reject the hy-

Table 3-4-A
95% Confidence Intervals for Hazard Ratios (Part 1)

ICD-9 Group	ln(E[Price])	Age	Service in Prefecture[a]	Male[b]	Dependent[c]
I	0.697–0.948	0.996–0.998	1.049–1.313	0.924–0.999	1.083–1.412
II	0.800–1.020	1.000–1.003	1.121–1.311	1.046–1.118	0.952–1.154
III	0.601–0.743	1.003–1.005	1.446–1.676	0.990–1.042	1.265–1.480
IV	0.645–1.163	0.999–1.003	0.933–1.417	0.887–1.056	0.842–1.415
V	0.631–0.869	0.996–0.999	1.075–1.261	0.972–1.061	1.119–1.451
VI	0.634–0.735	0.996–0.997	1.140–1.281	1.074–1.116	1.232–1.393
VII	0.561–0.629	1.005–1.006	1.103–1.229	0.963–0.986	1.361–1.474
VIII	0.659–0.777	0.999–1.000	1.082–1.240	0.972–1.018	1.217–1.396
IX	0.700–0.811	1.000–1.001	1.136–1.264	0.979–1.012	1.152–1.292
X	0.999–1.046	1.002–1.004	1.061–1.235	0.997–1.061	0.944–1.032
XII	0.656–0.855	1.001–1.002	0.981–1.204	0.989–1.054	1.096–1.372
XIII	0.834–0.932	1.001–1.002	1.219–1.373	1.041–1.075	1.007–1.106
XVI	0.668–1.032	0.997–1.001	0.855–1.137	0.951–1.065	0.933–1.342

Notes: [a] This hazard ratio is relative to patients who received services in hospitals located outside their home prefecture.
[b] This hazard ratio is relative to female patients.
[c] This hazard ratio is relative to nondependent plan enrollees.

Table 3-4-B
95% Confidence Intervals for Hazard Ratios (Part 2)

ICD-9 Group	ln(income)	Percent Urbanized	ln(population density)	Service in Hospital[a]
I	0.968–1.052	0.965–1.186	0.924–0.989	0.762–0.826
II	0.990–1.066	0.911–1.104	0.939–0.989	0.558–0.619
III	0.963–1.020	0.967–1.114	0.931–0.975	0.683–0.724
IV	0.927–1.068	0.814–1.203	0.937–1.053	0.671–0.775
V	0.968–1.051	0.865–1.064	0.945–1.007	0.691–0.776
VI	0.963–1.003	1.030–1.137	0.975–1.004	0.663–0.689
VII	0.960–0.987	1.032–1.104	0.971–0.996	0.762–0.785
VIII	0.983–1.015	0.967–1.058	0.968–0.993	0.751–0.774
IX	0.924–0.966	1.051–1.163	0.986–1.011	0.771–0.800
X	0.966–1.022	0.883–1.026	1.001–1.045	0.708–0.752
XII	0.984–1.057	0.917–1.100	0.934–0.984	0.869–0.927
XIII	0.974–1.011	1.065–1.162	0.981–1.007	0.837–0.863
XVI	0.924–1.044	0.897–1.213	0.943–1.033	0.761–0.862

Note: [a] The hazard ratios reported for this variable are relative to patients visiting clinics (institutions with fewer than 20 inpatient beds).

Table 3-4-C
95% Confidence Interval for Hazard Ratios (Part 3)

ICD-9 Group	Plan A[a]	Plan B	Plan C	Plan D
I	0.517–0.764	0.526–0.773	0.602–0.823	0.514–0.762
II	0.741–1.005	0.746–1.004	0.801–0.998	0.685–0.947
III	0.485–0.617	0.467–0.591	0.568–0.681	0.450–0.579
IV	0.517–1.075	0.521–1.106	0.577–1.059	0.485–1.035
V	0.433–0.643	0.429–0.638	0.492–0.673	0.417–0.624
VI	0.562–0.675	0.555–0.661	0.642–0.740	0.543–0.657
VII	0.473–0.536	0.455–0.517	0.585–0.636	0.458–0.513
VIII	0.571–0.692	0.543–0.667	0.628–0.737	0.551–0.665
IX	0.616–0.731	0.592–0.703	0.704–0.798	0.572–0.682
X	0.985–1.113	0.935–1.062	1.015–1.136	0.954–1.096
XII	0.558–0.780	0.569–0.787	0.643–0.832	0.537–0.752
XIII	0.780–0.897	0.777–0.898	0.836–0.929	0.764–0.886
XVI	0.535–0.922	0.534–0.914	0.633–0.953	0.487–0.842

Note: [a] All hazard ratios in this table are relative to plan E.

pothesis that it equals 1 at a 5% significance level.[17] Therefore, we conclude that, controlling for all other variables, increasing expected out-of-pocket expenditures results in a decreased probability of seeing the doctor on any particular day. This is consistent with the intuition that time between visits increases with price.

In addition to price, the disease type plays a crucial role in determining the utilization interval between outpatient visits. Table 3-5, which gives the results of the simulation experiments of changing everyone's expected price, demonstrates this point. For example, at the average expected price, patients with an endocrine disorder (ICD-9 code III), typically a chronic disorder such as type II diabetes, have longer utilization intervals than patients with an infectious disease (ICD-9 code I) at three times the average expected price. Even though aggregated major ICD code is a crude measure of disease acuity, these results can provide some insight into the relationship between it and the demand for outpatient services. Roughly, patients with acute diagnoses seem to have less price sensitivity than those with chronic diagnoses. Confirming the truth of this observation requires thorough analysis of further disaggregated disease categories, which is beyond the scope of this chapter.

The simulations illustrate the impact of raising the price of services. In every ICD-9 category, except genitourinary disorders (ICD-9 code X), raising the price leads to fewer outpatient visits per

Table 3-5-A
Simulation Results—Changing the Price for Everyone (Part 1)

ICD-9 Group	Out-of-Pocket Expenditures	Mean Number of Yearly Visits (standard error)	Mean Number of Weeks to New Visit (standard error)	Median Number of Weeks to Next Visit	Percent Censored Simulated Spells
I	0.5*E[Price]	8.4 (0.09)	5.2 (0.04)	4	4.3%
	1.0*E[Price]	7.2 (0.07)	5.8 (0.06)	4	5.8%
	2.0*E[Price]	6.3 (0.06)	6.5 (0.07)	5	7.1%
	3.0*E[Price]	5.8 (0.05)	6.9 (0.08)	5	8.0%
II	0.5*E[Price]	13.4 (0.25)	3.5 (0.02)	3	5.1%
	1.0*E[Price]	12.5 (0.24)	3.7 (0.02)	3	5.6%
	2.0*E[Price]	11.5 (0.21)	4.0 (0.03)	3	6.1%
	3.0*E[Price]	11.0 (0.19)	4.2 (0.03)	3	6.3%
III	0.5*E[Price]	7.3 (0.09)	5.8 (0.05)	4	2.7%
	1.0*E[Price]	5.7 (0.05)	6.9 (0.08)	6	7.1%
	2.0*E[Price]	4.6 (0.03)	8.1 (0.11)	8	10.2%
	3.0*E[Price]	4.1 (0.03)	8.7 (0.12)	9	14.1%
IV	0.5*E[Price]	11.3 (0.17)	4.1 (0.03)	3	2.5%
	1.0*E[Price]	10.1 (0.14)	4.5 (0.03)	3	3.1%
	2.0*E[Price]	9.1 (0.12)	4.9 (0.04)	3	3.7%
	3.0*E[Price]	8.5 (0.11)	5.1 (0.04)	3	4.1%
V	0.5*E[Price]	10.8 (0.11)	4.2 (0.03)	3	1.5%
	1.0*E[Price]	8.8 (0.09)	5.0 (0.04)	4	3.6%
	2.0*E[Price]	7.2 (0.06)	5.8 (0.05)	4	4.2%
	3.0*E[Price]	6.4 (0.05)	6.4 (0.06)	5	6.0%

year and longer interval times until the next outpatient visit on average. The anomalous result of a near zero elasticity for patients with genitourinary disorders is not too surprising given that a large portion of that group requires frequent hemodialysis to survive, and thus would be expected to show little price sensitivity. For the other diagnostic categories, the effect is sometimes so strong that nominal price increases lead to large increases in the time between outpatient visits. For example, for endocrine disorders (ICD-9 code III), raising the expected price from ¥4810 = 1.0*E[Price] to ¥14,430 = 3.0*E[Price], an increase of approximately $100, results in a three-week increase in the median interval time to the next outpatient visit. For reasons outlined in the "Methods" section, this result is not biased by the censoring of the dependent variable.

The data censoring problem does mean that the estimate of mean utilization interval should be viewed as a lower bound on the actual value, while the mean number of yearly visits is an upper bound. Furthermore, the absolute difference between the bounds and the

Table 3-5-B
Simulation Results—Changing the Price for Everyone (Part 2)

ICD-9 Group	Out-of-Pocket Expenditures	Mean Number of Yearly Visits (standard error)	Mean Number of Weeks to Next Visit (standard error)	Median Number of Weeks to Next Visit	Percent Censored Simulated Spells
VI	0.5*E[Price]	6.0 (0.05)	6.7 (0.07)	6	6.1%
	1.0*E[Price]	4.8 (0.03)	7.9 (0.10)	7	8.8%
	2.0*E[Price]	3.9 (0.02)	9.0 (0.13)	8	10.2%
	3.0*E[Price]	3.6 (0.02)	9.6 (0.15)	9	13.8%
VII	0.5*E[Price]	8.9 (0.10)	4.9 (0.04)	3	3.5%
	1.0*E[Price]	6.2 (0.06)	6.6 (0.07)	5	5.6%
	2.0*E[Price]	4.6 (0.03)	8.2 (0.11)	7	7.3%
	3.0*E[Price]	3.9 (0.02)	9.0 (0.13)	8	9.9%
VIII	0.5*E[Price]	11.8 (0.15)	3.9 (0.02)	3	2.4%
	1.0*E[Price]	9.1 (0.10)	4.8 (0.04)	3	3.9%
	2.0*E[Price]	7.2 (0.07)	5.9 (0.06)	4	5.0%
	3.0*E[Price]	6.3 (0.06)	6.5 (0.07)	5	5.9%
IX	0.5*E[Price]	8.2 (0.08)	5.3 (0.04)	4	3.1%
	1.0*E[Price]	6.7 (0.06)	6.2 (0.06)	5	5.1%
	2.0*E[Price]	5.6 (0.04)	7.0 (0.08)	6	7.4%
	3.0*E[Price]	5.1 (0.03)	7.6 (0.09)	7	8.2%

Table 3-5-C
Simulation Results—Changing the Price for Everyone (Part 3)

ICD-9 Group	Out-of-Pocket Expenditures	Mean Number of Yearly Visits (standard error)	Mean Number of Weeks to Next Visit (standard error)	Median Number of Weeks to Next Visit	Percent Censored Simulated Spells
X	0.5*E[Price]	20.7 (0.41)	2.4 (0.01)	2	3.4%
	1.0*E[Price]	20.8 (0.42)	2.3 (0.01)	2	3.2%
	2.0*E[Price]	20.9 (0.46)	2.3 (0.01)	2	3.1%
	3.0*E[Price]	21.1 (0.47)	2.3 (0.01)	2	3.0%
XII	0.5*E[Price]	8.9 (0.09)	4.9 (0.04)	3	3.2%
	1.0*E[Price]	7.3 (0.06)	5.8 (0.05)	4	4.3%
	2.0*E[Price]	6.0 (0.05)	6.7 (0.07)	5	5.6%
	3.0*E[Price]	5.4 (0.04)	7.3 (0.08)	6	6.2%
XIII	0.5*E[Price]	17.0 (0.27)	2.8 (0.01)	2	2.5%
	1.0*E[Price]	15.0 (0.23)	3.2 (0.02)	2	2.9%
	2.0*E[Price]	13.3 (0.20)	3.5 (0.02)	2	3.2%
	3.0*E[Price]	12.3 (0.18)	3.8 (0.03)	2	3.4%
XVI	0.5*E[Price]	7.2 (0.06)	5.9 (0.06)	4	4.6%
	1.0*E[Price]	6.3 (0.05)	6.5 (0.07)	5	5.6%
	2.0*E[Price]	5.6 (0.04)	7.0 (0.08)	6	6.4%
	3.0*E[Price]	5.3 (0.04)	7.4 (0.09)	6	7.0%

actual values increases with the price because more people reach the censoring point at higher prices. Estimates of price sensitivity using these figures tend to underestimate the impact of price on frequency of outpatient visits. Consequently, censoring cannot be used to explain away the result that these variables are negatively related.

Table 3-6 presents the results of two policy experiments that are more realistic than those in Table 3-5. In the first experiment, everyone's copayment rate is set at 10%; in the second, the copayment rate is raised to 30%. In both experiments, plan E enrollees' expected price is not changed. As expected, the former scenario results in more frequent visits, and the latter has the opposite effect. For most ICD-9 categories, changing the copayment rate to 10% does not decrease the utilization interval as much as cutting everyone's expected price in half. Raising everyone's copayment rate to 30% does not decrease the yearly utilization as much as doubling everyone's expected price.

Table 3-7 presents the estimates of price elasticity of demand for outpatient services we obtain using Equation 3-6. The result of a downward-sloping, generally inelastic demand curve correlates roughly with studies on the U.S. health care system, including the Rand health insurance experiment. They are close to the elasticity estimates obtained by Senoo (1985) and Kupor et al. (1995) for Japan as well. For reasons already enumerated, using censored data means that these estimates should be viewed as a lower bound on the actual elasticity. In other words, the demand curve is even more elastic than these estimates indicate. The fact that the divergence between the bound and the actual value increases with price helps explain why the elasticity decreases with price in nearly all ICD-9 categories. Of course, with our estimates, one can neither rule out nor accept the proposition that the demand curve for outpatient visits is more elastic at lower prices than at higher prices, though such a result does not seem likely.

Patients who visit an institution within their own prefecture have a higher probability of seeing the doctor on any given week than those leaving their home prefecture. This is true for every ICD-9 category and significantly true, at the 5% level, in most. There is a cost to travelling a far distance to get services, even if the services are of better quality. Therefore, all other things being equal, one would expect a large utilization interval for people who leave the prefecture in light of this extra cost.[18]

Ceteris paribus, dependents have a significantly higher hazard

Table 3-6-A
Results of Policy Experiments (Part 1)

ICD-9 Group	Policy Experiment	Mean Number of Yearly Visits (standard error)	Mean Number of Weeks to Next Visit (standard error)	Median Number of Weeks to Next Visit	Percent Censored Simulated Spells
I	10% Copayment rate for all	8.4 (0.11)	5.2 (0.04)	3	4.7%
	30% Copayment rate for all	6.8 (0.07)	6.1 (0.06)	4	6.5%
II	10% Copayment	13.1 (0.23)	3.6 (0.02)	3	5.3%
	30% Copayment	12.1 (0.23)	3.8 (0.02)	3	5.8%
III	10% Copayment	6.8 (0.07)	6.1 (0.06)	5	4.0%
	30% Copayment	5.3 (0.06)	7.3 (0.08)	6	8.9%
IV	10% Copayment	11.1 (0.16)	4.1 (0.03)	3	2.7%
	30% Copayment	9.7 (0.14)	4.6 (0.03)	3	3.4%
V	10% Copayment	10.9 (0.13)	4.1 (0.02)	3	1.3%
	30% Copayment	8.2 (0.08)	5.2 (0.04)	4	3.9%
VI	10% Copayment	5.9 (0.07)	6.8 (0.08)	6	7.3%
	30% Copayment	4.5 (0.03)	8.2 (0.11)	8	9.3%
VII	10% Copayment	7.6 (0.10)	5.6 (0.05)	4	4.0%
	30% Copayment	5.8 (0.06)	6.9 (0.08)	5	6.1%

Table 3-6-B
Results of Policy Experiments (Part 2)

ICD-9 Group	Policy Experiment	Mean Number of Yearly Visits (standard error)	Mean Number of Weeks to Next Visit (standard error)	Median Number of Weeks to Next Visit	Percent Censored Simulated Spells
VIII	10% Copayment	12.3 (0.21)	3.7 (0.02)	2	1.9%
	30% Copayment	8.5 (0.10)	5.1 (0.04)	3	4.5%
IX	10% Copayment	7.8 (0.09)	5.5 (0.05)	4	4.2%
	30% Copayment	6.1 (0.05)	6.6 (0.07)	5	6.6%
X	10% Copayment	20.7 (0.41)	2.4 (0.01)	2	3.3%
	30% Copayment	20.8 (0.44)	2.3 (0.01)	2	3.1%
XII	10% Copayment	8.8 (0.09)	5.0 (0.04)	3	4.2%
	30% Copayment	6.7 (0.06)	6.2 (0.06)	5	5.2%
XIII	10% Copayment	16.1 (0.26)	3.0 (0.01)	2	2.6%
	30% Copayment	14.3 (0.23)	3.3 (0.02)	2	3.2%
XVI	10% Copayment	7.0 (0.06)	6.0 (0.06)	4	5.0%
	30% Copayment	6.0 (0.05)	6.7 (0.07)	5	6.3%

Table 3-7
Estimated Price Elasticity of Demand[a]

ICD-9 Group	Price Elasticity Evaluated at:		
	0.75*E[Price]	1.5*E[Price]	2.5*E[Price]
I	−0.22	−0.21	−0.19
II	−0.12	−0.12	−0.12
III	−0.37	−0.33	−0.28
IV	−0.16	−0.16	−0.15
V	−0.31	−0.30	−0.28
VI	−0.33	−0.29	−0.25
VII	−0.54	−0.45	−0.38
VIII	−0.38	−0.35	−0.32
IX	−0.29	−0.27	−0.25
X	0.0052	0.0071	0.028
XII	−0.31	−0.28	−0.27
XIII	−0.19	−0.19	−0.18
XVI	−0.19	−0.18	−0.17

Note: [a] Demand is measured as the number of outpatient visits in a given year.

rate than nondependent enrollees in most ICD-9 categories; holding all else constant, dependents have shorter utilization intervals than heads of households in seeing the doctor.[19] Presumably, the daily schedule followed by dependents is more flexible than that followed by heads of households, for whom the cost of perturbing their schedule by going to see the doctor is higher. Increased time between physician visits allows for rescheduling appointments and taking other measures to facilitate the visit, thus mitigating the cost of changing the schedule quickly. Including this variable and insurance plan dummies in the analysis effectively controls for unobserved time available to see the doctor.

Patients who receive services in a hospital tend to have longer utilization intervals than patients going to a clinic to see a physician. This empirical regularity is significantly true for all ICD-9 groupings. In interpreting this result, one must remember that the sample excludes seriously ill patients who present at a hospital and are subsequently admitted as inpatients. Because of this, we rule out the explanation that people who wait longer become more ill and thus are forced to go to the hospital. If such an effect were true, we would not be able to detect it in our sample. One possible explanation for the result, consistent with the value-of-time argument, is that the density of hospitals in a given area is less than the density of clinics; thus, travel time to hospitals is higher on average. Another possibility is that patients spend more time waiting at hospitals than at clinics, which deters them from visiting the former. Finally, such a result may reflect practice pattern differences between hospital-based physicians and clinic doctors.

Increased population density in a prefecture leads to a lower probability of a doctor visit each day in most ICD-9 groups. We must regard this result with caution because population density is poorly measured. Prefectures encompass large land areas with heterogenous population densities. This local variation means that population density is subject to measurement error. Despite this caveat, this result is consistent with the observation that waiting room times in hospitals in densely populated areas are high. Other explanations are possible, but these data cannot distinguish among them.

Patients enrolled in insurance plans A, B, C, and D are all significantly more likely to have longer utilization intervals than patients in plan E. This is not surprising in view of the makeup of the insurance plans. Plan E consists entirely of elderly people, who are considered the most frequent users of outpatient services. Among the other plans, plan C has the lowest probability of long utilization intervals for all the ICD-9 categories, though calculation of appropriate likelihood ratio statistics results in the nonrejection at the 5% level of the hypotheses that the hazard ratios are the same among plans A and C, B and C, and D and C. This is true for all the ICD-9 categories.

Variables that do not have hazard ratios significantly different from 1, or have parameter estimates below zero for some ICD-9 subgroups and above zero for others, include age, gender, percentage urbanized, and ln(income). In the case of ln(income), this can likely be attributed to poor measurement of the variable because the income imputed to each patient is the prefectural average. Also, total family income is probably more relevant than individual income to the decision to see the doctor. Percent urbanization also suffers from measurement problems because a gross measure of urbanization within a prefecture inaccurately measures local conditions. The presence of the population density variable, with which the percent urbanization is positively correlated, also reduces this variable's power in forecasting the hazard rate. Despite the poor performance of these variables, their use is justified by the theoretical presumption that they measure some costs of a visit (e.g., travel time to the doctor's office) and thus belong in a demand function.

For many of the ICD-9 categories, age is not significant. However, much of the predictive power of the age variable is coopted by other variables included in the model, especially the insurance plan, which is significantly correlated with age (see Table 3-1). Additionally, one would not expect the hazard function to change dramatically, holding all else constant, when a patient ages by one year. Therefore, the hazard ratios presented do not provide intuition into the strength of the age effect, though they do properly report its direction. Sex, like age, is correlated with insurance plan. That the effect of gender on the hazard rate varies by ICD-9 code is not surprising. This is what one would expect if males were more concerned about some illnesses than females and less concerned about others or, alternatively, if there were no systematic sex differences.

Model Diagnostics

Goodness of Fit

We use the validation sample to evaluate the fit of the model for each ICD category. Given the diagnosis, we further break each sample into cells by deciles of age denoted $k = 1 \ldots 10$. We conduct an asymptotic χ^2 test of the joint hypothesis that each unconditional predicted probability from the Cox model equals the corresponding empirical probability observed in the data using the validation sample only.[20]

To construct this test statistic, using the parameter estimates β derived from the estimation sample, we calculate the distribution of predicted utilization interval for each individual i:

$$Pr(t = T|X_i, \beta) = \lambda_i(T)S(T|X_i, \beta) \quad \forall T \tag{3-8}$$

where $S(T|X_i\beta) = Pr(t >= T|X_i, \beta)$ is the survivor function. We then calculate the distribution of predicted utilization interval within each age cell as follows:

$$Pr(t = T) = \frac{1}{N_k}\sum_{i-1}^{N_k} Pr(t = T|X_i) \quad \forall T, k \tag{3-9}$$

where N_k is the size of cell k and i indexes over individuals in cell k. Let $N_{t,k}$ $t = 1 \ldots 9$ be the number of people in cell k who have a utilization interval of t weeks, and $N_{10,k}$ be the number of people in cell k with a utilization interval of 10 or more weeks. Define

$$Q_k = \sum_{T=1}^{10} \frac{(N_{T,k} - N_k Pr(t = T))^2}{N_k Pr(t = T)}. \tag{3-10}$$

Then $Q = \sum Q_k$ can be shown to be asymptotically χ^2.[21] We find the following for the joint hypothesis of equality between predicted and corresponding observed probabilities in the validation sample: For ICD groups II, III, VI, VIII, IX, and XIII, $p > 0.10$; for ICD groups I and VII, $0.05 < p < 0.10$; and for the remaining ICD categories, $p < 0.05$.

Patient Heterogeneity

Estimates from the Cox proportional hazard are susceptible to bias due to unobserved individual heterogeneity. In order to test for the possibility of patient preference heterogeneity due to differences in disease type, we estimate the model at two levels of diagnostic category aggregation in addition to the major ICD-9 code category breakdown described previously. We estimate the model using the whole sample while requiring price elasticities to be constant across different diagnostic categories, and we estimate the model at the lowest level of diagnostic disaggregation permitted by the data set. In particular, we examine the model for all such categories with at least 10,000 patients, of which there are three: diabetes mellitus, essential (primary) hypertension, and spondylosis and associated disorders.

For the whole sample, ignoring all diagnostic information, one obtains a price elasticity estimate of -0.22 evaluated at 1.5*E[Price]. Using the fine-level diagnostic information, one obtains the following price elasticity estimates, each evaluated at 1.5*E[Price]: diabetes mellitus, -0.41; essential hypertension, -0.57; spondylosis, -0.23. Whatever the level of diagnostic heterogeneity is allowed,[22] one obtains the result that the demand for outpatient visits is downward-sloping. Qualitatively similar price elasticity estimates across these different levels of aggregation provide some evidence that at least the qualitative conclusions about price effects are not sensitive to heterogeneity due to unobserved diagnostic status.

Discussion

Our results demonstrate that the interval between outpatient visits in Japan is sensitive to expected out-of-pocket expenditures. The average expected expenditure for different ICD-9 groups, which ranges from ¥670 (less than $10) to ¥9680 (more than $100), is quite small relative to average monthly income. Yet doubling or tripling the copayment can lead to a significantly increased utilization interval. Although the Cox proportional hazard model we use precludes a direct structural interpretation of these numbers, they strongly suggest a downward sloping demand curve for outpatient services; increased price leads to a decreased frequency of doctor visits. Though this has been demonstrated before in the U.S., ours is the first microeconomic evidence that such an effect holds in Japan, even with its universal health insurance system.

Previous studies holding the choice of insurance plan to be exogenous find a large price elasticity of demand in the U.S., up to -2.1 in some (Manning et al., 1988). Our results are more in line with studies that account for the endogeneity of plan choice. Estimates that concur with the latter group of studies are not surprising, even though we do not explicitly recognize plan membership as endogenous. Assuming insurance plan enrollment to be exogenous is more appropriate in Japan than in the U.S., because insurance plan membership is determined entirely by broad category of employment, age, retirement, and dependency status, and there is a significantly lower rate of job turnover in Japan (Aoki, 1988). Unlike U.S. workers, Japanese employees are not given a choice among several health plans, each with different benefits. Instead, coverage is universal, and Japanese workers must accept the plan offered by their employer, or the government plan if they are self-employed or unemployed. Minimum benefit levels are mandated by the government.

Although the hazard ratios for changes in expected out-of-pocket expenditures in different diagnosis groups seem to indicate that the price effect is strongest for patients who are seeing their physician for chronic illnesses, this finding is not definitive because the groupings by two-digit ICD-9 codes are too broad. Obviously, these categories contain both chronic and acute illnesses. Further study analyzing finer ICD-9 categories is required to examine the impact of illness acuteness on frequency of visits.

Our results indicate that price sensitivity for outpatient care exists in Japan, but we cannot conclude that it is all due to the patient's decision to put off a visit. An alternative explanation, also consistent with our results, is that doctors function as price agents for their patients. In other words, when doctors make recommendations about the time until the next visit, they incorporate information about the patient's price elasticity and choose a time that maximizes patient utility. Further study is needed to illuminate the locus of decision-making.

The most fruitful direction for further research on this topic, barring a Rand-type health insurance experiment in Japan, involves structural modelling of the determinants of time between doctor visits, starting with demand for outpatient services as the base of analysis. Also important and of independent interest are studies examining the extent of the selectivity bias introduced by this sampling mechanism, perhaps via Monte Carlo methods. A study that introduces a correct sample selection correction in the context of a structural model would answer most questions on the matter. Related questions that are also important to pursue include determination of income elasticities, the sensitivity of price elasticity to income, different price elasticities for acute and chronic illnesses, and price responsiveness estimates for inpatients.

Our results suggest that prices are an important factor to consider in analyzing a system with universal health insurance. The demand curve for medical care, although inelastic compared to other goods, is undoubtedly downward-sloping. Changing the copayment rate can be regarded as an effective measure to control utilization of outpatient medical services.

Appendix 3-1: Glossary of ICD-9 Codes

ICD-9 Code	Description of Category
I	Infectious Diseases
II	Neoplasms
III	Endocrine, Nutritional, Immune System, and Metabolic Disease
IV	Diseases of Blood and Blood Forming Organs
V	Mental Disorders
VI	Diseases of the Nervous System and Sense Organs
VII	Diseases of the Circulatory System
VIII	Diseases of the Respiratory System
IX	Diseases of the Digestive System
X	Diseases of the Genitourinary System
XI	Complications of Pregnancy, Childbirth, and the Puerperium
XII	Diseases of the Skin and Subcutaneous Tissue
XIII	Diseases of the Musculoskeletal System and Connective Tissue
XIV	Congenital Anomalies
XV	Certain Conditions Originating in the Perinatal Period
XVI	Symptoms, Signs, and Ill-Defined Conditions
XVII	Injury and Poisoning

Notes

[1] Sloan and Bentkover (1979) review part of this literature.

[2] Kupor et al. (1995) provide an estimate of the coefficient on average copayment level, β, in a regression of utilization by prefecture on a vector of explanatory variables. We obtained the mean value of the utilization rate, Y, from the paper and the

mean price, p, via direct communication with the lead author. We calculate the price elasticity of demand implied by their regression estimate as follows:

$$estimated\ elasticity = \frac{\partial \ln Y_t}{\partial \ln p_t} \approx \frac{p}{Y}\frac{\partial Y_t}{\partial p_t} = \frac{p}{Y}\beta$$

where Y_t is the utilization rate in prefecture t, and p_t is the average copayment level in prefecture t.

[3] Whether or not elasticities vary across diagnostic categories is an empirical issue that can be settled only if the estimation technique used to measure elasticities is flexible enough to allow for differing elasticities.

[4] We exclude patients who are members of the smaller insurance plans, such as Seamen's Insurance, because those plans are indistinguishable in the data. Together, these patients make up less than 5% of the original sample.

[5] Utilization interval measures time between visits to the same facility and thus does not preclude the possibility of a visit to another facility in the intervening period.

[6] One plausible hypothesis is that physicians act as the patient's agent and therefore consider their costs, as well as clinical factors, in formulating their recommended utilization interval.

[7] Indexing by prefecture of the facility rather than by the patient's home prefecture appropriately accounts for regional price variation regardless of the source of this variation.

[8] Other private information may be available to patients, though the cost of attaining it is likely to be high. Although we do not observe directly the patients' retirement status, we assume that people in plan C over 65 years old are retired in order to calculate their copayment rate.

[9] Because prefectures are large regions, these values are not well measured with respect to any particular individual in the sample, but finer data on patient location are not available.

[10] The average value reported for time is calculated by imputing censored observations with the least number of weeks past the censoring point, 14 weeks, and therefore is an underestimate.

[11] See Kalbfleisch and Prentice (1980) or Amemiya (1985) for details on this procedure.

[12] Given the definition of price, we must note the sources of variation that identify the price elasticity estimates that are the central focus of this chapter. The price will vary for patients by their dependency status, insurance plan membership, diagnosis, and prefecture of residence. However, the first two variables are included in the model as separate controls and copayment rates across insurance plans tend not to vary. Because we run the model separately for patients in different diagnosis groups, the identification of price effects comes from geographic variation in expected out-of-pocket expenditures, arising perhaps from exogenous variation in disease severity within diagnosis groups. Such variation would induce differences in prices because points are calculated based on procedures performed as well as diagnosis.

[13] We are indebted to an anonymous referee for suggesting cross-validation to evaluate the performance of this model. Cross-validation has been used extensively in the statistical literature to determine good values for smoothing parameters in spline fitting and for testing model performance. See Efron (1979) for a brief review of the cross-validation technique in statistics.

[14] We thank a referee for pointing out that if outpatient demand comes in bundles

of visits that arise from a single episode of illness and if price changes impact the probability of such a bundle, rather than its size, then the analysis will underestimate the price elasticity. The cross-section data set we use is not sufficient to address this issue, though population-based studies on Japanese outpatient demand, such as Kupor et al. (1995), essentially take this effect into account in their measurement because they estimate demand curves with utilization within a given period as the measure of quantity. The fact that they obtain price elasticity estimates similar to ours indicates that this demand measurement issue does not induce a large bias.

[15] There are theoretical reasons to believe that the elasticity will be biased toward zero (relative to the structural elasticity). With the cap on monthly out-of-pocket expenditures, the budget set for consumers choosing between outpatient visits and other goods is kinked, with the usual downward-sloping portion and a flat portion past a given point determined by the cap. Consider a small price increase from P to P'. There are three groups of consumers to consider. First is the group operating on the linear, "normal" part of their budget constraint under both P and P'—their elasticity is measured correctly. Second is the people past their cap (consuming at zero price) at both P and P'—their elasticity is measured to be zero. Third are people who move from the downward-sloping portion of the budget constraint to the flat portion—their demand is measured to be upward sloping. An analysis of the budget constraint in light of standard utility theory reveals that no consumer will move from the flat portion to the downward-sloping portion of the budget constraint. Because no group has a measured elasticity biased away from zero, and two groups have elasticity biased toward zero, we conclude that the likely bias is toward zero.

[16] If the patient has not seen the doctor past the censoring point we assume that he goes on week 13. Although this leads to an overestimate of the number of visits per year, the bias is not large because the percentage of censored spells, which we report, is generally small.

[17] Point estimates are available upon request from the authors.

[18] Generally, one cannot rule out the possibility that patients who cross borders are merely seeking immediate care away from home. However, since we exclude first time visitors to a facility from the analysis, such a possibility does not seem likely.

[19] Of course, this effect is mitigated by the higher copayments that dependents generally pay.

[20] In order to limit the number of categories, we group $Pr(t = 10)$, $Pr(t = 11)$, $Pr(t = 12)$, and $Pr(t > 12)$ into a single $Pr(t \geq 10)$ category.

[21] The proof makes use of the i.i.d. assumption across individual observations, and the fact that β is estimated without the validation sample.

[22] Of course, there may be other sources of unobserved heterogeneity present which may effect the parameter estimates and standard errors. In general, one can not sign the direction of the bias.

4

Inpatient Hospital Choice

Over the past several decades, the health services research community has become very interested in developing appropriate definitions of the quality of hospital care and in the role of competition among hospitals in influencing the provision of quality care. As discussed by Donabedian (1987), hospital quality is a multidimensional attribute, and no single statistic can capture it fully. Furthermore, hospital quality likely means different things to different people; physicians, patients, hospital administrators, and regulators all have their own ideas of what constitutes high-quality care.

Because the patient is the ultimate consumer of care, the patient's perception of the quality of care is of particular interest. A widely held belief is that patients are best able to assess the interpersonal aspects of care but less able to assess its technical aspects. Our primary focus in this chapter is to identify and measure the aspects of quality that patients are sensitive to. We explore three issues in this chapter: the determinants of Japanese patients' perceptions of hospital quality; the implications of these assessments for the structure of demand for hospital care and therefore for the competitive environment hospitals face; and the role of the availability and quality of hospital care in influencing access to care.

There are important institutional differences between the U.S. and Japan that make Japan a particularly relevant context in which to ask these questions. In the U.S., patients are highly heterogeneous and face a very complicated decision when choosing among health care providers. Japanese patients are homogeneous in important ways, and their decision-making environment is much simpler.

This chapter is based upon: Vogt, W.B., Bhattacharya, J., Yoshikawa, A., and Nakahara, T. 1995. "Hospital Choice in Japan," *Occasional Paper Series*, Asia/Pacific Research Center, Stanford University.

Four factors combine to make the modelling of American patients' choices among providers difficult. Different patients have different levels of insurance coverage, and considerations of coinsurance and deductibles have been shown to influence their choices (Manning et al., 1987). In fact, Phibbs et al. (1993) and Dranove, White, and Wu (1993) both show that insurance coverage has an impact upon choice of hospital. Second, there is wide variation in the fees charged by physicians and hospitals. Third, patients' managed care plans often place constraints upon their choice of provider and/or treatment. Finally, patients' physicians typically hold admitting privileges at only a few hospitals, limiting the patients' choice even further. Burns and Wholey (1992) and Folland (1983) both document the influence of physicians upon hospital choice. These sources of heterogeneity (price variability, insurance variability, managed care restrictions, and physician practice and referral patterns) are unobservable or imperfectly observable, and thus are difficult to analyze or control for.

By comparison, Japanese patients face a relatively simple environment. It is free from these confounding considerations, leaving them free to choose their health care providers only upon the bases of convenience and perceived quality. Insurance coverage in Japan is universal and very similar across plans. All health insurance in Japan is based on fee for service; deductibles and copayments are low, and the conventional wisdom is that effects of variations in these variables upon choice are modest (Okimoto and Yoshikawa, 1993). Prices for all health services in Japan are fixed by the government through the national fee schedule set by the Ministry of Health and Welfare (*Koseisho*); thus, there are no differences, observed or unobserved, in fees among providers. Patients are free to choose any provider they like; indeed, it is sometimes suggested that Japanese patients have too much freedom of choice, because many go to university hospitals for relatively uncomplicated conditions. Finally, physicians' role in directing patients among hospitals is very different in Japan. Community-based physicians in Japan almost without exception do not have admitting or other privileges to practice at hospitals. When patients go to hospitals, they are treated exclusively by physicians employed by the hospital. Conversely, physicians who practice in hospitals do not maintain practices outside the hospital. This division between community and hospital-based physicians mitigates the confounding influence of physicians in Japan relative to the U.S. These features together make Japan an attractive environment in which to answer questions about the determinants of perceived quality and its influence on patient choice.[1]

Two primary methodologies have been employed in exploring the determinants and influence of quality on patient choice of hospital. The first is to conduct a survey of patients to elicit from them directly their perceptions of quality of care. For example, Okorafor (1983) conducted a survey of several hundred patients and physicians in Indianapolis. Respondents were asked to rate the importance of several factors in influencing their choice of hospital. For both physicians and patients, the most important factors were reported to be quality of nursing staff, availability of medical technology, and quality/friendliness of non-nursing staff.

In the second methodology, patients' choices among providers are used to infer their preferences and thus their evaluations of quality. There have been a substantial number of studies in this vein. These studies rely upon a multinomial logit model of hospital choice (McFadden, 1973), and they are estimated with either maximum likelihood or minimum chi-square techniques.

The first wave of these studies (Erikson and Finkler, 1985; Folland, 1983; Lee and Cohen, 1985; McGuirk and Porell, 1984) uses a multinomial logit model of demand and estimates via various versions of Theil's (1969) minimum chi-squared estimator. These studies come to similar conclusions regarding the important influences on patient choice. Distance or time from the patient's home to the hospital, availability of physicians, complexity of clinical services offered, and medical school affiliation all influence patient choice strongly. It is difficult to conclude whether the patterns of preferences exhibited in these studies are the result of patients' preferences or those of physicians.

A second wave of studies (Adams et al., 1991; Burns and Wholey, 1992; Dranove, White, and Wu, 1993; Garnick et al., 1989; Luft et al., 1990; Phibbs et al., 1993) utilizes maximum likelihood estimation of the conditional logit model. These studies explore a number of issues relating to patient choice, and several themes emerge, including: (1) patients are extremely sensitive to distance between their residence and the hospital in their choices, and (2) they prefer larger and more specialized hospitals. The effect of insurance on choice has been modeled as well. Dranove, White, and Wu (1993) and Phibbs et al. (1993) both find that Medicaid patients are significantly less likely than privately insured patients to receive care in hospitals with highly specialized services. Several authors have explored the effect of charges and outcome-based quality on choice of hospital, with mixed results.

In summary, survey evidence and common wisdom argue that both clinical and personal aspects of quality should have important influences on patient choice. To date, studies of patient choice in the U.S. have examined the effects of clinical outcomes and techno-logical structure measures of quality on patient choice and have not examined personal aspects of quality. Also, the results of patient choice are difficult to interpret, given the important and unobserved or imperfectly observed influence of physician admitting privileges, insurance type, price, and managed care restrictions. The observed patterns of choice represent a complex interaction among these several influences and are not directly interpretable as representing patient preferences.

We seek to extend previous work in this area in several ways. We are better able to isolate the influence of quality attributes from other determinants of patient choice because of the particular structure of the Japanese health care system. Due to our large sam-ple of hospitals, we can identify the effects of a large number of variables and include many variables that have shown evidence of being important in prior survey work but have, because of the limited number of hospitals in typical samples, been neglected since. We are also able to generalize to a larger patient population, because our data set covers all of Japan, rather than a single county or state.

Data

Our primary data source is the Ministry of Health and Welfare's 1990 Facility Survey (*Iryo Shisetu Chosa*). We use information on the number of inpatients, the number of beds, staffing levels, and the availability of various items of equipment and specialized facilities.

The patient flow data used in our definition of markets (described in the "Market Definition" section) are derived from the Ministry of Health and Welfare's 1990 Patient Survey (*Kanja Chosa*). The patient survey is a random sample of inpatients and outpatients who are using the health care system at any clinic or hospital on the day of the survey. Data on population and age structure in the various markets for hospital care in Japan are derived from the 1990 Population Census of Japan (Management and Coordina-tion Agency). We use two sources of supplementary data. Data on average revenue per patient are derived from the *Chiiki Iryohi Soran* (edited by *Koseisho*, 1991). Data on wages are taken from the *Chingin Sensasu* (Ministry of Labor, 1990).

Method

Model

Three aspects of the demand for hospital care are relevant to our research goals. To examine the influence of perceived quality on choice, we model patients' choices among hospitals. To examine the competitive structure of hospital markets in Japan, we model patients' choices among different types of hospitals. To examine the impact of quality and availability on access, we model patients' decision to seek care. A patient's decision to seek care depends upon the characteristics of the patient (health status) and the number and quality of available hospitals in the patient's market. Having decided to seek care, the patient must decide what type of hospital (large or small, teaching or nonteaching) at which to seek care. Again, the type of hospital chosen will depend upon the number and quality of the various types of hospitals available to the patient. For example, in a market with many high-quality teaching hospitals, one expects patients to be more likely to choose a teaching hospital. Finally, having decided, say, to seek care at a teaching hospital, the patient must determine which one to use. To make this choice, the patient must weigh the characteristics of the various teaching hospitals and choose the one with the most desirable combination. We model the process in three stages in order to separate the effects of availability and quality on access (the first stage), the degree of market segmentation (the second stage), and the factors influencing the determination of which hospital the patient perceives as the best (the third stage). This model explicitly incorporates the dependence of the decisions in each of the early stages upon the choices available to patients in the later stages and upon heterogeneity in patient preferences over different hospitals and types of hospitals. The primary improvement of this model over multinomial logit is that it accounts for the fact that the unobserved components of patients' utility for different hospitals are correlated.

In order to estimate this staged choice, we utilize the nested logit model (McFadden, 1981). In our setting, the model is described by three conditional probabilities. The first of these is the probability of choosing a particular hospital, given that the patient has decided to seek care and has chosen to use a hospital of a particular type.

This probability is hypothesized to depend upon the characteristics of the hospitals available to the patient. Thus, the probability of a patient choosing hospital j given that he or she chooses from a hospital of type n is:

$$P(j|B_n) = \frac{\exp(X_j\beta)}{\sum_{j'\in B_n} \exp(X_{j'}\beta)} \tag{4-1}$$

where $j = 1, 2, \ldots, J_i$ is hospitals in market i; $n = 1, 2, \ldots, N$ is types of hospitals; $B_1, \ldots, B_N$ is B_n, the set of hospitals of type n; X_j are the characteristics of hospital j; and Y_i are the characteristics of individual i.

The left-hand side of Equation 4-1 is the probability of seeking care at hospital j, given that the patient has decided to seek care at a hospital of type n. This part of the model is similar to those used in previous work on hospital choice. A patient's probability of choosing a particular hospital depends both on the characteristics of the hospital chosen and on the characteristics of the hospitals rejected.

The second conditional probability is that, having chosen to seek care, a patient chooses a particular type of hospital n. This probability is:

$$P(B_n|\text{seek}) = \frac{a_n\{\sum_{j\in B_n} \exp(X_j\beta)\}^{\rho_n}}{\sum_{n'=1}^{N} a_{n'}\{\sum_{j'\in B_{n'}} \exp(X_{j'}\beta)\}^{\rho_{n'}}} \tag{4-2}$$

In this expression, the left-hand side is the probability that the patient chooses a hospital of a particular type (say a teaching hospital), given that the patient has chosen to seek care. The term in brakets is essentially an index of the aggregate quality of the hospitals of a particular type. So a patient's probability of choosing a particular type of hospital depends on the number and quality of the hospitals of that type and on the quality of the other types of hospitals available. The a's and ρ's are parameters to be estimated. The parameters ρ_n deserve special attention. They are a measure of how similar or dissimilar the various categories of hospitals appear to patients. A ρ_v close to 1 indicates that patients perceive hospitals in different categories to be close substitutes for one another.

Conversely, a ρ_n less than one indicates that hospitals in different categories are not close substitutes. Categories of hospitals that are close substitutes compete directly with one another for patients. In this context, the parameters ρ_n will enable us to examine whether or not, for example, patients view teaching and nonteaching hospitals as close or distant substitutes and, therefore, whether there are likely to be important competitive effects among the two groups.

The third probability is that a patient seeks care. The probability of a patient i with characteristics Y_i seeking care is

$$P(\text{seek}|Y_i) = \frac{a_{\text{seek}}(\sum_{n=1}^{N} a_n \{\sum_{j \in B_n} \exp(X_j \beta)\}^{\rho_n})^{\rho_{\text{seek}}}}{\exp(Y_i \theta) + a_{\text{seek}}(\sum_{n=1}^{N} a_n \{\sum_{j \in B_n} \exp(X_j \beta)\}^{\rho_n})^{\rho_{\text{seek}}}}$$

(4-3)

Y_i is a vector of characteristics of an individual considering the decision to seek care. Again, the term in brackets is effectively an index of the availability and quality of hospital care in the patient's market, and a_{seek}, ρ_{seek}, and θ are parameters to be estimated. The parameter ρ_{seek} measures the responsiveness of access to the availability of care—a positive value indicates that a greater number of hospitals in a market enhances access. In our data, we do not observe individual decisions to seek care; we observe only aggregate counts. Thus, we must integrate Equation 4-3 over the unobserved patient characteristics Y_i in each market in order to estimate the model:

$$P(\text{seek}) = \int_Y P(\text{seek}|Y)dF(Y).$$

(4-4)

$F(Y)$ is the distribution of Y in the population (in our case, the age distribution in each market for hospital care). Graphically, our model is represented in Figure 4-1.

Estimation Technique

The estimation technique operates in two steps. In the first step, we use Theil's (1969) estimator to estimate the third stage of the model, choice of hospital within each category.[2] Observe that:

$$\ln(P(j|B_n)) - \ln(P(j'|B_n)) = (X_j - X_{j'})\beta.$$

(4-5)

To implement this model, we take the log of each hospital's market share within its category. Then, within each category of each market, we choose the median hospital (in terms of bed size) to be the contrast hospital. We regress the difference of the log market share between each hospital and the contrast hospital upon the difference in characteristics between each hospital and the contrast hospital. We use generalized least squares regression to account

PATIENT BEHAVIOR

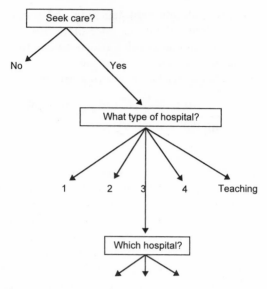

Figure 4-1
Patient Choice of Hospital

for the covariance among the choices. This produces a consistent, asymptotically normal, efficient estimate for b that is asymptotically equivalent to the (conditional) maximum likelihood estimate.

With the estimate of β in hand, the second step of the estimation algorithm proceeds to estimate the first and second stages of the demand model via maximum likelihood methods, after substituting the estimated value for β into the likelihood function. To wit, the contribution to the likelihood function of someone who chooses to seek care at a hospital in category n is:

$$P(B_n|\text{seek})\,P(\text{seek}) \tag{4-6}$$

The contribution of a person who does not seek care is:

$$1 - P(\text{seek}) \tag{4-7}$$

The forms of these functions were previously given. We model the distribution of ages in the population with a multinomial distribution having age categories 0–29, 30–44, 45–64, and 65+ as points of support. We enter the dependence on age of the decision to seek care in our model via dummy variables for each of the four age categories; this functional form can be interpreted as a spline approximating the true age-response function. In Equations 4-2 and 4-3 above, we substitute the estimated value for β for the true value. Using estimated values in this way does not affect the consistency of the estimates (McFadden, 1981).

Variables

As already described, the dependent variable in the third stage of the model is the difference between each firm's log market share and the log market share of the contrast firm in it its category. For the upper levels of the analysis, the technique is maximum likelihood, so the dependent variable is each patient's choice of hospital category. We construct five categories of hospitals: 20–49 beds, 50–99 beds, 100–199 beds, 200+ beds, and all teaching hospitals. We divide hospitals on the basis of size because of the frequently reported result that patients are more likely to prefer large to small hospitals. Furthermore, we put teaching hospitals in a separate category because they have a different role than nonteaching hospitals and there is a widespread perception in Japan that teaching hospitals provide higher quality care than nonteaching hospitals.

The independent variables at each stage are hospital characteristics. A number of considerations guided our choice of independent variables. In previous work, such variables as the size, ownership, teaching status, and complexity of clinical services offered have been found to influence choice. The survey evidence we describe indicates the importance of including measures of staffing, and the facility survey provides several such measures. We also solicit opinions from many Japanese physicians, administrators, health economists, and regulators. The most commonly mentioned influences on patient choice are reputation, level of personal service, comfort of surroundings, and ability to offer sophisticated clinical services.

To capture the effect of the level and quality of service on demand, we include a number of staffing measures: registered nurses (RNs) per bed, practical nurses (PNs) per bed, nurse aides per bed, and other staff per bed. Of the quality variables we include, staffing levels are the ones most easily generally observable by patients. Room size is another quality variable easily observed by patients. To capture patients' likely preference for hospitals with more comfortable rooms, we include a measure of the floor area of the wards divided by the number of beds in them. We capture reputation crudely by variables measuring the teaching status, ownership, and

Table 4-1
Variable Definitions

Variable	Definition
c	Constant term
Pub	1 if the hospital is owned by the government
NPO	1 if the hospital is owned by a charitable institution
Ins	1 if the hospital is owned by an insurance society
Prv	1 if the hospital is privately owned (omitted contrast)
bed	Natural log of the number of beds
area	Natural log of ward area per bed
RN	Natural log of the number of RNs per bed
PN	Natural log of the number of PNs per bed
NA	Natural log of the number of nurse aides per bed
oth	Natural log of the number of other staff per bed
labs	Numer of laboratory facilities the hospital reports
fiber	1 if the hospital provides gastrointestinal endoscopy
CT	1 if the hospital has a CT scanner
MRI	1 if the hospital has an MRI machine
MCR	1 if the hospital performs microsurgery
ESWL	1 if the hospital has an ESWL
EEG	1 if the hospital has an electroencephalograph
ICU	1 if the hospital has an intensive care unit

number of beds in the hospital. The conventional wisdom is that public hospitals, teaching hospitals, and bigger hospitals have the best reputation. We model the complexity of the services offered at the hospital by including dummy variables for a wide variety of medical technologies. All continuous variables are entered in logs. Those chosen for inclusion in the analysis are summarized in Table 4-1.

Market Definition

Because our approach depends upon identifying the differences in market share among competing hospitals, our definition of market must include all of a hospital's competitors and not include extraneous, noncompeting hospitals. Distance has been shown, very robustly, to be a major determinant of hospital choice, so a geographical definition of markets is appropriate here.[3]

To construct our markets, we use the algorithm introduced by Elzinga and Hogarty (1973). In this technique, product (in our case, patient) flow data are used to construct markets. This algorithm constructs markets that have the property that few patients who live inside each market leave the market to seek care elsewhere. The algorithm operates as follows: We begin with a set of proposed markets and examine the number of patients who live in each one who seek care in their home market and the total number who seek care in that market; the ratio of the second to the first is called LOFI. We also consider the ratio of the number of patients who live in each proposed market who seek care in their home market to the total number of patients who seek care from the market; this ratio is called LIFO. Any market for which either LIFO or LOFI is below 0.90 is too small, and it is combined with adjacent markets. This process of making markets larger proceeds until no market remains with either LOFI or LIFO less than 0.90. This algorithm produces a set of markets with the property that very few patients who live in one market seek care in any other market.

Koseisho has divided Japan into 345 "medical zones." These are administrative areas intended to represent markets for hospital care; they are used to regulate such things as hospital bed supply and ambulance service. The patient flow data we have access to via the patient survey are based upon medical zones, so medical zones are our proposed markets for the first iteration of the Elzinga-Hogarty algorithm. At the termination of the algorithm, we are left with 61 markets for inpatient medical services in Japan. Within these markets, we select for analysis the Japanese equivalent of community hospitals.[4]

Results

The results of the hospital-level regressions (stage 1) appear in Table 4-2. Across the top of the table are the various categories of hospitals, and the variables are down the side. Positive coefficients indicate that an increase in the variable increases the hospital's market share.

The first interesting result is the effect of ownership on market share. Public ownership in the small hospitals is associated with low market share, and public ownership of larger hospitals is associated with higher market share. This accords well with intuition. The large public teaching hospitals and large public nonteaching hospitals in Japan have the best reputation; the smaller public and private hospitals enjoy weaker repute.

The next rows down from the ownership rows are numbers of beds and area/bed. As expected, both of these variables enter strongly and significantly positive. Patients prefer larger hospitals, either *per se* or because size and reputation are related, as discussed

Table 4-2
Hospital-Level Market Share Regressions

| Variable | Hospital Category | | | | |
	20–49	50–99	100–199	200+	Teaching
c	−0.013	0.002	−0.012	0.006	−0.059
Pub	−0.109[†]	−0.183**	−0.118**	0.014	0.066
NPO	−0.256**	0.036**	−0.024	0.017	N/A
Ins	−1.053**	−0.312**	0.023	0.077**	N/A
bed	1.384**	1.264**	1.050**	0.982**	1.086**
area	0.141**	0.059**	0.113**	0.049**	0.035**
RN	0.132**	0.056**	0.034**	0.073**	0.231**
PN	0.233**	0.173**	0.110**	0.008	0.027
NA	−0.009	0.042**	0.029**	0.056**	0.020
oth	0.0165**	0.192**	0.040**	−0.078**	0.137**
labs	−0.002	−0.007	−0.020	0.081	−0.315*
fiber	0.037[†]	0.017	−0.0113**	−0.106**	−0.024
CT	0.033	−0.002	0.099**	−0.100**	−0.053
MRI	0.189[†]	−0.015	0.040[†]	0.051**	−0.009
MCR	−0.148**	−0.037	0.030*	0.082**	0.049*
ESWL	−0.319*	−0.062	0.044*	0.001	−0.017
EEG	0.179**	0.034**	0.027**	−0.083**	−0.055
ICU	−0.104**	−0.012	−0.029**	0.052**	−0.010
R^2	0.372	0.593	0.576	0.878	0.959
Staff χ^2 (4)	295.5[†]	543.5[†]	166.4[†]	131.4[†]	77.6*
eqpt χ^2 (8)	107.5[†]	18.7	137.8[†]	244.5[†]	10.1
N	1763	2088	1717	1503	235

* denotes significance at the 10% level.
** denotes significance at the 5% level.
[†] denotes significance at the 1% level.

earlier. The results for the area variable also accord well with our intuition. Patients are very sensitive to the spaciousness of their accommodation while in the hospital.

The next group of variables is the staffing group. As with area, there is a positive relationship between staffing ratios and demand— patients prefer hospitals with high ratios of staff to beds and thus more intensive personal services. The striking thing about the staffing variables is the uniformity with which they are positive and significant. We find this result in every specification of the model we estimate. This result can also be seen in the third to last row of the table, where the χ^2 statistic for the joint null that all staffing variables have coefficients of zero is reported.

The pattern of the coefficients as one moves across the table is also interesting. The ratio of the coefficient on RN to that on PN is low for the smaller hospitals and high for the larger ones. This says that patients have a stronger preference for being served by RNs (relative to PNs) in larger hospitals and a weaker preference for such service in smaller hospitals. This likely reflects the higher marginal value to the patient of the RN's additional training when the patient is more ill. Because sicker patients tend to go to larger hospitals and to teaching hospitals, it is natural that patients would express stronger preferences for skilled staffing at these hospitals. The larger hospitals and teaching hospitals employ more RNs relative to the number of PNs, reflecting the demands of a more severely ill patient population.

In sharp contrast to the results with staffing, there is no clear and consistent positive relationship between possession of medical technology and demand for the hospital. In many cases, there are positive coefficients: MRI, microsurgery, and EEG show positive coefficients more often than negative. But there is no overall pattern of positive influence of technology possession upon demand. Although the joint null hypothesis that the technology variables do not enter can be rejected for most of the models, comparing the magnitudes of the staffing and technology χ^2 statistics reveals the greater explanatory power of the staffing variables. Hospitals with a large investment in high-tech equipment have, on average, much greater market share than their competitors. However, after we control for the influence of size, staffing, and ownership, the relationship between medical technology and demand disappears. At first blush, this result is quite surprising, given our review of the literature and discussions with Japanese researchers and health care experts. However, given that technical aspects of quality are more difficult for patients to observe and to evaluate and given the smaller role played by physicians in directing patients to hospitals in Japan, it is perhaps not so surprising that demand is more responsive to interpersonal aspects of care than to the possession of medical technology.

In Table 4-3, the coefficient estimates for the market demand structure (Equations 4-2 and 4-3) appear. The coefficients ρ_1 through ρ_t reveal that the various types of hospitals are close substitutes for one another. This means that changes in behavior by hospitals in any of the categories we consider will affect the decisions of each of the other types of hospitals (i.e., that there are competitive interactions among the decisions of firms in these different categories). The coefficient ρ_{seek} is small and negative, indicating that the availability of hospitals in a market does not have

Table 4-3
Market Demand Structure

Parameter	Estimate	Standard Error
p_1	0.955	0.004
p_2	0.945	0.003
p_3	0.962	0.002
p_4	0.956	0.002
p_t	0.977	0.002
p_{seek}	−0.032	0.001
θ_{65}	−3.097	0.013
θ_{45}	−0.272	0.018
θ_{30}	−0.129	0.035

Table 4-4
Median Elasticities and Marginal Revenues

Variable	Elasticity	Marginal Revenue (¥)
beds	0.7237	65,464
area	0.0486	280
RN	0.0561	34,418
PN	0.1723	51,018
NA	0.0295	27,629
other	0.1640	28,592

any large influence upon access. This is largely as one would expect, given the universality and relative homogeneity of health insurance coverage and of prices in Japan. Negative coefficients for the age categories indicate that people in those categories are more likely to seek care. The largest negative coefficient is for people aged 65 years and over, yielding the conclusion that demand for medical care is highest for that group. The coefficients for age categories 45–64 and 30–44 are lesser in magnitude than the coefficient for the elderly category.

Table 4-4 contains the median estimated value of the demand elasticities with respect to each of the inputs and the median estimated value for the marginal (monthly) revenue associated with increasing each of the inputs.[5] We find that demand is fairly responsive to the size of the hospital, with a median elasticity of 0.72. Each of the labor inputs has substantially lower elasticities, ranging from 0.03 to 0.17.

The second column of Table 4-4 reports the (monthly) marginal revenue associated with an increase in the level of each of the inputs.[6] From these figures, we can assess the degree to which hospitals can influence their revenues by creating the perception of high quality in consumers' minds. By adding a bed, a hospital expects a demand increase equivalent to about ¥65,000; the marginal revenue associated with increasing the amount of space around a bed by one square meter is approximately ¥280 per month. The cost of building a square meter of hospital floor space is estimated at ¥240,000 on average. The revenues associated with hiring additional RNs and PNs are approximately ¥34,000 and ¥51,000 respectively. These compare with monthly wages of about ¥315,000 and ¥263,000, respectively.

Conclusions

We estimate a model of demand for inpatient care in Japan, finding that Japanese patients are consistently sensitive to the interpersonal and physical aspects of quality of care and hospital size. We find much less evidence that they are sensitive to more technical aspects of care. The magnitudes of the effects in the case of staffing are large enough that staffing strategies should be expected to be important strategic variables of these firms (i.e., quality competition should be expected to be mediated at least in part through staffing levels). We also find that markets for inpatient hospital care are not segmented to a significant degree; different categories of hospitals are substitutes for one another. Finally, we find that the availability of hospital care in a market is not an important determinant of access to care.

These findings have several implications for health care policy in Japan. First, given that access is not significantly affected by availability of care, controlling for a population's age indicates that rural patients are not greatly underserved, at least to the extent that they are equally able to obtain care. This is likely due to the success of Japan's policy of universal insurance. Second, the finding that hospitals have strong and consistent incentives to compete on the interpersonal aspects of care provision has implications for regulatory policies. Japan has relatively low hospital nursing staff levels, compared with other countries, and some policy measures have been taken in order to raise these levels (Okimoto and Yoshikawa, 1993). Our results indicate that it may be worthwhile to explore the possibility of raising these staffing levels by fostering competition among hospitals on this basis. One possible policy instrument available for this use is the restrictive limitations on hospital advertising now in place.[7] By selectively relaxing these restrictions, Japanese policy-makers may be able simultaneously to increase staffing levels, improve the public's information regarding their health care options, and improve the public's satisfaction with its quality of care.

Notes

[1] For a more complete description of the Japanese health care system, see Okimoto and Yoshikawa (1993). Several caveats are pertinent to our discussion of the differences in financing regime and institutional structure between Japan and the U.S. Although patients in Japan are free to choose any hospital at which to consume care, their particular condition and the facilities available at hospitals affect their choices. By our use of the nested logit model, we control for this confounder—by separating hospitals on the basis of complexity (size and teaching role), we allow sicker patients to have higher valuation for more complex hospitals through the correlation in the structural utility function errors (McFadden, 1981). Also, some physicians in large public hospitals do "moonlight" in community clinics. However, this exception to the general rule of separation between hospital and community practice applies to relatively few hospitals and physicians. Finally, in some cases, there are (illegal) payments from patients to physicians and to hospitals; however, this practice is prevalent to a much greater degree in geriatric hospitals (removed from our sample) than in others.

[2] In much previous work, models of this type are implemented via maximum likelihood techniques, using patient-specific information. A consistent finding is that distance to the hospital is an important determinant of hospital choice. Unfortunately, our data consist of aggregate counts of patients at hospitals, so this technique may not be applied here. Garnick et al. (1989) provide a discussion of issues of estimation technique in hospital choice models. They point out that Theil's estimator, like other minimum chi-squared estimators for discrete data, suffers from considerable difficulties when there are cells with no observations. Our data do not suffer from this problem, because they are aggregated to a level precluding zero observations in any cell.

[3] Market definition has been discussed extensively in the health services research literature. Previous market definitions have been based upon U.S. counties, Standard Metropolitan Statistical Areas, fixed radii around hospitals, zip codes, and patient flows. Our market definition technique is most similar to that used in Garnick et al. (1989). Our markets, however, are smaller than are those constructed therein.

[4] Our goal in selecting hospitals for analysis is to restrict our analysis to short-term general hospitals, similar to the set of community hospitals defined in the U.S. by the American Hospital Association and frequently used for analysis in similar studies. To select for the equivalent of community hospitals in Japan, we begin with the full sample of 10,096 hospitals and eliminate all tuberculosis and leprosy hospitals. To eliminate hospitals whose primary patient load is psychiatric, we select out all hospitals whose case load is comprised of more than 50% psychiatric patients. To eliminate the many hospitals in Japan that are effectively nursing homes, we remove all hospitals that have allocated more than 50% of their beds for geriatric care. This selection leaves a sample of 7,599 hospitals.

[5] We use medians rather than means because of the skewed distribution of these variables. Because the inputs were log-transformed, very small values of an input lead, in several cases, to very high estimates for the elasticities and for the marginal revenues.

[6] We construct the data on marginal revenue by multiplying the derivative of each hospital's demand function by the average inpatient reimbursement for the prefecture in which the hospital is located.

[7] Japanese hospitals are currently forbidden to advertise any aspect of their services other than their hours of operation.

Part II

Provider Ownership and Performance

Japan's hospital sector is characterized by a diversity of ownership arrangements. The 10,096 hospitals in Japan are owned by governments, nonprofit organizations, insurance societies, and individual physicians. These ownership arrangements give rise to discussions of possible differences in treatment at the various types of hospitals. Hospitals in separate categories may provide dissimilar types, quantities, or qualities of care, or they may provide this care at varying levels of efficiency.

This section focuses on differences in efficiency between government-owned and privately owned hospitals. This issue is of interest in the context of Japan's health care system because of the extensive system of subsidies for government hospitals. Japanese public hospitals frequently run operating losses, which are made up by generous government subsidies. These amounted to approximately ¥560 billion in 1991.

Several explanations for these subsidies have been given. Some suggest that government hospitals are inefficiently run, that they pay their staff excessively, and that they consequently run large deficits. Another possible explanation is that government hospitals provide higher quality (hence more expensive) care than their private counterparts. A third potential explanation is that government hospitals treat the most difficult caseload of patients, and because the fee schedule does not adjust for severity, this leads to the losses.

Technical inefficiency (or X-inefficiency) occurs if a firm could have produced the same outputs (here, patient care) with fewer inputs (capital, labor, materials, etc.) than it did. A firm exhibits allocative inefficiency (but not technical inefficiency) if it could produce the same level of outputs at a lower cost by substituting one type of input for another.

113

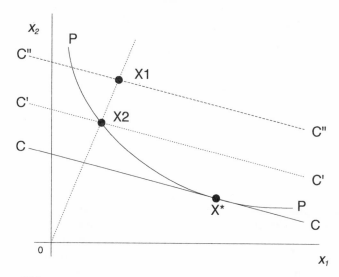

Figure II-1

Koopmans (1951) defines technical efficiency as follows: A producer is technically efficient if an increase in any output requires a reduction in at least one other output or an increase in at least one input and if a reduction in any input requires an increase in at least one other input or a reduction in at least one output.

Allocative efficiency results when hospitals do not exhibit cost minimization behavior at the point on the isoquant at which they are producing. In other words, if the marginal rate of substitution is not equal to the relative price of inputs, the hospital can reduce cost by changing the combination of inputs at the given output level.

Economic inefficiency (EI) can be divided into technical and allocative inefficiencies. To understand this, consider Figure II-1. The two axes X_1 and X_2 represent amounts of two inputs, say MDs and RNs. The curve PP is an isoquant of the production function and represents all the different combinations of the two inputs that will produce the same level of output (a given quantity of patient care). Because each input must be paid a wage for its use, the curves C, C', and C'' represent quantities of the inputs that can be purchased at the given cost level.

X^* is the economically efficient production level because it produces the output at the least cost. Production at X2 would be technically efficient (because it is on PP) but not allocatively efficient (because it requires C' more than C to be spent to purchase inputs). Point X1 is technically inefficient (because it is not on PP). Let the actual production be at point X1. Economic inefficiency is measured as the ratio of C'' to C:

$$EI = C''/C. \tag{II-1}$$

Technical inefficiency (TI) is measured as the movement from point X1 to X2:

$$TI = C''/C'. \tag{II-2}$$

Allocative inefficiency (AI) is measured as the movement from point X2 to X*:

$$AI = C'/C. \tag{II-3}$$

There is the following relation among the three efficiency measures:

$$EI = TI * AI. \tag{II-4}$$

The preceding discussion implicitly holds output quality constant. Although these concepts are readily extended to consider quality as well, in practice it is often difficult to measure quality. Apparent differences in efficiency may reflect only differences in quality—that is, a firm producing a high-quality output may appear inefficient relative to one producing a low-quality output if it is impossible to distinguish their relative quality levels.

The three chapters in this section explore differences in efficiency from three different methodological and theoretical perspectives. In Chapter 5, we examine differences in input use (labor and technology) relative to outputs produced in order to draw inferences indirectly about differences in behavior between government and private teaching hospitals. The technique described in Chapter 5 permits examination of differences in the use of technology and the employment of skilled staffing between government and private sector hospitals. It is possible to quantify differences in technology acquisition, technology use, and staffing directly between the two sectors.

Chapter 6 provides a measure of allocative efficiency in labor, assuming that no technical inefficiency exists. In this chapter, we identify differences in staffing between government and private hospitals and draw inferences about efficiency and about differences in the objective functions being pursued by hospitals in the two sectors. The advantage of this approach is that it permits inferences to be drawn about the hospitals' underlying preferences.

In Chapter 7, a data envelopment analysis (DEA) is reported of differences in technical efficiency between government and private hospitals. It examines the potential technical inefficiency of hospitals and allows examination of differences in technical efficiency between categories of hospitals. Unlike that in Chapter 5 and 6, the analysis in Chapter 7 requires no assumptions on the functional forms of hospitals' production functions.

Several unmeasured factors may be important in interpreting the analyses. First, in none of the studies is there a good control for the case mix of the hospitals. This means that a hospital may appear to be inefficient when it simply has a more difficult than average case mix. Second, hospitals are complex institutions that use many inputs, and some of these cannot easily be measured or incorporated into the analyses. Again, a hospital may appear by our measures to be inefficient if it is using more of the inputs we can measure to substitute for fewer of the inputs we cannot measure. Third, the quality of care hospitals provide is heterogeneous, and we cannot control for these differences in our analyses.

5

Technology and Staffing in University Hospitals

One striking feature of the health care industry is the diversity in the ownership of hospitals. In the U.S., for example, 17% of the hospitals are private for profit, 51% are private nonprofit, and 32% are government owned (American Hospital Association, 1986). Similarly, in Japan, 77% of hospitals are privately owned,[1] 8% are owned by nonprofit organizations or insurance societies, and 15% are government-owned. Those formulating policy for the hospital sector must understand differences in behavior among the various classes of ownership.

It has been suggested that private hospitals engage in prestige-building acquisitions of medical technology (Kopit and McCann, 1988; Lee, 1971; Newhouse, 1970; Robinson and Luft, 1985) or of nursing staff (Lee, 1971; Robinson, 1988). This could conceivably lead to excess employment of labor and/or overinvestment in capital in private hospitals (Valdmanis, 1992). Private hospitals may be more efficient than government hospitals because they pay more attention to profit (Register and Bruning, 1987). Understanding the magnitudes of and interplay among these effects is crucial to developing health care policies aimed at minimizing cost without sacrificing quality.

Hospitals owned in the private and public sectors may behave differently for two basic reasons. First, they may have different objectives. This potential difference is particularly compelling when examining private, for-profit hospitals versus government-owned

This chapter is based upon: Vogt, W.B., Kupor, S., Bhattacharya, J., Yoshikawa, A., and Nakahara, T. 1996. "Technology and Staffing in Japanese University Hospitals: Government vs. Private," *International Journal of Technology Assessment in Health Care* 12(1). This revised version is published with the permission of the Cambridge University Press.

hospitals. Government hospitals and government-owned organizations in general seem unlikely to pursue profit as their primary objective. Indeed, objectives such as budget maximization or output maximization have been posited as more plausible (Newhouse, 1970; Niskanen, 1971; Sloan and Steinwald, 1980). By contrast, for-profit institutions consider profit (and, by implication, efficiency) to be a primary goal.

Second, private and government hospitals may face different constraints. Because government and private hospitals receive dissimilar levels of compensation, treat varying case mixes of patients, face unlike regulatory requirements, and have various input costs, it is reasonable to believe that their behavior will differ as well.

This chapter examines behavior disparities among Japanese government-owned and privately owned university hospitals and draws inferences regarding the likely causes of these differences. Government hospitals in Japan receive substantial subsidies, and our primary focus is upon the effects of these subsidies. Specifically, government hospitals run under a nominal global budget; however, when they suffer a loss, the government reimburses them for it. We hypothesize that, other things being equal, the presence of subsidies in government hospitals ameliorates the cost pressures facing administrators in these hospitals and may lead to less cost-conscious purchasing and utilization strategies.

We focus specifically on university hospitals to mitigate the effect of a number of possible confounding influences. To quantify variations in behavior between government and private hospitals, we examine staffing levels, acquisition of a number of medical technologies, and rates of utilization for those technologies. These variables are relevant measures of behavior because technology and staffing policies contribute to the prestige, teaching efficacy, and cost of care at hospitals. In our analysis, we adjust for disparities in patient loads and case mix. Our analysis also accounts for the truncation of the utilization variable (that is, utilization is zero if a hospital does not possess a particular technology).

Several authors have explored differences in the diffusion of technology among hospitals in various ownership categories. For example, a number of studies focus on the diffusion of technology in U.S. hospitals, using ownership variables as controls. These studies generally find that government hospitals are less likely to adopt technologies (Luft et al., 1986; Russell, 1979; Sloan et al. 1986) or that government hospitals are slower to adopt new technologies (Duffy, 1992; Lee and Waldman, 1985; Russell, 1979). These results are often explained by the less lucrative insurance mix or the controls on capital expenditure typical of government hospitals in the U.S. Sloan et al. (1986) also find differences in volume between private and government hospitals. Government hospitals perform fewer procedures than do their private counterparts.

There has also been work on differences in staffing patterns among government and private-sector hospitals in the U.S. Robinson (1988) includes ownership dummies as controls in an analysis of the effects of competition upon staffing patterns. Robinson finds that government hospitals have lower demand for nursing staff and tend to employ a less rich staffing mix, because they employ a greater ratio of practical to registered nurses. Sloan and Steinwald (1980) also find that government hospitals employ a lower staff mix; however, they find that government hospitals employ more practical nurses and other staff than do their private counterparts.

There is also a substantial literature concerned with the relative efficiency of government and private hospitals. This literature is divided into two strands: the cost-based approach and the data envelopment analysis (DEA) approach. In cost regressions, dummy variables are often included as either controls or objects of interest. The results of these studies are inconclusive, with some authors finding that government hospitals have higher costs (Fournier and Mitchell, 1992; Robinson and Luft, 1985; Sloan and Steinwald, 1980), others finding them to have lower costs (Cowing and Holtman, 1983; Granneman, Brown, and Pauly, 1986), and still others finding little difference (Becker and Sloan, 1985). There are similarly mixed results in the DEA branch of the literature. Some authors find evidence that government hospitals are more efficient while others find no difference (Grosskopf and Valdmanis, 1987; Valmanis, 1990, 1992).

Our study adds to this body of evidence in two ways. First, to date, these questions have been posed primarily in the context of U.S. hospitals, and our study broadens this empirical base to Japanese hospitals. Second, the particular structure of health care financing and provision in Japan, in conjunction with a judicious choice of hospitals for analysis, allows us to control for a wide variety of possibly confounding influences and to draw conclusions regarding the likely cause of the differences we observe.

University Hospitals in Japan

University hospitals are the most prestigious hospitals in Japan. As a group, they are similar to the members of the Council of Teaching Hospitals in the U.S. They are large, tertiary care facilities that produce patient care, training for residents, and research. They are more expensive, offer a greater range of clinical services, and employ more staff than their nonteaching counterparts. They are important in determining the patterns of practice and medical technology diffusion throughout the Japanese hospital system (Holt et al., 1992).

Of the 164 university hospitals, 67 are owned by the Ministry of Education and are affiliated with public university medical schools, and 88 are owned by various private universities and are affiliated with those universities' medical schools. The financial environments these two groups face are quite different. All hospitals in Japan are reimbursed for patient care from the same nationally set fee schedule, so this reimbursement is the same across the two groups. Both the private university and the Ministry of Education hospitals receive subsidies from the national government to defray the costs of education. However, the teaching subsidies provided to the government hospitals are greater in extent and amount. Government hospitals receive additional subsidies to offset operating losses which they consistently incur. These factors combined create a considerably more relaxed financial environment for government hospitals than for private hospitals. For a detailed description of the system of teaching hospitals in Japan, see Holt et al. (1992).

We focus on university hospitals in Japan to control for a number of confounding influences and to enhance our ability to draw conclusions from the differences we find. Two important features distinguish government from private university hospitals. The first is in ownership and control, which may imply a difference in the objectives hospitals pursue. By our narrow focus upon university hospitals for analysis, we hope to minimize this difference. The second important difference is in financing. Government hospitals receive a substantial annual subsidy; private university hospitals do not. These subsidies constitute a difference in the constraints facing the government hospitals; they have less incentive to economize in their operations, because their government owners underwrite their losses.

Data and Methods

Our data source is the 1990 Facility Survey (*Iryo Shisetsu Chosa*), collected in September of each year by the Japanese Ministry of Health and Welfare (*Koseisho*). In our analysis, we focus upon 12 medical technologies and upon staffing variables. The technologies we consider (and their mnemonic abbreviations) are gastrointestinal

(GI) endoscopy, ultrasound (US), head computed tomography scanning (HCT), body computed tomography (CT scanning), magnetic resonance imaging (MRI), extracorporeal shock-wave lithotripsy (ESWL), dialysis (DIA), intensive care unit (ICU), digital angiography (DIGA), cine angiography (CINA), and electroencephalography (EEG). These technologies run the gamut from common and relatively inexpensive (GI endoscope and US) to rarer and relatively expensive (MRI and ESWL). Many of these technologies, especially HCT, MRI, and ESWL, have been singled out in Japan as having diffused too quickly and into extensive use (Niki, 1985; Yoshikawa, 1993). The five staffing variables we measure are the numbers of registered nurses (RN), practical nurses (PN), nurse aides (NA), full-time MDs (FTMD), and part-time MDs (PTMD). As described in Chapter 1, in Japan hospitals have closed medical staffs, and those physicians who practice in a hospital are employed directly by that hospital. Few physicians have both community practices and admitting privileges at a hospital.

Because we are interested in measuring differences in adoption rates and in utilization of the various technologies, we model each hospital's decision to purchase or not to purchase each technology. We also model the utilization of each technology, given that a hospital has adopted it. To assess adoption and utilization rates, we examine raw and adjusted frequencies of adoption and raw and adjusted utilization rates for adopters. We adjust for patient load and case mix. We develop the case mix measure from information on the number of cases in several diagnostic and procedure categories. To construct the case mix measure, we weight each diagnosis or procedure by its average reimbursement rate nationally. The list of diagnoses and procedures reported in the facility survey is not exhaustive, and cancer diagnoses are heavily represented. So the case mix measure we use is fairly crude and likely overemphasizes cancer patients.

We make the adjustment via a Tobit model, described in Greene (1993) and Tobin (1958). It is appropriate here because the utilization measure is truncated. That is, when a hospital does not possess, for example, a CT scanner, we may not observe what its utilization would have been had it possessed one. To make the adjustments we refer to in the text, we estimate the Tobit model separately for government and private hospitals. We then take the (pooled) average case mix-adjusted levels of inpatients and outpatients and use the coefficients from the two estimated Tobit models to predict the probability of adoption and the expected utilization for the two groups. To interpret the adjusted probabilities and utilization rates, consider the case of CT scanning. The adjusted probability of adoption for a private hospital (for example) is the probability of a private hospital adopting CT scanning, given that it has the pooled average patient volume. The use of the pooled average volume allows for valid intergroup comparisons.

In addition to the technology variables, we assess staffing levels. Again, we examine raw and adjusted staffing levels for RN, PN, NA, FTMD, and PTMD. Because many hospitals employ no part-time MDs, some employ no PNs, and some employ no NAs, and because we wish the adjustment methodology to be comparable with that used with the technologies, we employ the Tobit methodology with the staffing variables as well.

The ownership variable in the data set permits Ministry of Education and private university hospitals to be selected. In order to ensure a homogeneous sample, we remove psychiatric facilities from the group of selected hospitals. This leaves us with 66 Ministry of Education and 86 private university hospitals. The private university hospitals have an average bed size of 535, and the Ministry of Education hospitals have 502 beds on average. The two groups are also similar in the numbers of patients they treat, with the Ministry of Education hospitals treating an average of 4,559 outpatients per week and having an average census of 421 inpatients, and the private university hospitals treating 6940 outpatients, on average, and having an average census of 448 inpatients.

Results

Figure 5-1 plots the frequency of adoption for each of the technologies for government and private university hospitals. The results in this plot are mixed, with the private sector exhibiting higher adoption in some technologies and the government sector in others. Particularly striking is the difference for ESWL, with the private sector showing an adoption rate of 23% versus the government-owned adoption rate of 6%.

However, there are differences in patient load between government and private hospitals because government hospitals have fewer (case mix-adjusted) patients overall and a higher ratio of inpatients to outpatients. Figure 5-2 shows the differences in adoption probabilities after adjusting for these potential confounders. With the exception of lithotripsy and CT scanning, the adjusted probability of adoption for every technology is lower for private

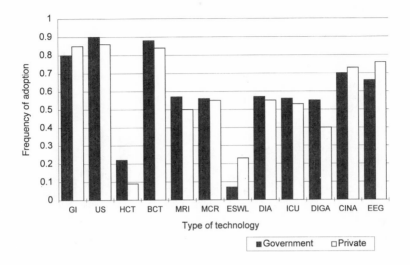

Figure 5-1
Unadjusted Frequency of Adoption

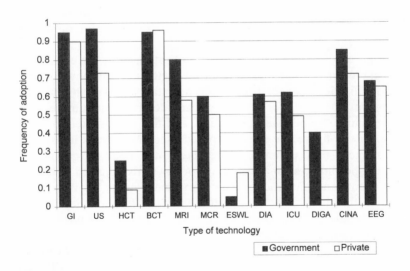

Figure 5-2
Adjusted Frequency of Adoption

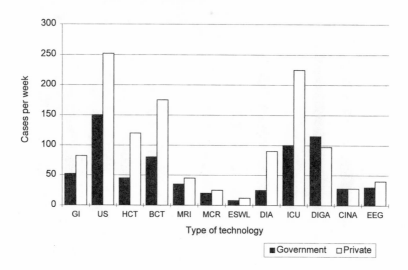

Figure 5-3
Unadjusted Utilization Level for Adopters

than for government hospitals. The differences between the groups are significant (at the 5% level) for all technologies other than microsurgery.[2]

Figure 5-3 presents the average utilization level for each of the technologies for adopters. Except for digital angiography, the average utilization rate for the private hospitals is above that for government hospitals. For reasons already described, it is more useful to examine the adjusted utilization, and this is presented in Figure 5-4. In this figure, we see that private sector hospitals utilize what equipment they purchase more intensively than do government sector hospitals, after controlling for case mix-adjusted volume of inpatients and outpatients. The story that Figures 5-1 through 5-4 tell is that private hospitals tend to adopt technologies less frequently and tend to utilize them more intensively than their government-owned counterparts.

Figure 5-5 shows the adjusted staffing levels for government and private hospitals. Government hospitals employ more MDs and fewer PNs and NAs, and the two types of hospitals employ roughly the same number of RNs, controlling for case mix-adjusted volume. For equivalent caseloads, government hospitals employ a more "skills-intensive" mix of personnel, favoring MDs, whereas the

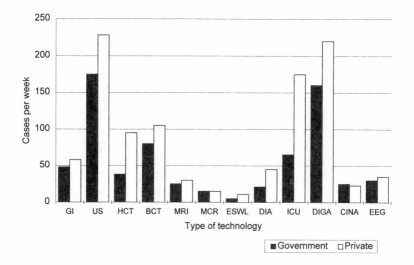

Figure 5-4
Adjusted Utilization Level for Adopters

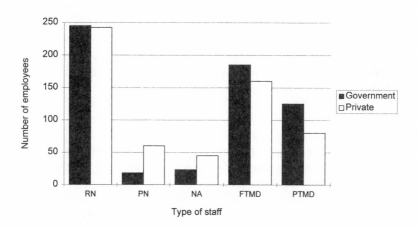

Figure 5-5
Adjusted Staffing Levels

private hospitals favor PNs and NAs. These results are statistically significant (at the 5% level) in every category.

Discussion

Our results sharply contrast with previous work in the U.S. They indicate that government university hospitals employ a more skills-intensive staffing mix, are more likely to acquire medical technologies, and utilize those technologies less intensively than do their private counterparts. Previous work finds government hospitals employing less skills-intensive staffing mixes and adopting medical technologies less frequently. This contrast is likely explained by differences in budgetary constraints arising in the Japanese and U.S. systems. In Japan, government hospitals operate in a more relaxed financial environment than do private hospitals; in the U.S., the opposite is typically the case.

Because we argue that the differences in adoption rates and utilization patterns between government and private hospitals are most likely due to the government hospitals' subsidy, it is important to consider the possible influence of confounding factors. First, although the ownership of the two groups of hospitals differs, their missions are substantively the same. Both the Ministry of Education and the private university hospitals are affiliated with medical schools. Both groups comprise tertiary care facilities, holding patient care, education, and research as their primary missions (Holt et al., 1992).

The two groups of hospitals are similar in a number of other dimensions as well. Both have about the same number of beds and similar patient loads (obviously, there are some differences in patient load, leading to the need to adjust). Government and private hospitals have similar geographical distributions, so the differences in utilization and costs among regions of Japan do not explain our findings. Furthermore, government and private university hospitals are subject to the same staffing regulations, and there is no certificate of need or similar regulation on technology diffusion.

In the U.S., one of the important differences between government and private hospitals is that the former support more indigent care. In Japan, however, this is not an issue, because of its system of universal insurance, which ensures that hospitals receive compensation for every patient treated. Although the benefits are not completely standardized, the provisions of the various insurance plans are both generous and similar to one another.

Another potential difference among these hospitals is the price they pay for the various technologies. In Japan, the prices of medical equipment diverge widely from the manufacturers' list prices. If government hospitals are able to extract a lower price from the manufacturers than are private hospitals, then the variations in adoption rates may flow from these price differences. Because the adoption of a particular manufacturer's device at university hospitals is used by the manufacturer to promote its products in other Japanese hospitals, it is important for manufacturers to penetrate the university hospital market. Thus they give substantial discounts to university hospitals. Because government university hospitals are generally considered to be more prestigious than private university hospitals (and because price data are difficult to come by in the private sector), we cannot rule out the possibility that government hospitals receive greater discounts. However, the disparity in prestige between private and government hospitals is small, so that any additional discount afforded to government hospitals is likely more than made up for by their tendency to purchase top-of-the-line equipment.

Many of the technologies we consider are not homogeneous. For example, there are large differences in the price and performance characteristics among various models of CT or MRI. If government hospitals consistently purchased lower-cost units than private hospitals, this could call into question our finding that government hospitals' purchasing strategies are more aggressive. However, previous work has shown that, at least in the case of CT and MRI, Japanese government hospitals purchase more expensive, higher-performance units than do private hospitals (Niki, 1985; Yoshikawa, 1993).

An important limitation of our study is our inability to determine the relative levels of efficiency of government and private hospitals. That is, we are unable to say whether the private hospitals are operating at their efficiency frontier (and thus that government hospitals are inefficient) or the government hospitals are behaving relatively efficiently (and thus that private hospitals are being overly cost-conscious). Though we have no reason to believe that there are substantive quality differences between the two groups, we cannot rule out this factor in explaining our results.

Conclusions

In our analysis, we compare the levels of adoption and utilization of a number of technologies in Japanese government and private university hospitals. We also compare staffing levels in these hospitals. Adjusting for case mix and volume, government-owned hospitals adopt technologies more readily and utilize them less than do their private sector counterparts. Government hospitals also employ a more highly skilled staffing mix. We interpret these differences as arising from the subsidy that government hospitals receive. Because concerns with prestige, quality of care, quality of teaching, and research motivate the purchase of technologies and employment of skilled staff, both groups of hospitals have similar incentives for purchase, utilization, and staffing. Because of their subsidies, government hospitals do not have the same degree of cost disincentive against purchase and hiring. The subsidies also mitigate the incentive to utilize each technology once it is acquired. Our findings are consistent with the hypothesis that the more relaxed financial constraints government hospitals face lead them to more aggressive technology purchase, less aggressive utilization, and employment of more highly skilled staff.

Notes

[1] Japan's hospitals are prohibited by law from disbursing profits to shareholders; therefore, there are no for-profit hospitals, at least nominally, in Japan.

[2] The test performed is a likelihood ratio test. The null hypothesis is that the coefficients of the Tobit models for the government and private hospitals are the same.

6

A Utility-Maximizing Model of Input Demand

Over the past several decades, many researchers have investigated production relationships in hospitals. Understanding concepts such as scale economies, input substitutability, and hospital efficiency is useful to policymakers as they contemplate antitrust enforcement and price regulation. Scale economies are an important factor in making good decisions regarding entry, exit, investment, and mergers in the hospital industry. Policymakers interested in hospital cost containment need information on elasticities of factor substitution because these indicate the degree to which cost inflation can be avoided by substituting away from the factor whose price has increased.

Despite the voluminous literature estimating hospital production relationships, two related problems persist. First, although researchers have proposed numerous theoretical models of hospital behavior that suggest nonminimum cost allocation of inputs in the provision of hospital services, few empirical studies measure this allocative inefficiency. The problem of inefficiency is affected by the organization of the industry, the market structure of labor inputs, and principal-agent problems.[1] Second, because cost minimization may not be the appropriate behavioral assumption for hospitals, measuring economies of scale and elasticities of factor substitution correctly is difficult. Eakin and Kniesner (1988) respond to these problems by introducing a nonminimum cost function in the analysis of U.S. hospitals.[2]

This chapter is based upon: Nakanishi, S., Bhattacharya, J., Vogt, W. B., Yoshikawa, A., and Nakahara, T. 1995. "Measuring Misallocation of Labor Inputs in Japanese Hospitals: Public vs Private Hospitals," *mimeo*. Asia-Pacific Research Center, Stanford University.

In this chapter, we measure misallocation of labor inputs, elasticities of factor substitution, and economies of scale in Japan's hospital industry, utilizing a nonminimum Generalized Leontief (GL) cost function. We use microdata from 741 public and private general hospitals (*sogo byoin*). Whereas Eakin and Kniesner (1988) report underemployment of MDs in U.S. hospitals, our empirical results indicate overemployment of MDs and registered nurses (RNs) and underemployment of practical nurses (PNs) in Japan. This misallocation of labor increases labor costs by approximately 39.8% in Japanese hospitals over cost minimization. In addition, our research focuses on assessing the relative efficiency of public and private hospitals. Our estimation results suggest that public hospitals are more efficient than private hospitals in that they have a more efficient labor allocation.

Labor Allocation in Japanese Hospitals

In 1990, Japanese hospitals received ¥1,263.2 trillion ($92.3 billion) for inpatient and outpatient medical care, such hospital care being the largest single category of medical care spending (Nakanishi et al., 1993b). Between 1962 and 1990, spending for hospital services increased at an annual rate of 14.6%, slightly higher than the 13.6% growth rate for total medical expenditures. As a result, spending for hospital services as a percentage of total medical expenditures increased from 48% in 1962 to 61.3% in 1990. Thus, while Japan's medical expenditures accounted for 4.9% of GDP in 1990, the hospital industry alone absorbed 3.0%. Even though Japan's national spending on health care is rather limited, especially in comparison with the U.S., Japanese health care policymakers have been paying closer attention to the hospital industry and its increasing share of medical expenditures.

The percentage of medical expenditures devoted to labor in 1989 was 48.0%: 24.8% paid to MDs, 9.9% to nurses, and the remaining 13.3% to other employees (Nakanishi et al., 1993b). Salaries comprised the largest share of expenditures for both public and private hospitals. Salaries occupied 53.9% of hospital expenditures in local government public hospitals and 47.5% in private (*iryo-hojin*) hospitals in 1991 (*Iryo Keizai Jittai Chosa*, Ministry of Health and Welfare). Whereas the difference in wages for doctors is relatively small between public and private hospitals, wage differentials for both RNs and PNs are large. Nurses in public sector hospitals earn a significantly higher wage than those in private sector hospitals. Somewhat surprisingly, in public hospitals, the wages for PNs are higher than those for RNs. This might be partially due to the seniority system in public hospitals; practical nurses have greater seniority than registered nurses. On the other hand, RN wages are higher than PN wages in private hospitals. The mix of labor differs widely between private and public hospitals.[3] Given the importance of labor in health care services and the large contribution of medical and professional staff to costs, we focus on the allocation of MDs and nurses in public and private hospitals and the subsequent efficiency resulting from different labor allocations.

Estimating a Nonminimum Variable Cost Function

Allocative inefficiency results from the technically efficient employment of inputs in a combination that does not produce an equality between marginal rate of technical substitution and the ratio of observed market factor prices. A firm may select a noncost-minimizing set of inputs if it evaluates the shadow prices of inputs as being different from observed market prices. A shadow price is the firm's internal perception of the unit price of input if, for example, the level of input enters directly into the firm's utility function. The existence of monopsony power in factor markets also causes divergence between observed market prices of inputs and their perceived prices (marginal factor costs). Firms are hypothesized to minimize shadow or perceived cost. The nonminimum cost function is a generalization of the traditional minimum cost function that allows for systematic allocative inefficiency.

Standard cost function analysis requires a number of assumptions. One of these is that firms are constantly employing the (shadow) cost-minimizing levels of all inputs, given prevailing output levels and (shadow) prices of factors. However, one might believe that firms cannot quickly adjust all inputs in response to changes in output levels or factor prices. Regulatory restrictions, for example, may hinder the adjustment of capital stock. If so, the firms in that industry will, at any given moment, employ the optimal quantities of the variable inputs (e.g., labor), given the probable existence of nonoptimal levels of fixed inputs (e.g., capital). To deal with these issues, a variety of short-run cost functions has been proposed and estimated. Short-run cost functions of hospitals were estimated by Cowing and Holtmann (1983), Vita (1990), and Fournier and

Mitchell (1992). Long-run cost functions have been proposed by Conrad and Strauss (1983) and Eakin and Kniesner (1988).

To derive the nonminimum cost function, consider a firm with the general production function

$$T(X, Y) \leq 0 \tag{6-1}$$

where X is a vector of inputs, Y is a vector of outputs, and $T( )$ is differentiable, increasing in Y and decreasing in X. Cost minimization requires that the firm hire inputs X_i and X_j in a combination such that their price ratio equals their marginal rate of technical substitution,

$$w_i/w_j = T_{Xi}/T_{Xj}. \tag{6-2}$$

Now, to introduce the possibility of allocative inefficiency, we rewrite Equation 6-2 as

$$w_i^{sh}/w_j^{sh} = T_{Xi}/T_{Xj} \tag{6-3}$$

where w_i^{sh} is the firm's shadow or perceived price of the ith input such that[4]

$$w_i^{sh} = w_i + \theta_i^k. \tag{6-4}$$

θ_i^k is the ith shadow price divergence parameter of the kth ownership type. The shadow prices divergence parameter may be different for various forms of ownership. We estimate twin price divergence parameters: θ_i^{public} and $\theta_i^{private}$. The firm's shadow variable cost function, which is dual to Equation 6-1, takes the form

$$C_v^{sh} = C_v^{sh}(Y, w^{sh}, K) \tag{6-5}$$

where K is a fixed input. The demand function of factors is related to the shadow cost function by Shephard's lemma, such that

$$X_i^* = X_i(Y, w^{sh}, K) = \partial C_v^{sh}/\partial w_i^{sh}. \tag{6-6}$$

The observed variable cost is, in turn,

$$C_v^{obs} = C_v^{obs}(Y, w^{sh}, w, K) = \sum w_i X_i. \tag{6-7}$$

Of course, shadow variable cost is unobserved. However, because factor input use is observed, we can estimate shadow cost from parameters and observables. We are interested in allocative inefficiency as well as elasticities of factor substitution, so we estimate both a minimum and a nonminimum cost function.

We are interested not only in allocative distortion brought about by noncost-minimizing behavior, but also by variations in this distortion associated with market structure. Under price competition, more efficient firms drive less efficient firms out of the industry. Thus, increasing competition may induce cost-minimizing behavior and reduce labor costs in hospitals. This would indicate a negative relationship between the level of competition and the level of labor inputs. However, as shown in Chapter 5, there is a positive relationship between staffing levels and demand for hospital care. Hospitals in very competitive markets may attempt to attract more patients by increasing their staffing. Under nonprice competition, the relationship between competition and labor inputs might be positive. Fournier and Mitchell (1992) report that competition among hospitals based upon nonprice considerations (i.e., quality of care, service intensity, and resource availability) tends to raise costs relative to purely competitive, market price-taking firms. However, they do not identify relationships between nonprice competition and the employment levels of each input. We do this by estimating the effects of the market structure on hospital labor demand.

To estimate the shadow cost function, one must select an explicit functional form; we choose a Generalized Leontief (hereafter GL) cost function. The traditional GL cost function is a functional form in a single output and the square root of prices. Beyond this point, several generalizations have been added to account for technical change and returns to scale (Berndt and Khaled, 1979; Diewert and Wales, 1987; Parks, 1971; Woodland, 1975); for fixed inputs (Morrison, 1988); and for allocative inefficiency (Toda, 1976). These factors vary, depending on the method used for "generalizing" the GL cost function. We extend the standard GL form to allow for multiple products, returns to scale, fixed inputs, competitive strategy, and allocative inefficiency. Such a GL shadow variable cost function can be written

$$C_v^{sh} = Y \cdot \sum_i \sum_j B_{ij} \sqrt{w_i^{sh}} \sqrt{w_j^{sh}} + \sqrt{Y} \sqrt{K} \sum_i D_i w_i^{sh}$$

$$+ \sum_i G_i w_i^{sh} K + \sum_i H_i w_i^{sh} HI \qquad (6\text{-}8)$$

$$Y = \left(\sum_i A_i y_i \right)^\alpha$$

where y_i is the hospital's production of the ith output, w^{sh} is the price of variable input i, K is the stock of fixed input, and A_i, B_{ij}, D_i, G_i, and H_i are parameters to be estimated. We proxy competitive environment by the Herfindahl index of bed size (HI), which we calculate with data from the Facility Survey for each of 345 "medical zones." A medical zone is a geographical area used by the Ministry of Health and Welfare as a market area for hospital care.

Demand equations for empirical implementation may be derived from Equation 6-8 based on Shephard's lemma. The derived demand functions of the ith input may be written as

$$X_i^* = Y \cdot \left[B_i + \sum_j B_{ij} \sqrt{w_i^{sh}} / \sqrt{w_i^{sh}} \right] + D_i \sqrt{Y} \sqrt{K} + G_i K + H_i HI.$$

$$(6\text{-}9)$$

It is clear from Equation 6-9 that zero-degree homogeneity in shadow prices of the input demand function is satisfied. In other words, although demand equations include the "demand" for fixed input, demand for variable inputs remains constant if all shadow prices increase equiproportionally. However, this demand system is not zero-degree homogeneous in observed prices. This failure of zero-degree homogeneity is the reason the divergence factors are identified.

We model the hospital as a firm producing four outputs with four inputs (three variable and one fixed). The variable inputs are the number of physicians, registered nurses, and practical nurses. We use the number of beds as a proxy for capital stock, the fixed input. The outputs are the number (per day) of outpatient visits, surgical inpatients, internal medicine inpatients, and inpatients of all other types. We assume the number of beds is fixed and exogenous in the short run because under the 1989 Regional Health Care Plan, the government restricts the number of hospital beds.

Following Conrad and Strauss (1983), we drop the demand equations for supplies in our estimation model. We exclude the price of purchased supplies from the list of independent variables included in the labor input demand equations. If purchased supplies such as syringes, sheets, and scalpels are sold in a national market, then the prices will be the same at every hospital. Supplies are easily transported commodities, so it would be reasonable to assume that they would not have radically different prices at different hospitals, an assumption we adopt from Cowing and Holtmann (1983), Vita (1990), and Eakin and Kniesner (1988).

Data

We limit ourselves to the set of all general hospitals (*sogo byoin*) in Japan; we describe general hospitals in Part I. This selection is motivated by two considerations. First, we wish to ensure a homogenous sample of hospitals. Second, general hospitals are required to maintain surgery and internal medicine departments, and because these patients are included in our analysis as outputs, it is desirable to guarantee the existence of these departments. With this selection in place, we are left with 394 public hospitals and 582 private hospitals.

From the 1990 Facility Survey, we obtain data for four outputs: outpatient visit (OUTVISIT#), surgical inpatients (SURG#), internal medicine inpatients (INT#), and all other inpatients (OTHER#). From this same survey, we also obtain data for four inputs: number of physicians (DOC#), number of RNs (RN#), number of PNs (PN#), and number of beds (BED#).

For input price (wage) data, we use prefecture-level market wages for doctors, registered nurses, and practical nurses. A prefecture is roughly the size of a county in California, and prefectural boundaries reflect longstanding, geographically distinct areas; thus, they are appropriate markets for labor inputs. Prefectures vary greatly in size. In Japan, wages reflect the seniority system: The greater the seniority of a worker at a hospital, the higher is his or her wage. Furthermore, the average age of staff members differs widely between hospitals. Therefore, information regarding the average age of doctors and nurses is necessary to assess why wages are higher in one hospital than in another. Unfortunately, the Facility Survey, which provides various facility-specific data, does not provide this information. We obtain such data from the Wage

Table 6-1
Variable Definitions

Variable	Definition
OUTVISIT#	Average number of outpatients per day
SURG#	Average number of surgical inpatients per day
INT#	Average number of internal medicine inpatients per day
OTHER#	Average number of other inpatients per day
DOC#	Total number of doctors
BED#	Total number of beds
RN#	Total number of registered nurses
PN#	Total number of practical nurses
DOC¥	Average monthly wage of doctors (×¥1,000)
RN¥	Average monthly wage of registered nurses (×¥1,000)
PN¥	Average monthly wage of practical nurses (×¥1,000)
HI	Herfindahl index of bed size

Census (Ministry of Labor, 1990). For each of the 394 public sector hospitals, we obtain wages of doctors (DOC¥), RNs (RN¥), and PNs (PN¥) from the 1991 *Koei Kigyo Nenkan* (Ministry of Local Government, 1990), and calculate the prefectural averages from them.

Prior to transforming to the square root of all explanatory variables, we divide each by its sample mean for the purpose of normalization. Table 6-1 summarizes the variable definitions, and Table 6-2 provides descriptive statistics for these variables.

Empirical Results

Maximum likelihood estimates of the parameters of the nonminimum and standard minimum GL cost functions are found in Table 6-3. In both models, all output parameters (i.e., the A_i) and scale parameters (α) are positive and significant. These results coincide with theoretical predictions. A high degree of competition (indicated by a low HI) has a positive effect on employment levels of doctors and registered nurses, but a negative effect on practical nurse employment. These results support the conclusion in Chapter 5 that the staffing of hospitals plays a role in nonprice competition among Japanese hospitals.

Public hospitals perceive higher shadow prices of inputs relative to market prices. However, these differences are not statistically significant. In the private sector, the shadow prices of RNs and PNs are significantly higher than market prices. These estimation results suggest the existence of allocative inefficiency in private hospitals relative to cost-minimizing hospitals.

There are no drastic differences in output estimates among the estimated parameters in the nonminimum specification compared to the standard GL cost function specification. However, relatively large differences in wage-related parameters exist between two models. In the nonminimum cost model, some estimated parameters (i.e., B1, B12, B13, D2, and D3) have opposite signs compared to the result from the standard minimum cost model. From these estimated parameters, we can see that standard cost function estimation may calculate erroneous elasticities of factor substitution.

Measuring Misallocation

In this section, we calculate the allocative inefficiency of private and public hospitals implied by the parameter estimates. We obtain an

Table 6-2
Sample Means of Variables

Variable	Public Hospital	Private Hospital	All Sample
OUTVISIT #	704.97	739.30	725.44
SURG #	66.67	68.23	67.60
INT #	102.52	111.20	107.70
OTHER #	150.96	163.31	158.32
DOC #	45.54	64.10	56.61
RN #	162.01	158.85	160.12
PN #	42.57	49.21	46.53
BED #	394.38	424.68	412.44
DOC¥	1,121.42	924.02	1,003.71
RN¥	415.29	336.26	368.16
PN¥	463.72	287.02	358.35
HI	0.13	0.07	0.10

Table 6-3
Estimated Demand Function Parameters

Variable		Parameter	Nonminimum	Standard Minimum
Divergence factor of DOC	(public)	θ_{md}^{public}	0.393	
	(private)	$\theta_{md}^{private}$	−0.165	
Divergence factor of RN	(public)	θ_{rn}^{public}	0.523	
	(private)	$\theta_{rn}^{private}$	1.572**	
Divergence Factor of PN	(public)	θ_{pn}^{public}	1.488	
	(private)	$\theta_{pn}^{private}$	2.331[†]	
SURG #		A1	0.794[†]	0.743[†]
INT #		A2	0.474[†]	0.482[†]
OTHER #		A3	0.636[†]	0.627[†]
Scale factor		α	1.458[†]	1.463[†]
DOC¥		B1	−2.878	28.297[†]
RN¥		B2	−45.851	−15.732**
PN¥		B3	−56.699**	−30.776[†]
DOC¥*RN¥		B12	−12.502*	18.593[†]
DOC¥*PN¥		B13	21.100**	−11.270[†]

Table 6-3 (continued)

Variable	Parameter	Nonminimum	Standard Minimum
RN¥*PN¥	B23	57.083**	26.575†
Y.5*K.5*DOC¥	D1	−10.446	−96.174†
Y.5*K.5*RN¥	D2	23.992	−40.080
Y.5*K.5*PN¥	D3	−33.835*	45.630**
K*DOC¥	G1	8.169	97.204**
K*RN¥	G2	37.002	103.597†
K*PN¥	G3	94.330†	11.461
HI*DOC¥	H1	−2.802**	−4.973†
HI*RN¥	H2	−5.553†	6.116†
HI*PN¥	H3	5.272†	6.602†

* denotes significance at the 10% level.
** denotes significance at the 5% level.
† denotes significance at the 1% level.

estimate of the cost-minimizing level of inputs $\{X_i^o\}$, by evaluating the estimated demand function of input factors at $w_i^{sh} = w_i$ for all i, that is,

$$\hat{X}_i^o = \hat{X}_i^*(Y, w : w_i^{sh} = w_i) \qquad (6\text{-}10)$$

where $\hat{X}_i^*$ is the fitted value of optimal labor demand and $\hat{X}_i^o$ is the fitted value of labor demand, evaluated with all shadow price divergence terms set equal to zero. Similarly, the standard minimum cost function $\hat{C}^{min}$ can be obtained by substituting Equation 6-10 into Equation 6-7:

$$\hat{C}^{min} = \hat{C}^{obs}(Y, w : w_i^{sh} = w_i). \qquad (6\text{-}11)$$

If $w_i^{sh} = w_i$ for each input, then shadow costs C^s and observed costs C^{obs} coincide. If any $w_i^{sh} \neq w_i$, there is systematic misallocation of inputs and excess cost occurs, $C^{obs} > C^{min}$.

The estimated misallocation of ith labor (ML_i) as a proportion of optimal employment is

$$ML_i = (\hat{X}_i^* - \hat{X}_i^o)/\hat{X}_i^o. \qquad (6\text{-}12)$$

UTILITY-MAXIMIZING MODEL OF INPUT DEMAND 139

Table 6-4
Misallocation of Labor Inputs

Variable	Public	Private	All Ownership	Est. at Sample Mean
DOC (ML1)	1.195	13.432	8.492	4.095
RN (ML2)	0.720	1.360	1.102	0.874
PN (ML3)	−0.583	−0.663	−0.631	−0.639†
Total (TML)	0.250	0.786	0.570	0.398

* denotes significance at the 10% level.
** denotes significance at the 5% level.
† denotes significance at the 1% level.

The total misallocation of labor (TML) is expressed by a proportion of minimum cost:

$$TML = (\hat{C}^{obs} - \hat{C}^{min})/\hat{C}^{min}. \tag{6-13}$$

Table 6-4 presents mean values of ML_i and TML for private, public, and all hospitals in our sample. We find that doctors and registered nurses are overemployed and practical nurses are underemployed in Japan's hospital industry. The misallocation of labor in private hospitals is larger than that in public hospitals. The total misallocation of labor in the hospital industry increases hospital labor costs by 39.8% for the average hospital. This misallocation is caused mostly by private hospitals.

Input Elasticities

One attractive feature of flexible functional forms, like the GL cost function, is that they place no *a priori* restrictions on substitution elasticities. We compute the Allen partial elasticities of substitution (AES_{ij}) and the own price elasticities of factor demand (ED_i^{sh}) for a general dual shadow cost function C^{sh} having n inputs:

$$AES_{ij} = \frac{C^{sh} \cdot C_{ij}^{sh}}{C_i^{sh} \cdot C_j^{sh}} \tag{6-14}$$

$$ED_i^{sh} = AES_{ij} M_i^{sh} \tag{6-15}$$

Table 6-5
Estimated Price Elasticities and Elasticities of Factor Substitution

	Nonminimum	Standard Minimum
Price Elasticities of Factor Demand (Shadow Price)		
S_EDdoc	−0.719[†]	
S_EDrn	−0.476[†]	
S_EDpn	−1.086[†]	
Price Elasticities of Factor Demand (Market Price)		
M_EDdoc	−0.635**	−0.337[†]
M_EDrn	−0.236**	−0.712[†]
M_EDpn	−0.377**	−0.810[†]
Elasticities of Factor Substitution		
DOC*DOC	−7.000**	−1.610[†]
RN*RN	−1.575*	−1.169[†]
PN*PN	−11.360**	−4.465[†]
DOC*RN	−1.312*	1.402[†]
DOC*PN	5.846**	−2.854[†]
RN*PN	4.030**	2.309[†]

* denotes significance at the 10% level.
** denotes significance at the 5% level.
[†] denotes significance at the 1% level.

where M_i^{sh} is the cost share of the ith input shadow cost, and subscripts on C^{sh} represent derivatives of the cost function. The own price elasticities have market price values that may differ from their associated shadow price values:

$$ED_i^{obs} = ED_i^{sh}/(w_i + \theta_i). \tag{6-16}$$

Table 6-5 contains estimated elasticities of factor substitution in the nonminimum cost and standard minimum cost models. The estimated own market price elasticity of input demand for RNs is 55% less than its shadow price elasticity.

There are relatively large differences in the estimated own price elasticities and substitution elasticities between the two models. In the nonminimum cost model, the price elasticity of input demand for doctors is twice as large as the one estimated in the standard model. Own price elasticities for nursing labor are overestimated by 300% in the standard model. Registered nurses and practical nurses are substitutes in both models. However, doctors and registered nurses are complements in the nonminimum cost model, and they are substitutes in the standard model.[5] The estimated elasticities of

Table 6-6
Elasticities of Labor Demand for Capital Growth

Variable	Nonminimum	Standard Minimum
DOC	−0.065	−0.136
RN	0.434[†]	0.405[†]
PN	1.250[†]	1.374[†]

* denotes significance at the 10% level.
** denotes significance at the 5% level.
[†] denotes significance at the 1% level.

doctors and practical nurses have opposite signs when using the nonminimum cost model and standard model. These results indicate the assumption that cost minimization can yield incorrect forecasts of a hospital's employment policy owing to a change in input prices.

Changes in capital stock influence labor demand. We obtain capital growth elasticities of labor demands (CEL):

$$CEL_i = \partial \ln X_i / \partial \ln K. \tag{6-17}$$

Table 6-6 presents capital growth elasticities of labor demand evaluated at the means of data. All estimated CELs are stable across model specifications. The estimated CEL for physicians is negative but not statistically significant. Other estimated CELs have positive signs. Therefore, capital stock is complementary to nursing staff, but not to doctors in our study.

Scale Economies

In the production context, the level of ray (overall) scale economies is defined as the proportional increase in all outputs that would result from a proportional increase in all inputs. When the production relationship is examined using the firm's freely varied inputs to minimize total (shadow) costs, the measure of ray scale economies is given by

$$S = \frac{1}{\sum_k (\partial \ln C^{sh} / \partial \ln y_k)}. \tag{6-18}$$

Caves, Christensen, and Swanson (1981) show that when ray scale economies are analyzed via a variable cost function, the measurement of ray scale economies (S) is given by

Table 6-7
Labor Demand Elasticities for Outputs and Scale Economies

Variable	Nomninimum	Standard Minimum
DOC	1.635[†]	1.373[†]
RN	0.881[†]	0.854[†]
PN	−0.531[†]	−0.765[†]
Ray scale economies	0.662[†]	0.669[†]

* denotes significance at the 10% level.
** denotes significance at the 5% level.
[†] denotes significance at the 1% level.

$$S = \frac{1 - \partial \ln C^{sh}/\partial \ln K}{\sum_k (\partial \ln C^{sh}/\partial \ln y_k)}. \tag{6-19}$$

Ray scale economies are present when the calculated value of S exceeds one. Similarly, we can obtain output elasticities of labor demands (EOi):

$$EO_i = \sum_k \partial \ln X_i/\partial \ln y_k. \tag{6-20}$$

Table 6-7 presents estimated output elasticities of labor demand (EO_i) and the measurement of ray scale economies (S) at the means of data. Every estimated EOs and S is stable across model specifications. With the exception of practical nurses, medical staff inputs are normal. When all outputs increase by 1%, the employment level of PNs decreases by 0.53%.

At the mean output vector for the entire sample, the calculated value of S is 0.662. This implies the existence of decreasing returns to scale among the hospitals studied. Increasing all "average" hospital outputs by 1% induces a labor cost increase of approximately 1.51%. Vita (1990) finds a similar result for American hospitals— decreasing returns to scale with an S value of 0.79 inducing a 1.26% increase in variable cost. Table 6-8 reports estimates of the marginal labor costs (MLC_i) of the four outputs. We evaluate each MLC_i at the sample mean of all dependent variables. Each estimated MLC_i appears reasonable.[6]

Conclusions

We estimate misallocation of medical labor resources in hospitals in our sample. Our empirical results indicate that physicians and RNs

Table 6-8
Marginal Labor Costs

	Nonminimum	Standard Minimum
Outpatient	$14.54	$16.12
Surgery	3,730.18	3,991.12
Internal medicine	1,392.71	1,573.15
Other inpatient	1,302.13	1,423.40

are overemployed and PNs are underemployed in Japanese hospitals. This misallocation of labor increases total labor costs by approximately 39.8%. However, public hospitals exhibit less labor misallocation than private hospitals. Contrary to the conventional belief that private sector hospitals are more cost-conscious and more efficient, we find that public hospitals operate more efficiently than private ones.

The degree of monopsony power may be one reason for the discrepancy in operating efficiency between public and private hospitals. The existence of monopsony power causes a difference between the marginal productivity (the shadow price) of labor and its market wages.[7] In the public sector, nursing labor is more unionized than in the private sector. These nurses' strong bargaining power reduces the monopsony power of hospitals and decreases the divergence of shadow and market prices. If nurses can move among hospitals quickly, the difference in operating efficiency disappears among hospitals. However, there is a wage differential between public and private hospitals (see Table 6-2) that suggests that the nursing labor market is segmented. To better understand the wider divergence between market and shadow prices in private hospitals, a study considering labor market structure for hospitals staff would be useful.

Our estimation results indicate that a high degree of competition encourages hospitals to employ more doctors and registered nurses and to reduce practical nurse employment. If hospitals engage in nonprice competition, the ensuing competitive environment forces them to increase skilled medical staff to improve the quality of hospital services. Our results suggest that nonprice competition exists in the hospital industry.

We find no scale economies at the sample mean. The growth of production increases the employment of doctors and registered nurses and decreases the employment of practical nurses. Capital growth has positive effects on practical nurse and registered nurse employment. We find a negative relationship between capital and doctor employment, but it is not statistically significant. These results are stable across model specifications.

There are relatively large differences in estimates of own market price elasticities and substitution elasticities between the two models. In the nonminimum cost model, the price elasticity of input demand for doctors is twice as large as that estimated in the standard model. Our results indicate that the assumption of cost minimization in the hospital industry can yield incorrect forecasts of hospital employment policies subject to changes in the market conditions of inputs. We must consider allocative inefficiency in order to estimate elasticities of factor substitution correctly.

We illustrate the importance of considering the deviations from cost-minimizing behavior by hospitals when formulating policy in the health care sector. In particular, the use of a nonminimum cost framework provides substantially different estimates of demand elasticities from the standard framework. The importance of these deviations from cost-minimizing behavior indicates the usefulness of a further exploration of imperfections in the labor market for medical staff and of nonprice competition.

Notes

[1] For representative economic models of hospital behavior, see Newhouse (1970), Lee (1971), and Pauly and Redisch (1973). Phelps and Sened (1989) and Pope (1989) study monopolistic competition in the hospital industry. For imperfect competition of the labor market, see Yett (1970) and Sullivan (1989). Harris (1977) presents the first study of the internal organization of hospitals. See also Sloan (1980) and Dranove and White (1987).

[2] Lau and Yotopoulos (1971) wrote a seminal paper on nonminimum cost function estimation. See also Toda (1976) and Atkinson and Halvorsen (1984).

[3] For differences in labor mix in private and public teaching hospitals, see Chapter 5.

[4] If the utility-maximizing entrepreneur faces an imperfect market, divergence between shadow and observed input prices becomes additive such as in Equation 6-4. See Thornton and Eakin (1992) for details.

[5] We mean substitutes in production in the technical economic sense here; this does not imply that MDs and nurses literally substitute for one another in the same tasks in the hospital.

[6] Our MLC_i estimates are comparable in magnitude to values obtained in previous studies. The marginal labor cost of an outpatient visit, for example, is about \$15, though Grannemann, Brown, and Pauly (1986) and Vita (1990) report its marginal cost at \$83 and \$74, respectively.

[7] Grosskopf, Margaritis, and Valdmanis (1990) provide an empirical study of the relationship among the monopsony power and labor misallocation.

7

Technical Efficiency of Hospitals

In this chapter we estimate technical inefficiencies in Japanese hospitals utilizing the data envelopment analysis (DEA) method. There is a growing literature applying these methods to the health care industry. Grosskopf and Valdmanis (1987), Register and Bruning (1987), and Valdmanis (1990, 1992) analyze hospital efficiency with DEA. Fizel and Nunnikhoven (1992) utilize the DEA method to measure inefficiencies among nursing homes in the U.S.

Our main interest is to determine whether private hospitals are more efficient than public hospitals. Using data from 17 public hospitals owned by regional governments in Japan, Minami and Gunji (1994) measure relative technical inefficiencies of these public hospitals utilizing the DEA method. However, they do not compare the technical efficiencies of public and private hospitals and thus do not address the question we are most interested in. Aoki and Urushi (1994) measure the technical inefficiencies of private and public hospitals, and find that public hospitals are more technically efficient. However, they collect the private hospital data through an informal survey. Using data that may contain measurement errors is a serious problem when employing the non-stochastic DEA method. Our study builds upon previous work by using more reliable and detailed data than have been used in former studies. We also investigate the factors associated with the inefficiency level.

DEA is an appropriate method for analyzing the efficiency of enterprises that are not necessarily for profit. The method permits

This chapter is based upon: Aoki, K., Bhattacharya, J., Vogt, W.B., Yoshikawa, A., and Nakahara, T. 1995. "Measuring Technical Efficiencies of Japanese General Hospitals: DEA Analysis of Public vs Private Hospitals," *mimeo*, Asia/Pacific Research Center, Stanford University.

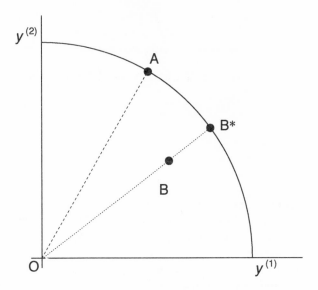

Figure 7-1
Production Frontier and Technical Efficiency Measure

us to compare a firm with a given input-output mix with other firms with similar mixes and to measure their efficiencies.

We conduct DEA estimations under several different technical hypotheses: constant returns to scale, nonincreasing returns to scale, and variable returns to scale. Under each of these conditions, we find that public hospitals are more efficient than private hospitals in Japan. Finally, by using a Tobit regression, we determine which factors are associated with the level of inefficiency.

Data Envelopment Analysis

If the actual production frontier could be observed,[1] one could measure technical efficiency of individual firms by comparing their position in input-output space to the frontier. Figure 7-1 graphically represents a production frontier with a given production process and inputs. Firms A and B are plotted in this output space. In this example, firm A is on the frontier and firm B is not. Firm A cannot proportionally expand its production level, but firm B can proportionally expand its production level to point B*. Following Debreu (1951) and Farrell (1957), we may use the ratio of the actual production level (OB) to the highest possible production level along a ray from the origin (OB*) as the technical efficiency measure.[2] This measure, OB*/OB, is called the output-oriented Debreu-Farrell technical efficiency measure. The greater this measure, the more technically inefficient the hospital is. Technically efficient firms have a measure of 1.

Measuring technical efficiency for firms using DEA involves constructing the frontier as a curve in input-output space that envelops all the data. DEA measures the relative efficiency of the firms in the sample. If every firm exhibits technical inefficiency, one cannot construct a theoretical frontier using this method. However, our main focus is comparing the technical inefficiency of private and public hospitals, for which we need to compare only relative efficiency between the two groups.

The actual production frontier is the set of highest output points that can be produced with the available technology and given inputs. Because all the real production points must be inside the actual production frontier, we are incapable of constructing it using real-world data. Thus, we need to construct an "estimated frontier" containing all the production points within its boundary, using a linear programming method. DEA uses the principle that firms on the frontier, described by intersecting hyperplanes for a multi-dimensional input-output space, must have production points that are orthogonal to the appropriate hyperplane. Firms on the interior will have production points that have a negative value for the inner product of the actual production point and the normal vector of the tangent hyperplane.

We now discuss the DEA model under three different technical hypotheses: constant returns to scale, nonincreasing returns to scale, and variable returns to scale. This discussion follows Lovell (1993).

Constant Returns to Scale (CRS)

N firms are plotted in input-output space as N points. If we could construct the surface that envelops all the data (N points), the surface would be regarded as the *production frontier* constructed from the actual data. In DEA, we construct the production frontier by a combination of hyperplanes.

Let $x \in R_+^m$, $y \in R_+^n$ denote the inputs and outputs, respectively. For simplicity, we first assume that all firms have technology that provides a constant return to scale (CRS). Under this assumption, if a firm is producing at (x, y), it can make goods at $(\alpha x, \alpha y)$ for an arbitrary positive α. In other words, we describe the technology a firm adopts by a hyperplane through the origin in input-output space.

The object of DEA analysis under CRS is to find a hyperplane whose normal vector is given by $\begin{pmatrix} -u \\ v \end{pmatrix}$, $u \in R_+^m$, $v \in R_+^n$, which goes through the origin and contains all the data points. In order for the estimated hyperplane to be the production frontier, the inner product of the normal vector and each data point in the sample must be negative or zero. However, because it is meaningless for us here to construct a production frontier in which no firm is efficient (when all inner products are negative), we introduce an additional condition that ensures at least one firm is efficient. Thus, the hyperplane satisfies:

$$\begin{pmatrix} x_i \\ y_i \end{pmatrix}^T \begin{pmatrix} -u \\ v \end{pmatrix} \leq 0 \quad i = 1, 2, \ldots, N \quad \text{and at least one firm } i_0$$

$$\begin{pmatrix} x_{i_0} \\ y_{i_0} \end{pmatrix}^T \begin{pmatrix} -u \\ v \end{pmatrix} = 0. \tag{7.1}$$

Figure 7-2 presents a simple example. Firm i's combination of input and output is given by (x_i, y_i). In this case, the inner product

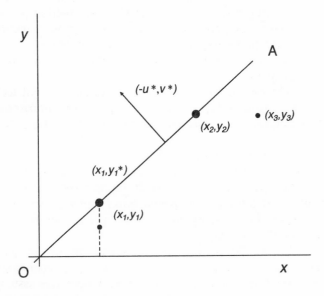

Figure 7-2
Hyperplane as a Production Frontier

of normal vector, $\begin{pmatrix} -u^* \\ v^* \end{pmatrix}$, and the input-output vector for Firm 1 and Firm 3 are clearly negative. The inner product of the normal vector and Firm 2's input-output vector are equal to zero. Therefore, the line OA whose normal vector is $\begin{pmatrix} -u^* \\ v^* \end{pmatrix}$ is the production frontier in this example.

Firm 1 can operate at (x_1, y_1^*) if it utilizes efficient technology. The technical efficiency measure of Firm 1 is measured by output ratio, $\dfrac{y_1^*}{y_1}$. When the normal vector to the hyperplane that represents the frontier is $\begin{pmatrix} -u^* \\ v^* \end{pmatrix}$, firm i can produce y_i^*, which satisfies the equation $u^{*T}x_i = v^{*T}y_i^*$. Therefore, Firm i's technical efficiency is measured by

$$\frac{v^{*T}y_i^*}{v^{*T}y_i} = \frac{u^{*T}x_i}{v^{*T}y_i}.$$

Clearly, in Figure 7-2, we can create a hyperplane that satisfies the condition (7.1) by selecting the flattest line, and this implies that the technical efficiency measure of the firm i is minimal. Therefore, the method of finding the hyperplane which satisfies condition (7.1) and measures the technical efficiency of firm i_0 is found by solving the following problem:

$$\min_{u,v} \frac{u^T x_{i_0}}{v^T y_{i_0}}$$

s.t.

$$\begin{pmatrix} x_i \\ y_i \end{pmatrix}^T \begin{pmatrix} -u \\ v \end{pmatrix} \leq 0 \quad i = 1, 2, \ldots, N \tag{7-2}$$

$$u, v > 0.$$

We assume that the minimum value of the objective function of Problem (7-2) is attained at (u^*, v^*). The optimized value of the objective function, $\dfrac{u^{*T}x_{i_0}}{v^{*T}y_{i_0}}$, is the technical efficiency measure of firm i_0. However, the optimal solution of problem (7.2), (u^*, v^*), is unique only up to a positive constant, so we impose the constraint, $v^T y_{i_0} = 1$. Let X, Y denote

$$X = \begin{pmatrix} x_1^{(1)} & \cdots & x_N^{(1)} \\ x_1^{(2)} & \cdots & x_N^{(2)} \\ \vdots & \ddots & \vdots \\ x_1^{(m)} & \cdots & x_N^{(m)} \end{pmatrix}, \quad Y = \begin{pmatrix} y_1^{(1)} & \cdots & y_N^{(1)} \\ y_1^{(2)} & \cdots & y_N^{(2)} \\ \vdots & \ddots & \vdots \\ y_1^{(n)} & \cdots & y_N^{(n)} \end{pmatrix}.$$

The superscripts index the m kinds of inputs and n kinds of outputs and the subscripts index the firms.

Then problem (7-2) is equivalent to the following linear programming problem:

$$\min_{u,v} \begin{pmatrix} x_{i_0} \\ 0 \end{pmatrix}^T \begin{pmatrix} u \\ v \end{pmatrix}$$

s.t.

$$v^T y_{i_0} = 1 \qquad\qquad (7\text{-}3)$$

$$X^T u - Y^T v \geq 0$$

$$u, v > 0.$$

In practice, we calculate the technical efficiency measure by solving the dual problem of (7-3). (See Appendix 7-1.)

Nonincreasing Returns to Scale (NIRS) and Variable Returns to Scale (VRS)

In the previous section, we assume that the technology each firm employs is characterized by constant returns to scale. This assumption is unrealistic, but is easy to modify. We need only modify the constraint to $X^T u - Y^T v \geq w\mathbf{1}$, where $\mathbf{1}$ is an N-dimensional vector of 1's.

$$\min_{u,v,w} \begin{pmatrix} x_{i_0} \\ 0 \\ 1 \end{pmatrix}^T \begin{pmatrix} u \\ v \\ w \end{pmatrix}$$

s.t. $\qquad\qquad\qquad\qquad\qquad\qquad (7\text{-}4)$

$$v^T y_{i_0} = 1$$

$$X^T u - Y^T v \geq w\mathbf{1}.$$

This constraint is equivalent to $\begin{pmatrix} -u \\ v \end{pmatrix}^T \begin{pmatrix} x_i \\ y_i \end{pmatrix} \leq w \quad i = 1, 2, \ldots, N.$
When this equation satisfies the equality, this indicates a hyperplane

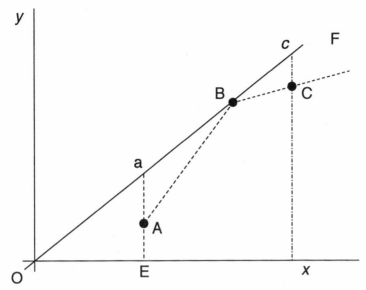

Figure 7-3
Production Frontiers under Different Technology Assumptions

that does not necessarily intersect the origin. Therefore, we can now construct the production frontier by a combination of hyperplanes which do not necessarily intersect the origin. In practice, we calculate the technical efficiency measure by solving the dual problem of (7-4).[3]

If we impose $w \geq 0$, then we have nonincreasing returns to scale (NIRS). In Figure 7-3, this means that any line representing the frontier intersects with the y axis in the non-negative range. However, if we allow w to be unrestricted, we have VRS. In Figure 7-3, this means that the line representing the frontier intersects with the y axis at any range. For example, in Figure 7-3, A, B, and C show the input-output combinations of three firms. Here, the line OBF is a frontier assuming CRS, the line OBC is a frontier assuming NIRS, and line EABC is a frontier assuming VRS.

DEA vs. the Cost Function Approach

Efforts to measure technical efficiency usually utilize either the DEA method or the cost function approach. In the cost function approach, cost functions and technical efficiency are estimated simultaneously.

There are both advantages and disadvantages to estimating technical efficiency with DEA rather than with a cost function. The first advantage is that DEA is a nonparametric method; the cost function approach is parametric. Any particular parametrization of a cost function may involve specification error. In contrast, DEA models the production technology far more flexibly. Although DEA may embody assumptions on returns to scale, it does not parametrically restrict any isoquant or substitution elasticity. Second, DEA embodies no behavioral assumptions (e.g., cost minimization) for a firm and thus is appropriate for studying nonprofit and "not necessarily for profit" organizations like hospitals. In contrast, the cost function approach generally assumes that hospital behavior is motivated by either profit maximization or cost minimization. (In Chapter 6, we utilize a nonminimum variable cost function in order to respond to this problem.) The third advantage is a pragmatic one. DEA is feasible in the absence of input price data; the cost function approach is not. To the extent that input price data are unreliable, the DEA method should be preferred.

Data Description

The Ministry of Health and Welfare (*Koseisho*) conducts an annual Facility Survey of all hospitals and clinics in Japan. In order to control for various conditions that may affect hospital efficiency, we focus our attention on general hospitals (*sogo byoin*). General hospitals are a relatively homogeneous group with similar production technology and patient case mix. They are also an important subset of Japanese hospitals, accounting for 11.2% of all hospitals, 28.7% of all beds, and 27.9% of all inpatients. In addition, this group includes most of the large, complex hospitals in the country.

Our primary interest is to compare the technical efficiency of public and private hospitals. From our sample of private hospitals, we eliminate "semi-public" private hospitals (hospitals owned by insurance associations). Similarly, we eliminate "other public hospitals" which include hospitals owned by quasi-private organizations such as the Japanese Red Cross. Although this differs from the sample of general hospitals considered in Chapter 6, these selections are appropriate for DEA. In particular, they assure to the extent it is possible that all the hospitals included in the analysis have similar production technologies. In the Facility Survey, there are four ward categories: psychiatric, tuberculosis, ordinary, and geriatric. Some general hospitals have multiple different categories of wards, and others do not. Because our main object is to compare the technical efficiency of public and private hospitals and differences in case mix may introduce differences in technology employed by hospitals, tending to bias our results, we restrict attention to hospitals that have only an ordinary ward.

After we eliminate hospitals with multiple ward types and those with missing values from the complete facility survey, the data used to estimate the technical efficiency measure come from a single cross-section of 412 general hospitals in Japan, including 159 public and 253 private hospitals.

We use the number of patients in specific departments (such as internal medicine, surgery, and ophthalmology) as output measurements. From the 1990 Facility Survey, we obtain five output figures for each hospital—outpatient visits per day (OUT), surgical inpatients (SURG), orthopedic inpatients (ORTHO), internal medicine inpatients (IM), and all other inpatients per day (Other IN)—and eight input figures—the number of full-time physicians (FullD), the number of part-time physicians (PartD), the number of residents (Resid), the number of registered nurses (RN), the number of practical nurses (PN), the number of office workers (Office), the number of other workers (Other), and the number of beds (Bed). Table 7-1 provides descriptive statistics for these variables.

In our sample, private hospitals employ more labor than do public hospitals, save registered nurses. Private hospitals employ more doctors (full-time, part-time, and resident) and have more administrative and other staff. With regard to outputs, public hospitals have fewer internal medicine inpatients and outpatient visits.

Estimated Results

The optimum technical efficiency measure of a hospital is 1. If the technical efficiency measure of hospital i_0 is 1.5, this means that hospital i_0 could treat 1.5 times the number of patients, given its input level, if it were as efficient as the other firms. In this sense, hospital i_0 is said to have a technical inefficiency of 50%. The higher the technical efficiency measure, the more inefficient that hospital is.

We calculate the technical efficiency measure of hospitals under three assumptions, CRS, NIRS, and VRS, and two different input-output specifications. The results using each specification are shown at the top of Table 7-2.[4] The results using the data that do not include office workers are shown in the "no office" section in Table 7-2. Under both specifications, the public hospitals are, on average,

Table 7-1
Descriptive Statistics of Inputs and Outputs

	Mean		Minimum		Maximum	
	Private	Public	Private	Public	Private	Public
Inputs						
FullD	41.13	34.54	4	9	538	115
	(53.57)	(20.49)				
PartD	63.53	46.19	0	0	2479	768
	(177.71)	(83.86)				
Resid	5.15	2.68	0	0	172	29
	(18.83)	(6.01)				
RN	106.26	133.52	5	28	615	408
	(89.58)	(78.54)				
PN	52.5	29.43	1	1	173	108
	(33.38)	(19.89)				
Other	100.66	70.82	12	19	434	210
	(62.82)	(33.98)				
Office	46.62	29.40	7	9	254	66
	(31.53)	(12.27)				
Bed	336.02	321.00	100	100	1154	810
	(161.21)	(138.60)				
Outputs						
SURG	51.94	57.70	0	2	266	166
	(41.00)	(34.46)				
ORTHO	37.62	45.23	0	0	154	205
	(26.00)	(31.20)				
IM	99.05	84.52	0	0	322	242
	(57.29)	(41.29)				
Other_IN	75.27	80.36	0	2	391	299
	(76.55)	(63.98)				
OUT	707.73	704.25	14	129	2464	1756
	(337.57)	(311.30)				

Note: The values in parentheses are standard deviations.

more technically efficient than the private hospitals. When we use every kind of input-output, under the constant returns to scale assumption, the level of technical inefficiency for private hospitals is 9.3%; it is 4.8% for public hospitals. Under the nonincreasing returns to scale assumption, it is 6.6% for private and 4.1% for public hospitals. Under the variable returns to scale assumption, it is 6.1% for private and 3.4% for public hospitals.

Under the constant returns to scale assumption, public hospitals are far more efficient than private hospitals; the difference in tech-

Table 7-2
Descriptive Statistics of Technical Efficiency Measure

	Mean		Minimum		Maximum	
	Private	Public	Private	Public	Private	Public
CRS	1.093	1.048	1	1	1.923	1.435
	(0.133)	(0.0924)				
NIRS	1.066	1.041	1	1	1.923	1.435
	(0.115)	(0.0872)				
VRS	1.061	1.034	1	1	1.923	1.416
	(0.110)	(0.0791)				
No office*						
CRS	1.100	1.063	1	1	2.065	1.438
	(0.139)	(0.102)				
NIRS	1.072	1.051	1	1	2.058	1.436
	(0.123)	(0.0967)				
VRS	1.067	1.045	1	1	2.058	1.436
	(0.118)	(0.0903)				

Note: The values in parentheses are standard deviations.
*For no office, we calculate the technical efficiency measure without using office workers as an input.

nical inefficiency level is 4.5%. However the differences between private and public hospitals in technical inefficiency are smaller for the nonincreasing returns to scale assumption and for the variable returns to scale assumption.

We now conduct two statistical tests to establish whether these differences in efficiency are statistically significant. We use both a two-tailed asymptotic t-test for difference in the mean and a nonparametric test, the Mann-Whitney U test. Table 7-3 presents the result of these tests.

The null hypothesis for the first test is that the mean efficiency level is the same for private and public hospitals. If the null hypothesis is rejected, then the private hospitals with the higher mean technical efficiency measure are on average more inefficient than the public hospitals. In the second test, the null hypothesis is that the distribution of efficiency measures or the median efficiency levels are the same for private and public hospitals. If this hypothesis is rejected, one group of hospitals has a distribution of efficiency measures that are everywhere greater than the other group's. Null hypotheses are rejected in both tests at the 5% level (except for NIRS in the no-office specification). Figure 7-4 shows the distribu-

Table 7-3
Hypothesis Tests: DEA Results

		No Office
Difference in Means (t-test)		
1. Private Mean vs. Public Mean under CRS	4.018[†]	3.108[†]
2. Private Mean vs. Public Mean under NIRS	2.564[†]	1.910**
3. Private Mean vs. Public Mean under VRS	2.871[†]	2.105**
Difference in Distributions (Mann-Whitney U test)		
1. Private vs. Public under CRS	−4.244[†]	−3.111[†]
2. Private vs. Public under NIRS	−2.535[†]	−1.833*
3. Private vs. Public under VRS	−2.862[†]	−2.076**

* denotes significance at the 10% level.
** denotes significance at the 5% level.
[†] denotes significance at the 1% level.

tion of technical efficiency measures under two assumptions: CRS and VRS. In both cases, the distribution of efficiency in private hospitals is in a position of first-order stochastic dominance with respect to the distribution in public hospitals.

Does this result mean that public hospitals are more technically efficient than private ones? When we compare the efficiency of the two groups, we can separate the inefficiency into two factors: individual inefficiency within groups and inefficiency caused by the difference in productivity between groups. For example, in Figure 7-5, the line OA shows the frontier of group A, and OB shows the frontier of group B. Suppose that hospital H belonging to group A is plotted as point H. Hospital H can provide service at point b if it employs the technology that is efficient in group A. The inefficiency measured by the ratio ab/aH is the within-group individual inefficiency of hospital H. An efficient hospital in group B can provide service at point c. Thus, the inefficiency measured by the ratio ac/ab reveals the difference in productivity between the two groups, and is constant over all (x, y) pairs as long as CRS is assumed.

In this example, if we use all the data to calculate the technical efficiency measure of hospital H, the measure is ac/aH. If we use only group A data to calculate the efficiency measure of hospital H, its measure is ab/aH. The former is called pooled technical efficiency; the latter is called separate technical efficiency. There is a relation, $\dfrac{ac}{ab} = \dfrac{ac}{aH} \Big/ \dfrac{ab}{aH}$, between the two measures, which means that we can obtain the productivity difference between the two

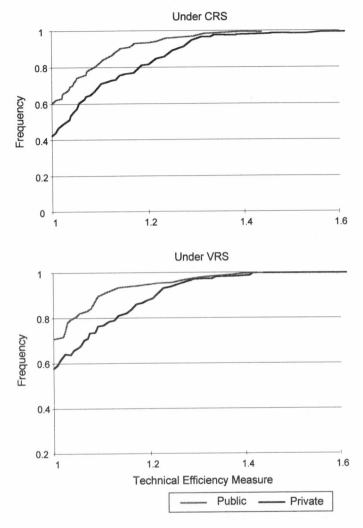

Figure 7-4
Distribution of Technical Efficiency Measure

groups by dividing the individual efficiency values. The measure that represents the difference of productivity between the two groups is labeled ratio in Table 7-4.

Table 7-4 presents the mean value of pooled, separate, ratio, and scale efficiency measures. For each measure, private hospitals have larger values than do public hospitals. However, there is little dif-

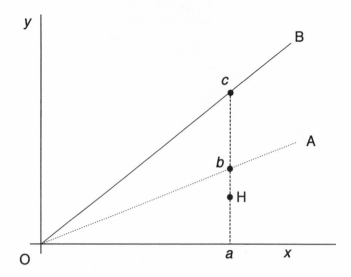

Figure 7-5
Comparative Productivity of Two Groups

Table 7-4
The Mean Value of Other Efficiency Measures

	Pooled*		Separate		Ratio		Scale	
	Private	Public	Private	Public	Private	Public	Private	Public
CRS	1.0923	1.048	1.067	1.030	1.023	1.018	1.030	1.014
	(0.133)	(0.0924)	(0.111)	(0.0738)	(0.0502)	(0.0425)	(0.0548)	(0.0332)
VRS	1.0607	1.034	1.044	1.020	1.015	1.014		
	(0.110)	(0.0791)	(0.0916)	(0.0635)	(0.0431)	(0.0376)		

Note: The values in parentheses are standard deviations.
* This value is the same as Table 7-3.

ference in this ratio between private and public hospitals, except in the separate case. Under separate CRS, the level of inefficiency for private hospitals is 6.7%, whereas it is 3.0% for public hospitals; under separate VRS, the level of inefficiency is 4.4% for private hospitals and 2.0% for public hospitals. Private hospitals are about twice as inefficient as public hospitals in the separate case. This result means that there is no difference between the best-practice technology employed by private and public hospitals. Moreover,

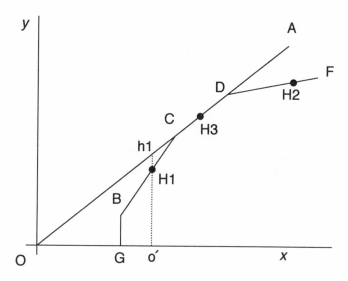

Figure 7-6
Scale Efficiency of Technology

there is a wider dispersion between the most and least efficient private hospitals compared to that between the most and least efficient public hospitals.

We can calculate the scale efficiency of technology and decompose the technical efficiency measure into two parts. For example, in Figure 7-6, the line OA shows the frontier under CRS, and the line GBCDF shows the frontier under VRS. The points H1, H2, and H3 represent the three hospitals. Hospitals H1 and H2 show inefficiency under CRS. If the technology is, in fact, not constant in terms of returns to scale, then differences in scale may show up as inefficiency. To avoid this potential problem, we may use VRS. However, by comparing the efficiency measures under CRS and VRS, we can gain insight into the scale effect. For example, the efficiency measure of hospital H1 is O'h1/O'H1 under CRS and O'H1/O'H1 under VRS. Therefore, we can determine the scale effect by dividing the measure under CRS by the measure under VRS. The measure that represents the scale effect is labeled scale in Table 7-4.

The scale measure is 3.0% for private and 1.4% for public hospitals. This result suggests that there are more private than public hospitals operating in regions with nonconstant returns to scale. As demonstrated in Figure 7-3 (relative to the CRS frontier), Firm A

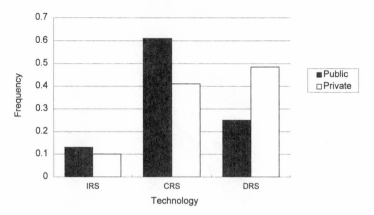

Figure 7-7
Distribution of Scale Economies

operates in the increasing returns to scale region, Firm B operates in the constant returns to scale region, and Firm C operates in the decreasing returns to scale region. There is a relationship between the firm's type of returns to scale technology and its technical efficiency measure. If firm i operates in the IRS region, it has the same technical efficiency measure under the CRS and NIRS assumptions, and this measure is bigger than that obtained under the VRS assumption. If firm i operates in the decreasing returns to scale (DRS) region, it has the same measure under the NIRS and VRS assumptions, and this measure is smaller than that obtained under the CRS assumption. If firm i operates in the CRS region, it has the same measure under any assumption. The distribution of the returns to scale measure in the data is shown in Figure 7-7.

Factors Associated with the Level of Inefficiency: Regression Analysis

The dependent variable here is the natural log of the technical inefficiency measure estimated previously. By the definition of the output-oriented technical efficiency measure, these measures are all greater than or equal to one. Therefore, the natural log transformation of the technical efficiency measure is greater than or equal to zero. The larger the value, the more inefficient the hospital is. In order to identify possible sources of inefficiency, we regress log of the hospital-specific estimates of technical inefficiency against hospital characteristics obtained from the Facility Survey. We perform regressions for both CRS and VRS. In order to account for the fact that log efficiency must be greater than or equal to zero (i.e., that log efficiency is truncated at 0), we use a Tobit regression.

Because our primary focus is the relationship between ownership arrangements (private vs. public) and efficiency, we introduce an ownership dummy (OWNER) that is equal to 1 if a hospital is public. Based upon our results up to this point, we expect a greater efficiency for public hospitals; thus, we expect a negative coefficient in the regression.

As already noted, out of 10,096 Japanese hospitals, we selected 412 general hospitals that have only ordinary wards for our analysis. Our purpose was to control for various factors affecting the technical efficiency of a hospital. Such factors include the case mix of patients and the intensity and quality of care provided. Our independent variables include hospital size, a dummy variable for teaching hospitals, and the level of competition in a hospital market.

We use the number of beds as a proxy of hospital size and introduce both the natural log and the square of the natural log of beds into the regression.[5] Because our sample is limited to the general hospital group, we have, to certain degree, already controlled for the impact of scale upon technical efficiency.

Because teaching hospitals have a different organizational structure, we also introduce a teaching hospital dummy (TEACH), which equals 1 if a hospital is affiliated with a medical school. There are 24 teaching hospitals in our sample. It may be argued that teaching hospitals provide more intensive care, to accommodate difficult case mixes and to serve educational missions. Thus, essentially, there is an unobserved output: teaching. This may indicate a higher level of technical inefficiency in teaching hospitals, other things being equal. In such a case, we expect a positive relationship between the teaching dummy and the degree of inefficiency.

In a competitive market, more efficient firms drive less efficient firms out of the industry. Thus, if the market is not competitive (e.g., because of a barrier to entry), inefficiencies in hospitals may persist. This would generate a negative relationship between the level of competition and the level of technical inefficiency. However, as shown in Chapters 4 and 8, we find evidence for the existence of incentives for nonprice competition among Japanese hospitals and argue that Japanese hospitals in a competitive market may attempt to attract more patients by increasing medical staff. In the case of nonprice competition, the relationship between competition and the level of technical inefficiency might be positive. A competitive environment is proxied by the Herfindahl index, which is the sum of squared market shares (in beds) of each hospital. When a market

Table 7-5
Tobit Estimation Results

Variable	CRS	VRS
Intercept	−2.798[†]	−9.795[†]
TEACH	0.068*	0.073*
OWNER	−0.059[†]	−0.043**
LBED	1.052[†]	3.568[†]
SQLBED	−0.094[†]	−0.321[†]
HERF	−0.026[†]	−0.025[†]
Log of likelihood	−44.69	−63.20

* denotes significance at the 10% level.
** denotes significance at the 5% level.
[†] denotes significance at the 1% level.

contains only one hospital, the Herfindahl index is at its maximum value of 1. We use the algorithm introduced by Elzinga and Hogarty (1973) to construct 61 markets for inpatient medical services in Japan using the government-defined medical zone as a starting point. If hospitals in a competitive market are competing for patients by increasing the staffing ratio, we expect to find a negative coefficient for the Herfindahl index. Table 7-5 presents the regression results.

As expected, the estimated coefficient for the ownership dummy is negative, and it is positive for the teaching dummy. Other things being equal, public hospitals are more efficient than private ones, and teaching hospitals are less efficient than nonteaching ones. In a market where competition is stronger (Herfindahl index is smaller), the level of technical inefficiency is higher. These results indicate that nonprice competition may induce hospitals to increase the employment of inputs.

For the size variable, we find a positive coefficient for the natural log and a negative value for the square value. Under the maintained assumption of constant returns to scale embodied in the CRS technique, the inefficiency measures may be polluted if, in reality, hospital returns to scale are not constant. Under the VRS assumption, we eliminate this pollution as a result of scale inefficiency. However, we obtain the same result under both assumptions.[6]

Conclusions

By using the DEA method, we measure and compare the technical inefficiency of private and public hospitals. We use a Tobit regression to explore factors associated with technical inefficiency. Our primary results are as follows:

1. Public hospitals are more technically efficient than private hospitals. This result does not change after excluding other factors that affect the technical inefficiency of hospitals.

2. Larger hospitals are more efficient than smaller hospitals.

3. Hospitals in more competitive markets are less efficient, consistent with nonprice competition via staffing levels.

4. There are more private hospitals than public hospitals operating in regions with nonconstant returns to scale.

It is important to keep in mind several caveats when interpreting this or any DEA paper. The DEA technique assumes that the inputs and outputs are all observed, are all precisely measured, and are all homogenous. Biases in intergroup comparisons can arise from differences in unmeasured inputs, unmeasured outputs, differences in the quality of inputs or outputs, or unobserved differences in type of the inputs or outputs between groups.

Of particular note in this context are potential quality differences and potential differences in unmeasured inputs between the public and private hospitals, neither of which we can explicitly treat. Public hospitals receive material and pecuniary subsidies which may function as unmeasured inputs, biasing upwards their technical efficiency. Alternatively, the conventional wisdom in Japan holds that public hospitals are, in general, higher quality providers than private; if this is true, it would tend to bias upward the efficiency of private hospitals. We leave to future research the extrication of these potential confounding influences.

Appendix 7-1

The dual problem of (7-3) is

$$\max_{\theta,\mu} \begin{pmatrix} 1 \\ 0 \end{pmatrix}^T \begin{pmatrix} \theta \\ \mu \end{pmatrix}$$

s.t.

$$X\mu \leq x_{i_0} \tag{A7-1}$$

$$y_{i_0}\theta \leq Y\mu$$

$$\mu > 0$$

where $\theta \in \boldsymbol{R}$, $\mu \in \boldsymbol{R}^{\mathrm{N}}$.

If firm i_0 employs firm j's technology and uses μ_j times the input of firm j, it can produce $\mu_j y_j$ goods. Likewise, if it combines the other firm's technology by the ratio $\mu = (\mu_1, \mu_2, \ldots, \mu_N)$, it can produce $Y\mu$ and reach the production point $(X\mu, Y\mu)$. The constraint of problem (A7-1) is transformed to Equations (A7-2) and (A7-3):

$$\sum_{j=1}^{N} \mu_j x_j^{(k)} \leq x_{i_0}^{(k)} \quad k = 1, 2, \ldots, m \tag{A7-2}$$

$$\theta y_{i_0}^{(l)} \leq \sum_{j=1}^{N} \mu_j y_j^{(l)} \quad l = 1, 2, \ldots, n \tag{A7-3}$$

Equation (A7-2) says that firm i_0 selects the combination of technology μ to be under the actual input level x_{i_0}. The right-hand constraint [Equation (A7-3)] is the output level when firm i_0 selects the combination μ. The larger the right-hand side value of Equation (A7-3) is, the larger the value of θ. We want to maximize θ. Therefore, in order to maximize the objective function of (A7-1), we must select the combination μ to be bigger than the level of output. The hyperplane is determined by the normal vector or by specifying the points on the hyperplane. Primal problem (7-3) determines the normal vector that determines the hyperplane; dual problem (A7-1) determines the points that determine the hyperplane.

By the duality theorem, the optimal value of the dual problem, θ^*, is the same as the optimal value of Equation (7-3) if (u^*, v^*) denotes the optimal solution of (7-3), $u^{*T} x_{i_0}$. Because $v^{*T} y_{i_0} = 1$ by the previous assumption and $u^{*T} x_{i_0} = v^{*T} y_{i_0}$, from the nature of

the frontier hyperplane, the relation $\theta^* = u^{*T} x_{i_0} = \dfrac{v^{*T} y_{i_0}^*}{v^{*T} y_{i_0}}$ is derived. In other words, θ^* is the technical efficiency measure of firm i_0.

Notes:

[1] We use the term "actual production frontier" to indicate the theoretical frontier; this is the maximum output for a given production process and inputs. This is different from an "estimated frontier," which is constructed from real data.

[2] Firm B can expand its production level in a nonradial direction and so it is possible to create another measure. However, we treat only radial expansion in measuring the technical inefficiency.

[3] The dual problem of Equation (7-4) is the following:

$$\max_{\theta,\mu} \begin{pmatrix} 1 \\ 0 \end{pmatrix}^T \begin{pmatrix} \theta \\ \mu \end{pmatrix}$$

s.t.

$$X\mu \leq x_{i_0}$$

$$y_{i_0}\theta \leq Y\mu$$

$$1^T\mu \leq 1 \quad \text{or} \quad 1^T\mu = 1.$$

When we choose $1^T\mu \leq 1$ as the additive constraint, the range of w is non-negative, $w \geq 0$. If we choose $1^T\mu = 1$, the range of w has no restrictions

[4] The owners of public hospitals, either the government or a local self-governing body, have administrative duties toward their hospitals. To fulfill these duties, the owners hire people to manage their hospital. We are unable to observe these administrative personnel. Public hospitals may be estimated to be more efficient than they really are due to this unobservable input. To counter this effect, we calculate the technical efficiency of the hospitals under the condition "no office" because the people in administration are categorized as office workers in private hospitals

[5] If hospitals can freely choose the number of beds, this is an endogenous variable. However, hospitals cannot, by law, freely change the number of beds. Therefore, we treat the number of beds as an exogenous variable.

[6] Under both assumptions, the efficiency measure is a decreasing function of number of beds in the range over 250 beds.

Part III

Product Choice of Hospitals

There is a wide variety in the services offered by different hospitals. Japanese hospitals range in size from 20 beds to nearly 2000 beds, the average being around 150. They differ in their patient mix. Some serve more inpatients; some serve more outpatients; some specialize in cancer; some treat mostly internal medicine patients. Hospitals also vary markedly in the range of clinical services they offer, from small and unsophisticated, offering basic diagnostic and laboratory services, to large and technically advanced, offering the latest diagnostic and treatment services. In this section, we explore the factors influencing a hospital's decisions concerning what services to provide its patients. We focus on economic influences upon these choices.

A hospital must consider a number of economic factors when deciding on a portfolio of services to offer. One of the important considerations is what competitors offer. In a market where competitors all provide many sophisticated services, a hospital may feel a stronger incentive to adopt similar services. Conversely, the duplication of services may instead lead a hospital to be more reticent toward such adoption if the market for the services in question is already divided among too many competitors. Chapters 8 and 10 focus primarily upon this issue, dealing with the effects of competition on the specialization and sophistication of the services provided by hospitals in a market.

Another important economic consideration that arises when a hospital is deciding to provide a new service is the effect of that new service on its existing product line. If introducing a new service will reduce demand for a preexisting one, a hospital may hesitate to adopt, even if the service is a money-making proposition on a stand-alone basis. But if the new service will tend to enhance demand for other services (e.g., by attracting more patients to the hospital), a hospital may be willing to adopt even a money-losing service. Of course, added to this already complex decision environment is the fact that many hospitals are motivated by factors other than profit, which may induce them to engage in different behavior. Chapter 9 discusses the issue of the effect of service provision on other services.

8

Diagnostic Technology and Competition

The role of technology in hospitals has been a subject of considerable and recurring interest to policymakers, hospital managers, health services researchers, and economists over the last two decades. Technological advances in the health care field have been trumpeted as revolutionary breakthroughs sure to provide great benefits to patients. At the same time, many health care technologies have been criticized for their role in driving up the costs of care. International comparisons have highlighted the fact that the U.S. has far higher health care costs than other countries and that the diffusion of many medical devices is far higher in the United States than elsewhere (Yoshikawa, Shirouzu, and Holt, 1991).

The role of technology and the health care financing system in competition among hospitals has been emphasized in explaining the high rate of diffusion in the U.S. and its possible implications for the costs of care. Historically, the financing system for U.S. health care has been thought to provide strong incentives for hospitals to compete on nonprice bases and relatively weaker incentives for them to compete on price. In the traditional U.S. system of fee-for-service payment by third-party payers, consumers' incentive to shop for low-price providers is blunted, and choices among providers may be based on nonprice factors. This situation furnishes incentives for investment in technologies that make hospitals relatively more attractive to patients (or to physicians who influence patients' decisions).

In industries where it is difficult or impossible for firms to com-

This chapter is based upon: Vogt, W.B., Bhattacharya, J., Kupor, S., Yoshikawa, A., and Nakahara, T. 1995. "The Role of Diagnostic Technology in Competition among Japanese Hospitals," *International Journal of Technology Management, Series on Management of Technology in Health Care*, No. 1. This revised version is published with the permission of Interscience Enterprises.

171

pete on a price basis, they often compete for customers on the basis of quality or other nonprice factors. When a firm cannot lure customers away from its competitors by offering a lower price, it will instead offer higher-quality products, more advertising, and so forth. A prominent example of this sort of competition occurred in the U.S. airline industry. Before its abolition in 1984, the Civil Aeronautics Board regulated U.S. airline ticket prices. The airlines, unable to compete with one another on price, competed by providing customers with more frequent flights, leading to many flights leaving airports with empty seats (Schmalensee, 1977). This wasteful competition, in part, led to the eventual deregulation of the U.S. airline industry.

In this chapter, we report on an investigation of the role of technology in competition among hospitals in Japan. The similarities and differences in financing and delivery systems in the U.S. and Japan provide an instructive case study in the influence of financing and competition on hospitals' behavior. Because of the financing arrangements of the health care system, Japanese hospitals are effectively barred from competing with one another on a price basis. As a result, we expect to observe competition on nonprice bases, and one possible avenue of this nonprice competition is through the provision of high-technology medical services. We examine two high-profile diagnostic technologies, computed tomography (CT) scanning (full body scanning) and magnetic resonance imaging (MRI). With respect to these technologies, we ask: Are Japanese hospitals' decisions to invest in medical technologies significantly influenced by their competitive concerns?

Technology and Competition among Hospitals

Several authors have commented upon the importance of a hospital's level of technology provision to its competitive position. Hillman et al. (1987) report a survey including providers, regulators, and manufacturers in which they find that competitive concerns are the most important influence upon providers' decisions concerning MRI acquisition. They also find that those considering acquiring MRI had acquired CT scanners for similar reasons. The impulse to acquire both diagnostic technologies is part of an overall strategy these providers pursue to be in the vanguard of technological advance; they hope to create "an advantageous niche in competing against other local providers."

Niki (1985) documents the rapid diffusion of CT scanners in

Japan. He concludes that Japan's high diffusion rate for CT technology is due to the entrepreneurial spirit of smaller private hospitals and the mix of public policies promulgated by the Japanese government. Other researchers in Japan have emphasized the competitive aspects of technology acquisition. Ushimaru (1988) argues that hospitals invest in medical equipment in order to attract patients and, thus, that medical technology serves a function similar to advertising in other industries, forming quality expectations in patients' minds and serving as a conduit for competition.

There have been a number of empirical investigations of the role of financing and competition in the technology policies of U.S. hospitals. Luft et al. (1986) find that several technologies exhibit evidence of quality competition among U.S. hospitals. For these technologies, they find that a hospital is more likely to adopt a technology if its neighbors have adopted it. By contrast, Sloan et al. (1986) find that hospitals in more competitive markets are less likely to provide certain surgical services. Sloan et al. do find that financing is an important influence on technology provision in hospitals, as hospitals in markets with many privately insured patients are more likely to provide services. Dranove, Shanley, and Simon (1992) find that the number of hospitals offering high-tech services is higher in more competitive markets, but the effect is small.

These studies point to the importance of technology in competition among U.S. hospitals and also to the influence of the financing system on that competition. Our study is of interest as part of a comparison of hospital markets in Japan and the U.S. But it is of particular interest as an investigation of nonprice competition in health care markets because the Japanese market for hospital services provides a particularly conducive environment for nonprice competition.

Hospital Behavior under the Japanese System

Understanding Japan's health care financing system is integral to understanding the diffusion of medical technology in Japan. Hospitals and clinics are paid on a fee-for-service basis. The fees for each office visit, procedure, and drug are set by the Japanese Ministry of Health and Welfare (*Koseisho*). When a new medical device is proposed for introduction to Japan, *Koseisho* decides whether to include it in the fee schedule and at what level its use should be reimbursed. Understandably, the diffusion of a medical device is very slow until it is added to the fee schedule.

As we have noted, there are 10,096 hospitals in Japan (compared to 6,780 in the U.S.), and they are, for the most part, privately owned. The private sector controls 83% of the hospitals, with the great majority of these owned by individual physicians. Private hospitals receive little or no subsidy from the government; they must finance their operations out of revenue generated by treating patients. Although hospitals are forbidden to disburse profits to shareholders, the fact that they depend for their existence on a steady stream of patients induces a substantial incentive to attract patients. Hospitals operate under very little regulation regarding their capital expenditures; there is no certificate of need[1] or similar regulation in Japan.

Government hospitals operate in a very different financial environment from those in the private sector. Government hospitals receive substantial subsidies from national and local governments. The effect of these subsidies on technology acquisition decisions is unclear, however. Because they do not have to break even, government hospitals have less incentive to compete with their private counterparts, which may reduce their incentive to innovate. Conversely, government hospitals' subsidies may enable them to procure new technology more easily, tending to increase their adoption rates. In Chapter 5, we compared private and public teaching hospitals and found some evidence that such governmental subsidies do promote the adoption of technology and richer staffing mix in public teaching hospitals.

Japanese hospital markets have many of the attributes associated with nonprice competition among firms. Consumers, because of generous and universal insurance, have little incentive to shop for inexpensive care; however, their incentive to seek out care of high (perceived) quality is unblunted. Even more important, hospitals are barred from engaging in price competition. It is not surprising, given an environment characterized by fixed prices, fee-for-service medicine, and large numbers of competitors, that several authors have observed the importance of competitive concerns to technology diffusion in Japanese hospitals.

The Two Technologies

The computed tomography scanner and the magnetic resonance imager each represent revolutionary advances in the field of diagnostic radiology. CT was invented in 1967 and began to be adopted by U.S. and Japanese hospitals in the mid-1970s. CT integrates X-ray technology with computer technology, allowing radiologists to construct three-dimensional images of structures within a patient's body. This ability represents a considerable advance over conventional X-ray technology and was heralded at the time of its invention as a breakthrough in diagnostic imaging. CT spread quickly in both the U.S. and Japan. Trajtenberg and Yitzhaki (1989) report that, of 20 technologies studied, CT has a diffusion speed in the top third and its speed of diffusion is three times as great as two other diagnostic technologies studied. In Japan, the CT scanner has seen even more extensive diffusion. As of 1982, Japan had 2,120 CT scanners, and the U.S. had 2,318. Japan's population is slightly less than half the U.S.'s, so Japan had twice the diffusion of the U.S. on a per capita basis (Okimoto and Yoshikawa, 1993).

MRI serves a similar role to CT, although it operates on different physical principles. MRI uses the magnetic properties of hydrogen atoms in the body to construct three-dimensional images of internal structures. Unlike CT, MRI does not expose the patient to radiation, and the MR imager is sensitive to differences in the chemical composition of the tissues it scans. It began to be used in medicine in the U.S. and Japan in the early to mid-1980s, and it has diffused rapidly since then. As in the case of CT, the diffusion of MRI in Japan has been more extensive than in the U.S.; the number of MRIs in Japan rivals the number in the U.S. in absolute numbers and dominates it on a per capita basis (Okimoto and Yoshikawa, 1993).

These two technologies have become symbols of high-technology, high-cost medicine and have shown very high diffusion rates in both the U.S. and Japan. CT is the more mature of the technologies; it has been available for two decades. Its real price has fallen, its quality has improved over the decades since its introduction, and it has become very widely diffused. Japanese patients and doctors have come to expect and value services from advanced medical devices, and CT particularly is valued because of its usefulness in diagnosing cerebrovascular disease, a prevalent condition in Japan (Niki, 1985; Okimoto and Yoshikawa, 1993). MRI, the more expensive and newer of the technologies, has seen far less diffusion (Figures 8-1 and 8-2) and may be integrated into Japanese patients' expectations to the same degree.

Hypotheses

The previously described considerations lead us to form a number of hypotheses. First, we hypothesize that diagnostic technologies are

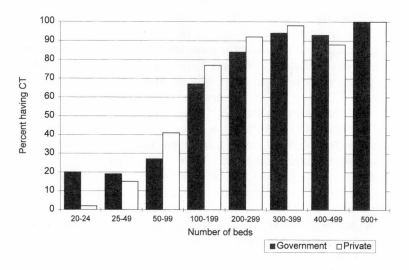

Figure 8-1
Diffusion of CT

an important instrument of competition among Japanese hospitals. Specifically, we hypothesize that when a particular hospital's rivals acquire a CT scanner (or MRI), that hospital is likely to respond to protect its competitive position by acquiring the same equipment. Second, we hypothesize that small and private hospitals respond more strongly to competitive pressures than do their larger and government-owned counterparts. This hypothesis is motivated by two facts: (1) In most markets, there are many small hospitals, and they therefore have a greater need to differentiate themselves from one another. (2) Government hospitals, by virtue of their subsidies, have less incentive to behave competitively, because they are shielded from the consequences of lax attention to their competitive position. However, as discussed previously, there is a rationale under which one might expect the converse from government hospitals. Third, we hypothesize that there may be important differences in the diffusion patterns of CT and MRI because these two technologies differ in a number of respects. It is an empirical issue whether MRI will prove to be a stronger conduit of competition, by virtue of its greater expense and prestige, or whether its much greater demands on space and finances will mitigate against its use in competition.

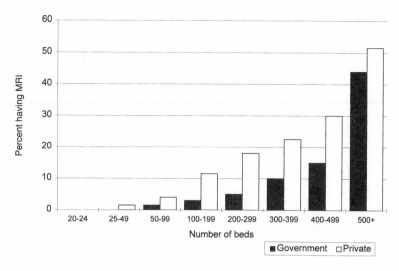

Figure 8-2
Diffusion of MRI

Data

We draw the hospital-specific variables used in our analysis from the Facility Survey, which allows us to determine which hospitals possess each of the technologies studied. We also observe the ownership of each hospital, whether or not it is affiliated with a medical school, how many beds it has, how many inpatients and outpatients it treated in the month of September, and its location. In our market definition, we use patient flow information contained in the Patient Survey.

Many of our data come from public sources. Data on population density, age structure, and population in urban areas are derived from the Management and Coordination Agency (1990). The data on income are derived from the Ministry of Home Affairs (1991). The price index and income data are recorded in Management and Coordination Agency (1990).

Methodology

The dependent variable in all our analyses is the presence of a technology (CT or MRI) at a particular hospital. The dependent variable takes a value of 1 if the hospital owns a CT scanner (MRI

Table 8-1
Variable Definitions

Variable	Definition
%CT	Proportion of a hospital's competitors with a CT scanner
%MRI	Proportion of a hospital's competitors with an MRI
INPT	Inpatients (in 100s) on the survey date
OUTPT	Outpatients (in 1,000s) in the survey week
INCOME	Per capita income in the hospital's prefecture (in ¥100,000s)
CPI	Consumer price index in the hospital's prefecture
DENSITY	Population (in 1,000s)/square kilometer
OLD	Proportion of population over 65 years of age in medical zone
URBAN	Proportion of population living in urban areas in medical zone
GOV	1 if the hospital is owned by the government
PRIVATE	1 if the hospital is private (individual, *iryo-hojin*, private corporation)
NPO	1 if the hospital is owned by a non-profit organization
Insurance	1 if the hospital is owned by an insurer (omitted contrast)
TEACH	1 if the hospital is affiliated with a medical school

machine) at the time of the survey. As such, the variable reflects each hospital's decision regarding whether to purchase a CT (MRI) by the time of the survey. Because the dependent variable is discrete, our estimation technique is probit maximum likelihood.[2] All the variables used in the analysis are described in Table 8-1.

The first independent variable is the percentage of a hospital's rivals that possess the technology in question (called %CT and %MRI in Table 8-1). We follow Luft et al. (1986) in this respect. We detail the construction of the variable %CT (%MRI is similar). Each hospital in our sample is located in a market for hospital care (the construction of markets is discussed later in this section). For each hospital, we count the number of other hospitals in its market that possess CT. We divide this number by the number of hospitals in the market and multiply by 100 to obtain %CT. In calculating both the numerator and denominator of this fraction, we are careful to exclude the hospital itself, so that %CT measures only the actions of a hospital's rivals and not the behavior of the hospital itself. Also, in calculating both numerator and denominator, we consider only hospitals meeting certain selection criteria (also detailed later). As already discussed in our first hypothesis, we anticipate a positive coefficient for this variable, because we hypothesize that hospitals react to purchases of technology by making purchases themselves.

In addition to analyzing the full sample, we analyze several subsamples to test our second hypothesis. We wish to explore differences in behavior between government and private hospitals, so we analyze these two groups separately. Similarly, we analyze large and small hospitals separately to model differences between their reactions to competitive pressures. In the subgroup analyses, we eliminate size from the sample.

We use several other independent variables to control for differences among hospitals and among markets. To account for differences in the caseloads of different hospitals, we enter the number of inpatients and outpatients they treated. Because a larger volume of patients provides the hospital with greater opportunity to use a CT scanner or MRI, we expect these variables to be significant. Furthermore, because both CT and MRI are used on both an inpatient and outpatient basis, we enter both inpatients and outpatients. We control for differences in demand at the market level by entering per capita income and the percentage of the population over the age of 65. Both variables affect the demand for medical care positively, so we anticipate a positive coefficient for both. We control for costs by entering the consumer price index at the prefecture level and the degree of urbanization in the hospital's medical zone. In markets with higher input costs, hospitals should be less likely to adopt either technology because operating the technology will be more costly in high-cost markets, but reimbursement is the same in all markets (because fees are fixed at the national level). Ideally, we would like to have an index of input costs; however, in its absence, we hope that consumer prices and degree of urbanization will serve as proxies for costs. To account for differences in behavior by ownership and role, we enter dummy variables for the major ownership categories and for clinical education hospitals.

To define a suitable and relatively homogeneous sample for analysis, we begin with the full sample of 10,096 hospitals and eliminate all tuberculosis and leprosy hospitals. To eliminate hospitals whose primary patient load is psychiatric, we select out all hospitals whose caseloads are more than 50% psychiatric patients. Also, many hospitals in Japan are effectively nursing homes. To eliminate these, we remove all institutions which have allocated more than 50% of their beds for geriatric care. In devising these selection criteria, we intend to create a sample similar to the sample of community hospitals used in similar research in the U.S.

To measure competition, we need to have an operant definition of markets. We begin by considering "medical zones." Japan's 345 medical zones are administrative areas the government created in order to delineate market areas for hospital care. Rather than taking these administrative areas as markets themselves, we utilize patient flow data from the Patient Survey to cast out those with inflows or outflows in excess of 25%. This market definition follows that described by Elzinga and Hogarty (1973). Although using flows to define markets is itself problematic, the lack of price variability in these markets precludes estimating cross-price elasticities (the preferred method of market delineation). After all of the selections, we are left with 3,307 hospitals in 148 markets. They account for 36% of the hospital-based CT scanners in Japan and 37% of the MRIs.

An important limitation of our analysis is the probable existence of simultaneous equations bias. The dependent variables measuring competition are determined by a simultaneous equations system, and this can induce biases in the estimated coefficients (Dranove, Shanley, and Simon, 1992; Working, 1926). In this case, the competition variables could be proxying for unobserved components of demand in these markets. This bias is mitigated to some extent in our case because we include firm-level output controls (number of inpatients and outpatients), which were absent in previous work.

Results

In our sample of 3,307 hospitals, 667 are governmental and 2,640 are private. Overall, 53.7% of the hospitals we examine possess a CT scanner, and 8.8% have an MRI. Figures 8-1 and 8-2 show the levels of diffusion by ownership and by size. As these figures and our analyses show, the most important predictor of adoption of either technology is the size of the hospital. This is as expected: Hospitals that treat more patients have greater opportunities to use either technology (generating greater revenue), making the technology more financially viable. When we control for size, private hospitals have a greater propensity to possess each technology. This is especially evident for the small to medium-sized hospitals—the ones with the greatest need to differentiate themselves from their rivals.

There are interesting differences between the diffusion patterns of the two technologies, however. The penetration of CT into medium-sized and small hospitals is nearly as high as for the largest hospitals. In the case of MRI, the diffusion rate falls off much more rapidly for smaller hospitals. This pattern is reasonable, given that CT is the more mature and less expensive technology. CT also demands far less physical space to operate than does MRI. Ground rent is very high in Japan, so hospitals (especially small ones) are tightly constrained in their use of space, exaggerating the cost differential between CT and MRI. Furthermore, some hospitals are so small that they essentially do not have the space to accommodate MRI.

Private hospitals, especially in the medium-sized range, are far more likely than their government counterparts to have each technology. Given these hospitals' relatively greater incentive to differentiate themselves, we take this pattern also to be broadly consistent with the existence of nonprice competition.

We turn now to our probit results for CT scanners, presented in Table 8-2. The column headings describe the sample of hospitals. For example, the last column contains the results for small private hospitals. The rows are the dependent variables in our analysis. The entries in the table are coefficient estimates, with significance level indicated.

In the first column, the results for the full sample are presented. Notice that the coefficient of the variable percent of competitors with CT (%CT) is significant and positive. Thus, firms in markets in which many of their rivals have CT scanners are more likely to adopt CT themselves. Measures of size—number of inpatients and number of outpatients—also have positive and highly significant coefficients, confirming our earlier finding that size (and thus demand for services) is important in purchasing decisions. Income per capita, population density, and percent of population over 65—all demand-side variables—operate in the expected direction; an increase in any one of them increases the probability of adopting CT. The consumer price index and the level of urbanization—cost variables—both operate as expected. Higher costs decrease the probability of adopting CT.

Looking across the rows in the table, two variables reveal systematic differences among groups of hospitals. The coefficients on %CT reveal that government hospitals are the least responsive to competitive concerns and small and privately owned hospitals are more responsive. The same pattern is apparent with the urbanization variable; private and small hospitals are more responsive to cost differences than are government hospitals.[3] Thus, all the hospitals in the sample show a response to competitive and cost pressures, but the response of the government hospitals is muted.

Figure 8-3 examines the magnitude of the competitive effect for CT scanners. This graph shows the probable response of an average

Table 8-2
Probit Results for CT Adoption

Variable	Full Sample	Government Hospitals	Private Hospitals	Small Hospitals	Small Private Hospitals
CONSTANT	0.33	−0.78	−0.39	1.18	0.34
%CT	0.93†	0.58	1.08†	0.92†	0.99†
INPT	0.97†	0.62†	1.24†	1.55†	1.69†
OUTPT	0.52†	0.78†	0.56†	0.50†	0.040†
INCOME	0.54†	1.13**	0.46**	0.74†	0.56†
CPI	−0.30*	−0.32	−0.19	−0.40**	−0.28
DENSITY	0.05	0.24	0.03	0.05	0.08
OLD	1.37	6.22	−0.17	1.50	−0.20
URBAN	−0.32	−0.09	−0.49**	−0.48**	−0.69†
GOV	0.00				
PRIVATE	0.27				
NPO	0.47				
TEACH	0.17				

* denotes significance at the 10% level.
** denotes significance at the 5% level.
† denotes significance at the 1% level.

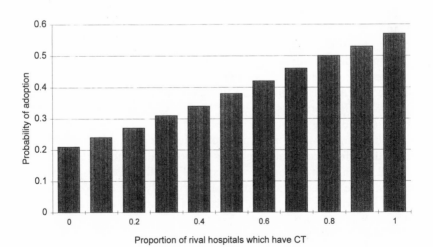

Figure 8-3
Competitive Effect of CT Adoption

Table 8-3
Probit Results for MRI adoption

Variable	Full Sample	Government Hospitals	Private Hospitals
CONSTANT	−2.94†	−2.14**	−3.45†
% MRI	−0.56	0.47	−1.63*
INPT	0.26†	−.06	0.45†
OUTPT	0.14†	0.34†	0.16†
INCOME	17.30	0.90*	−1.27
CPI	−0.01	0.01	−0.02*
GOV	−0.31		
PRIVATE	0.04		
NPO	−0.01		
TEACH	1.10†		

* denotes significance at the 10% level.
** denotes significance at the 5% level.
† denotes significance at the 1% level.

small, independently owned hospital to the actions of its rivals. In a market where no competitors have CT, the hospital would have only a 21% chance of purchasing a CT. However, in a market where all its competitors have CT, the same hospital is 57% likely to purchase a CT. So the measured effect not only is statistically significant, but also has considerable empirical relevance: Competition raises the probability that our average hospital has a CT by 36%.[4]

The results of the MRI analysis appear in Table 8-3, and they show a different pattern. Because many fewer hospitals have MRI, we remove several variables from the analysis to preserve degrees of freedom. For similar reasons, we perform subgroup analysis only for government and private hospitals. As with CT, the demand variables have a positive impact on the probability of adopting MRI. In contrast, however, the competition variable, %MRI, does not show the same pattern of affecting the adoption decision as it did for CT. There is no significant impact of competitors' decisions on purchasing decisions with respect to MRI. We conjecture that this is due to three factors. First, because the government made a conscious effort to set the fee for MRI very low, hospitals are under a strong incentive to ensure an adequate number of patients in order to break even on MRI utilization. Most hospitals must have referrals from other facilities to meet this need, and this may have led to some collusion, tacit or otherwise, blunting the competition in MRI acquisition. Second, MRI is more expensive than CT in terms of direct equipment costs, running costs, and demands for physical space. Third, the wide diffusion of CT may itself be blunting the competitive pressures for MRI diffusion, because CT and MRI are partial substitutes for one another.

One variable that is highly significant for MRI but not for CT is TEACH. Education hospitals are far more likely (14% on average) than noneducation hospitals to adopt MRI. This is consistent with the life-cycle explanation: Medical technologies typically penetrate teaching hospitals early in their life cycle, before they become objects of competition among hospitals at large (Niki, 1985; Okimoto and Yoshikawa, 1993).

Conclusions

Our results for CT scanners are consistent with the existence of nonprice competition among Japanese hospitals. Hospitals are significantly more likely to purchase a CT scanner if a large proportion of their neighbors have purchased one, after controlling for factors including demand for the hospitals' services and cost levels. By contrast, MRI diffusion was predicted primarily by the size and teaching role of a hospital, showing little evidence of being an instrumentality of competition.

The differences in the competitive patterns of these two technologies is likely due to differences in their maturity and costliness. MRI is a younger and more expensive technology, and, like other new medical technologies, it is penetrating clinical education hospitals first. However, in the last few years MRI has begun to diffuse rapidly among nonteaching hospitals (Okimoto and Yoshikawa, 1993). The rapid diffusion may indicate that MRI is now or soon will be an important instrument of competition among hospitals, and this possibility warrants further observation.

Our results have implications for policymakers in Japan as well as those in other countries. Japan's fixed-fee schedule was instituted as part of an extremely effective cost-control system. The fee schedule has succeeded in keeping Japan's aggregate spending on health care quite low, at only 4.9% of GNP (Okimoto and Yoshikawa, 1993). Like any policy, however, it may have unintended consequences. In particular, there is evidence that price regulation has led to aggressive nonprice competition among providers in several industries. Our analysis provides preliminary evidence that similar effects may be occurring in Japan's hospital market. In considering any policy for regulating health care costs, whether in Japan or elsewhere, one must carefully consider its effect on the behavior of key players in the marketplace.

Notes

[1] Certificate of need regulation in the U.S. consists of a variety of state laws constraining the diffusion of medical technologies by requiring hospitals and, in some cases, doctors to obtain permission before adopting a new device or service.

[2] In the probit model, the parameters, b, are estimated by maximizing the (log) likelihood function: $\ln L(\beta) = \sum_{i \in I_1} \ln \Phi(X_i\beta) + \sum_{i \in I_0} \ln(1 - \Phi(X_i\beta))$. I_1 is the set of hospitals having the technology. I_0 is the set of hospitals not having the technology. X_i are the characteristics of hospital i and Φ is the normal cumulative distribution function.

[3] It is not formally correct to compare coefficient estimates from separate probit equations directly; however, comparisons of probability derivatives yield the same qualitative results.

[4] There are hospitals in our sample for which all rivals have CT. There are other hospitals in our sample for which none of their rivals have CT. Thus, the predictions in Figure 8-3 are predictions inside the range of the data.

9

Substitution of MRI for CT

Over the last decade, magnetic resonance imaging (MRI) has diffused rapidly into use in a number of countries. The fastest and most extensive diffusion, in per capita terms, has occurred in Japan and the United States. In 1990, Japan had 733 MRIs installed, second only to the U.S. (Figure 9-1). This rapid diffusion of MRI has raised a number of questions among policymakers, researchers, and participants in the hospital industry about the relative costs and benefits of this technology.

MRI is an expensive technology. A single machine often costs more than $1 million, not including the substantial site preparation and training costs it occasions. Operating expenditures for MRI are also large (Evens and Evens, 1991; Muroff, 1992; Niki, 1993). Because of its great expense and rapid diffusion into use, MRI has attracted a considerable amount of public scrutiny, with many people believing that diffusion has been too rapid in Japan and elsewhere (Hisashige, 1994).

One potential factor that could mitigate the cost of MRI would be its substitution for older technologies. For example, if an MRI scan costs ¥21,000 to perform, but it replaces a computed tomography (CT) scan that would have cost ¥11,500, then the net cost of the MRI scan is only ¥9,500.[1] There is widespread agreement that MRI is superior to CT scanning for a variety of diagnostic tasks; however, MRI is often used in tandem with CT, rather than as a substitute for it (Boutwell and Mitchell, 1993). In evaluating the costs of MRI diffusion policymakers should understand the full effects of such diffusion, both in creating costs through the use of MRI imaging and in avoiding costs through substitution for older technologies (and

This chapter is based upon: Vogt, W.B., Bhattacharya, J., Yoshikawa, A., and Nakahara, T. 1995. "Substitution of MRI for CT," *mimeo*. Asia/Pacific Research Center, Stanford University.

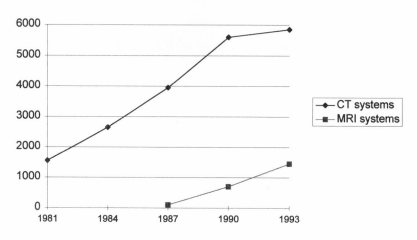

Figure 9-1
Diffusion of CT and MRI

potentially through its use in improving diagnostic accuracy and allowing earlier and more effective interventions). This chapter investigates the effect of MRI diffusion on the use of one older technology, CT scanning, and the effects of this substitution on the costs of medical care.

Background and Literature Review

Magnetic resonance imaging and computed tomography are both recently developed, sophisticated diagnostic imaging modalities. Commercial CT scanners were first marketed in 1973, and the first MRI units were sold in 1982. Like X-rays, both of these technologies permit physicians to "take pictures" of structures inside a patient's body without using probes or incisions. CT scanning is, in fact, a modern application of X-rays combined with computer reconstruction techniques that create a much more detailed image than can be constructed with traditional X-ray technology. MRI uses magnetic properties of hydrogen nuclei in a patient's body to create its images.

Although MRI and CT perform similar functions and although their images are superficially similar, there are a number of important differences between the two technologies. The signal in a CT scan is based upon the interaction between X-ray photons and tissue electrons; that is, an MRI image is determined by the magnetic resonance properties of the nuclei of tissues. CT typically provides better information about the structure of bones, and MRI provides more information concerning soft tissues. MRI allows images to be formed in any plane. In addition, MRI does not require subjecting a patient to ionizing radiation, as CT scanning does (Young, 1988).

There is widespread agreement that MRI is superior to CT for a number of indications and that there should be, over time, some substitution of MRI for CT in clinical practice (Feigenbaum, 1985; Kent et al., 1994; Young, 1988). Several previous studies have addressed the issue of whether or not MRI imaging has, in fact, substituted for CT scanning to any important degree. Peddecord, Janon, and Robins (1988) study the patterns of CT and MRI use in a freestanding imaging center in Southern California. They examine the percentage of patients undergoing an MRI of the head or spine who had previously undergone a CT scan. Over a two-year period, this percentage declined from about 50% to 16% for head CT and from 44% to 20% for spine CT. In addition, patients undergoing myelography (a spinal imaging procedure to which MRI is widely thought superior) dropped from 15% to 0% over the same period. The substitution of MRI for CT occurred most quickly among those physicians with the most experience with the new technology.

The findings in this early study contrast considerably with those of later studies. Doughty, Nash, and Gift (1992) utilize a statewide MRI data base in Michigan and ask a question similar to the one posed by Peddecord, Janon, and Robins. They find a modest substitution, with use of CT before head MRI studies declining from about 50% in mid-1988 to about 45% in early 1991. Similarly, the percentage of patients undergoing CT before MRI drops from roughly 35% to roughly 25% for spine MRI cases.

Bautz et al. (1992) explore the question of substitution of MRI for CT in a Washington, D.C., health maintenance organization. Over the study period, there was a 131% increase in the use of MRI while CT scans showed no decline; in fact, CT utilization actually rose by 27%. However, there was a 32% decrease in the rate of head CT scanning (from 7.55 per 1000 enrollees to 5.16) over the study period.

Boutwell and Mitchell (1993) examine CT and MRI utilization in the Medicare system between 1985 and 1989. The use of both procedures increased substantially over the study period, although the growth in CT scanning was slower. They find an overall prevalence of repeat scanning within six months (either with the same or different modality) of 13%, and they also find no change over time in this rate.

Hisashige (1994) discusses the substitution of MRI for CT in the Japanese context. From 1985 to 1991, there was a very large increase in the number of MRI scans performed, with no concomitant decrease in the number of CT scans. In fact, the number of CT scans increased by a large amount over the period.

Eisenberg et al. (1989) do not directly address the CT-MRI substitution issue, but they do examine substitution of newer for older diagnostic tests. Their data come from 63 American hospitals distributed in the eastern, southern, and midwestern portions of the United States and cover the years 1978, 1979, and 1980. For four of the five test pairs examined, no evidence of decreased use of the older test is associated with increased use of the newer test.

The weight of the evidence to date points to a small degree of substitution of MRI for CT in clinical practice. However, all the studies described above suffer from some weaknesses. Many use small or unrepresentative data sets. Others rely upon aggregate time series data and infer a lack of substitution from the fact that the number of CT scans does not fall as the number of MRI scans increases. This inference is problematic because there is ongoing research into the uses of and ongoing improvements in the technology of CT scanning that could lead to an increase in use, masking any substitution effect. In addition, many studies examine whether CT scanning is used in tandem with MRI scanning. Although the prevalence of this phenomenon is clearly related to a lack of substitution, it is not identical with it. For example, patients who previously would have had a CT scan only and who now have an MRI only do not show up as having been substituted in the methodology of Peddecord, Janon, and Robbins (1988); Doughty, Nash, and Gift (1992); and Boutwell and Mitchell (1993).

Our study contributes to this literature in a number of ways. First, unlike most of the previously cited studies, we examine a national, government-collected database. Second, because the decision to adopt technology is the decision of the hospital and decisions regarding test-ordering are made by physicians employed by the hospital, the appropriate unit of analysis is the hospital, and our data set permits us to perform analyses at this level. Finally, our study uses instrumental variables to account for the fact that the decision to adopt a new technology is endogenous—that is, that a hospital's decision to adopt a technology is influenced by its assessment of how much it will be utilized.

Model

In our model, a hospital is contemplating the purchase of an MRI scanner which will generate a stream of revenue determined by the number of scans the hospital will be able to order and by the price fixed by the government for scanning. The hospital will be required to pay a fixed cost of adoption to purchase and install the MRI scanner. However, the MRI scanner will affect other revenue streams of the hospital because services that are complements to and substitutes for MRI in the hospital's production process for health care will have their production altered. We assume that all these quantities are stable and deterministic (at least from the hospital's point of view) at the time the decision is made. We make this assumption because we are using cross-sectional data and cannot identify any dynamic effects as a result. Also, we assume (for simplicity of exposition) that an MRI scanner has an infinite effective lifetime. Finally, we assume that the hospital adopts an MRI scanner if the net present value of the adoption is positive.[2] The notation and then the model itself are presented below.

Notation:

X_i — Characteristics of hospital I
F_i — Fixed costs of adopting MRI
$AFC_{k,i}$ — Average variable cost of service k
p_k — Reimbursement for service k
$Q_{MR,i}$ — Number of MRI scans the hospital will perform if it adopts MRI
$Q_{k,i}^0$ — Quantity of service k the hospital will perform if it does not adopt MRI
$Q_{k,i}^1$ — Quantity of service k the hospital will perform if it does adopt MRI
β — Rate of time discounting
$R_{0,i}$ — Returns to nonadoption
$R_{1,i}$ — Returns to adoption

The discounted present value of the stream of returns to the hospital, given adoption and nonadoption, are given by:

$$R_{0,i} = \sum_k \frac{1}{1-\beta}(p_k - AVC_{k,i})Q_{k,i}^0$$

$$R_{1,i} = \frac{1}{1-\beta}(p_{MR} - AVC_{MR,i})Q_{MR,i} +$$

$$\sum_k \frac{1}{1-\beta}(p_k - AVC_{k,i})Q_{k,i}^1 - F_i.$$

Thus, the hospital adopts MRI if:

$$R_{1,i} - R_{0,i} \geq 0$$

$$\frac{1}{1-\beta}(p_{MR} - AVC_{MR,i})Q_{MR,i} +$$

$$\sum_k \frac{1}{1-\beta}(p_k - AVC_{k,i})(Q_{k,i}^1 - Q_{k,i}^0) - F_i \geq 0.$$

Relabelling the first two terms above yields:

$$R_{MR,i} + \Delta O_i - F_i \geq 0 \quad \text{implies adoption.} \tag{9-1}$$

We turn to modelling the components of Equation 9-1. First we consider the $Q_{k,i}$, the quantities of the hospital's services which are produced given either adoption or nonadoption of MRI. Economic theory dictates that these quantities be determined by the prices of the various services, the cost of producing the services, and the number of patients treated at the hospital. We model these as follows:

$$Q_{k,i} = X_i'\beta_k + \delta_k MR + \varepsilon_{k,i}. \tag{9-2}$$

MR is a dummy variable equalling 1 if the hospital has adopted MRI and zero if not. In this equation, the X_i contains hospital characteristics influencing the number of services performed at the hospital. Variables in X_i include number of patients, ownership of the hospital, and case mix. $\varepsilon_{k,i}$ is a random variable capturing such things as unobserved case mix and unobserved variations in the average variable cost of the service. In particular, we are interested in $Q_{CT,i}$ and $Q_{MR,i}$.

$Q_{k,i}$ enters Equation 9-1 through R_i and ΔO_i. Other variables entering R_i and ΔO_i are variables shifting marginal costs (and potentially reimbursement) for each hospital. The last term in Equation 9-1 is F_i, the fixed cost to the hospital of adopting MRI. The fixed cost of adopting an MRI depends upon a number of factors. The first of these is the cost of the machine; there is some reason to believe that this should vary for different ownership categories (see the discussion in Chapter 5 or in Niki (1993)). MRI is sold in a national market, so once ownership heterogeneities are taken account of, the cost of the machine itself should be similar across hospitals. However, other sources of fixed costs are often substantial. The scanner requires a large space, and the opportunity cost of this space can be quite high, especially in small hospitals or in those facing high ground rent. In addition, there is often a cost associated with preparing the site for the MRI scanner (which varies with hospital characteristics and the type of machine purchased). Thus, variables that shift the value of space in the hospital must be included in Equation 9-1.

Specification and Estimation

The parameter of central interest in our investigation is δ_{CT}, the number of CT scans a hospital forgoes if it adopts MRI. One might imagine estimating this parameter by running ordinary least squares (OLS) on Equation 9-2 for $k = CT$. However, the dummy variable for the adoption of MRI is endogenous in this equation because there is very likely to be correlation between $\varepsilon_{MR,i}$ and $\varepsilon_{CT,i}$; both of these error terms capture unobserved differences in case mix, and the two services have substantial overlap in terms of the patients they are useful for. This endogeneity biases the OLS parameter estimates (intuitively, the coefficient will be biased upward since the dummy for MRI adoption may be proxying for a more imaging-intensive case mix). Therefore, we need to perform some instrumental variables procedure to obtain consistent estimates. For these instruments, we need variables that affect the incentive to purchase an MRI scanner but which do not affect the number of CT scans done in the hospital. We previously identified such variables: those that shift the fixed cost of adopting MRI but not the marginal cost of operating CT. Potential instruments include the total area of the hospital (in square meters), the cost of new hospital construction in the hospital's prefecture, and the rental price of commercial real estate in the hospital's prefecture as shifters of F_i.

Our empirical methodology is as follows. We use ownership, patient volume, case mix, and the F_i shifters, Z_i, to predict the adoption and utilization of MRI. We then use the predicted values for the adoption probability as instruments for MR_i to perform instrumental variables estimation in Equation 9-2 for CT scanning. We compare these estimates to estimates obtained by ordinary least squares and explore the importance of the endogeneity of MRI adoption. The following are the equations for estimation:

$$X_i\gamma_i + Z_i\gamma_2 \geq 0 \quad \text{implies MRI adoption} \tag{9-3}$$

$$Q_{MR,i} = X_i\beta_1 + \varepsilon_{MR,i} \tag{9-4}$$

$$Q_{CT,i} = X_i\beta_2 + \delta_k d_{MR} + \varepsilon_{CT,i}. \tag{9-5}$$

Equations 9-3 and 9-4 are estimated jointly by a sample selection model (the Type II Tobit described in Amemiya [1985]), to provide more efficient estimates of γ. We then estimate Equation 9-5 by instrumental variables.

Data

Our primary data source for this analysis is the Facility Survey. To define a suitable and relatively homogeneous sample for analysis, we follow the procedure outlined in Chapter 8. We begin with the full sample of 10,096 hospitals and eliminate all tuberculosis and leprosy hospitals, all hospitals whose caseload is composed of more than 50% psychiatric patients, and all hospitals that allocate more than 50% of their beds for geriatric care. In devising these selection criteria, we intend to create a sample similar to that of community hospitals used in similar research in the U.S. In addition, to focus on the effects of MRI on CT use, we select only those hospitals in the sample that have a full-body CT scanner. Finally, we eliminate a number of hospitals whose scanning volume represents a probable coding error; these hospitals report performing more than 500 scans per week per machine (this volume would have them performing 6 scans an hour, 12 hours a day, seven days a week). After the various selections, we are left with 4,339 hospitals.

The dependent variables used in the analysis are a dummy variable that equals 1 if the hospital has an MRI, the number of MRIs performed in the hospital during the week of the survey, and the number of CT scans performed during the same week. Independent variables are the number of inpatients in the hospital at the time of the survey, the number of outpatients seen in the hospital during the survey week, an index of the number of cancer surgeries in the hospital, the number of neurology and neurosurgery patients (inpatient and outpatient), and the number of orthopedics patients (inpatient and outpatient). The last three are included as crude controls on case mix, as is a dummy variable for whether or not the hospital has an emergency room. MRI and CT are both frequently used in neuroimaging and in diagnosing cancer, so that we expect neurology/neurosurgery and cancer to affect positively both the volume of cases for the two technologies and the probability of adopting MRI. CT is important in diagnosing many types of trauma; hence, we expect the presence of an ER to affect positively the volume of CT scanning. MRI has shown itself to be useful in imaging joints in the extremities, hence the inclusion of orthopedics (Young, 1988; American College of Physicians, 1994; Eisenberg, 1988).

The factors used as independent variables capturing the fixed

Table 9-1
Variable Definitions

in	Number of inpatients in the hospital (in 100s)
out	Number of outpatients in the week of survey (in 1,000s)
er	Dummy variable equalling 1 if the hospital has an ER
can	Index of cancer cases
neu	Number of inpatients and outpatients in neurology department (in 100s)
ort	Number of inpatients and outpatients in orthopedics department (in 100s)
area	Number of square meters of floor space in the hospital (in 1,000s)
pr_cons	Price of hospital construction in the hospital's prefecture (in ¥1,000/sq m)
p_rent	Average commercial rent in the hospital's prefecture (in ¥1,000/sq m)
mr	Dummy variable equalling 1 if the hospital has an MRI
#ct	Number of CT scans performed during the week of the survey
#mr	Number of MRI scans performed during the week of the survey
npo	Dummy variable equalling 1 if the hospital belongs to the Red Cross or other nonprofit organization
ins	Dummy variable equalling 1 if the hospital is owned by an insurance society
gvt	Dummy variable equalling 1 if the hospital is owned by the government

cost of adopting MRI are the size of the hospital, the cost of hospital construction, and the average commercial rent in the hospital's prefecture. Hospital size comes from the Facility Survey; the rationale for including it is that, *ceteris paribus*, as the size of the hospital increases, the shadow price of floor space within it should fall. In order to capture probable differences in the effective prices facing government and private hospitals (due to differing subsidy regimes and goals),[3] we separate the sample into hospitals owned by the government and private hospitals (*iryo-hojin*, individually owned, and company owned). Table 9-1 contains variable definitions for the analysis.

Results

Table 9-2 contains the sample means for the various dependent and independent variables used in our analysis. This table shows that government hospitals are slightly more likely to have MRI scanners than are private hospitals and, given that they have them, to use them more. Similarly, government hospitals' use of CT scanners is considerably greater than is that of their private counterparts. However, this must be interpreted in the light of the substantial differences in the volume of cases treated at the two types of institutions. The 941 government hospitals treated 257 inpatients and

Table 9-2
Variable Means (standard deviation)

Variable	Overall	Government	Private
mr	0.13 (0.34)	0.14 (0.35)	0.12 (0.33)
#ct	44.88 (44.81)	60.58 (49.95)	34.97 (37.06)
#mr	4.64 (14.32)	4.92 (14.79)	4.43 (14.25)
in	1.62 (1.43)	2.57 (1.76)	1.14 (0.97)
out	2.10 (2.01)	3.30 (2.29)	1.44 (1.34)
can	4.07 (7.42)	8.72 (10.94)	1.75 (3.93)
neu	0.78 (1.73)	1.20 (1.89)	0.57 (1.60)
ort	3.22 (3.61)	4.59 (3.47)	2.39 (3.29)
area	8.46 (9.79)	16.44 (13.57)	4.87 (5.44)
pr_cons	25.81 (5.91)	24.81 (4.97)	26.10 (6.13)
p_rent	1.54 (2.05)	1.02 (1.56)	1.74 (2.15)
gvt	0.22 (0.41)		
npo	0.11 (0.31)		
prv	0.64 (0.48)		
N	4339	941	2794

3,300 outpatients each, on average, while the 2,794 private hospitals treated 114 inpatients and 1,435 outpatients each. Government hospitals also have a case mix more skewed toward cancer patients, as the cancer index shows. Finally, the physical plant of government hospitals far exceeds that of the private hospitals: The average government hospital is more than three times as large as the average private one.

First, we consider the estimation of Equations 9-3 and 9-4 via the sample selection model. The results of this analysis are reported in Table 9-3. Our hypotheses regarding the adoption and utilization of MRI described previously are largely borne out by this analysis. The floor space and the commercial rent are both significant predictors of the adoption of MRI; they both have the signs that would be expected under the interpretation that they represent shifting fixed costs of adoption. Additionally, the number of inpatients and outpatients and especially the number of patients in neurology and orthopedics are predictive of both the number of scans performed given that adoption occurs and the adoption decision itself. Once case load, some case mix, and cost variables are controlled for, government hospitals are less likely to adopt MRI than are their private counterparts, and they utilize the machines which they do adopt less. It is also interesting to note that the correlation between the adoption error term and the utilization error term is +0.94

Table 9-3
Sample Selection Model, Full Sample

Variable	Adoption Equation for MR	Utilization Equation for MR
constant	−1.746†	−36.36†
in	0.164†	7.99†
out	−0.093†	−1.88**
er	0.097*	2.21
can	0.007	0.10
neu	0.185†	6.42†
ort	0.041†	1.32†
gvt	−0.827†	−17.83†
npo	−0.413†	−12.90†
ins	−0.591†	−18.25†
pr_cons	0.003	
p_rent	−0.036**	
area	0.027†	
rho	0.942†	

* denotes significance at 10% level.
** denotes significance at 5% level.
† denotes significance at 1% level.

and is highly significant. This is certainly consistent with the view that different adoption and utilization rates at different hospitals are the result of unobserved case mix differences among the hospitals.

We run a number of other specifications to check the robustness of these results. The model was run separately for the government and private hospitals. There is no qualitative change in the results when the model is run this way. Furthermore, we run the model in its separate form without the area variable, since one could argue that it is endogenous. Again, very little of substance changes. The only major change resulting from the omission of the area variable is that r, the correlation coefficient between the error terms in Equations 9-3 and 9-4, is no longer precisely estimated and is actually slightly but not significantly negative for the private hospitals. To construct instruments for MR in Equation 9-5, we use the separate models for government and private hospitals. Also, out of concern over the potential endogeneity of area, we use both the versions with area and those without area.

We turn now to our investigation of the effect of MRI acquisition on the number of CT scans performed at a hospital. In hospitals without MRI, the average number of CT scans performed is 38;

Table 9-4
Regressions for Full Sample

Dependent Variable: #CT Variable	OLS	IV1	IV2
constant	9.44†	10.45†	9.86†
in	7.55†	11.62†	9.25†
out	5.74†	4.98†	5.43†
er	3.54†	4.29†	3.85†
can	0.34†	0.61†	0.45†
neu	9.69†	13.14†	11.13†
ort	−0.49†	−0.16	−0.35*
gvt	−3.61†	−11.87†	−7.06†
npo	5.32†	0.29	3.22*
ins	2.60	−4.46	−0.34
MR	10.98†	−55.69**	−16.85
R^2	0.62	0.46	0.59

* denotes significance at 10% level.
** denotes significance at 5% level.
† denotes significance at 1% level.

hospitals with MRI do an average of 90 scans per week. The most naive estimate of δ_{CT}, the effect of MRI acquisition on CT volume, would be that MRI adoption increases CT utilization by about 52 scans per week. Obviously, this estimate is unreliable because it accounts for neither differences in case load nor case mix; nor does it correct for the endogeneity of the adoption decision. We turn to each of these corrections in turn.

First, we correct for observable determinants of CT utilization. Table 9-4 contains the estimates for Equation 9-5 for the full sample of hospitals. In the first column are the results obtained simply by running ordinary least squares on Equation 9-5 for the 4,339 hospitals in the sample. In the third column are the results from running instrumental variables using the predicted adoption probabilities from the sample selection model reported in Table 9-3. In the second column are the instrumental variable estimates generated using instruments generated from the sample selection model without area. In all cases, the instrument for the dummy variable MR is the predicted probability of adoption using Equation 9-3. Again, in accord with our previous predictions, a heavy case load, many cancer and neurology patients, and the existence of an emergency room at the hospital all predict high utilization of the CT scanner. Also, like the results for MRI, the government hospitals tend to use their CT scanners more sparingly than do their private counter-parts, and this result comes through in each column of the table.

The striking difference between the OLS column of Table 9-4 and the other two columns is the sign and significance of δ_{CT}, the MR dummy variable. There are 11 extra scans per week at MRI-acquiring hospitals, lower than our naive estimation above, but still positive and contrary to the substitution hypothesis. In the OLS column, however, the endogeneity of MR is not corrected for. Once we correct for this in columns two and three, a different pattern emerges. In the last two columns, the substitution of CT scans for MRI scans begins to emerge, as the MRI scanner is estimated to replace 56 and 17 scans per week, respectively. The standard errors for MR are quite large in both columns, perhaps because the instruments for MRI acquisition are not terribly powerful. Indeed, the percentage of correct predictions from the probit equation of the sample selection model never exceeds 88%, and we could obtain an 87% rate by simply guessing that no hospital ever adopts.[4] Also, the narrowing of the standard error moving from column two to three must be due to the improvement when area is added to the instrument-creating model.

As already discussed, differences in subsidies and goals between government and private hospitals make separate analyses for the two groups attractive. Considering only the 941 government hospitals, those that have an MRI scanner perform 117 CT scans per week, and those that do not have an MRI scanner perform 52 scans, for a difference of 65 scans per week. As in the pooled analysis, this difference narrows to only 11 scans when other variables are included. Again, when the endogeneity of MR is accounted for, the substitution effect emerges, as the coefficients in columns two and three in Table 9-5 show a negative coefficient for MR. The standard errors for MR in both columns are very large, once again reflecting the relative weakness of the instruments. In our preferred specification in the third column, the acquisition of MRI results in a reduction of 30 scans per week in the number of CT scans performed.

The case for the private hospitals is similar. Looking only at sample means, adopters of MRI perform 74 scans per week; non-adopters perform 29, for a difference of 45 scans per week. In the OLS column of Table 9-6, we see that this total drops to only 8 additional scans per week when we include other relevant variables. As before, using instrumental variables to control for the endogeneity of MRI adoption results in estimates of a substitution of MRI for CT, but with very imprecise estimates.

Table 9-5
Regressions for Government Hospitals

Dependent Variable: #CT

Variable	OLS	IV1	IV2
constant	6.20†	0.02	3.77
in	6.65†	11.75†	8.65†
out	7.26†	8.29†	7.67†
er	1.96	−0.12	1.14
can	0.37†	0.94†	0.59†
neu	5.45†	8.37†	6.60†
ort	0.15	−0.52	−0.12†
MR	10.96†	−92.35†	−29.55**
R^2	0.64	0.39	0.59

* denotes significance at 10% level.
** denotes significance at 5% level.
† denotes significance at 1% level.

Table 9-6
Regressions for Private Hospitals

Dependent Variable: #CT

Variable	OLS	IV1	IV2
constant	7.43†	7.02†	7.24†
in	6.53†	7.96†	7.20†
out	6.94†	6.97†	6.95†
er	4.01†	4.21†	4.10†
can	0.78†	0.84†	0.81†
neu	11.19†	12.63†	11.87†
ort	−0.56†	−0.40	−0.49**
MR	8.41†	−13.39	−1.74
R^2	0.58	0.55	0.57

* denotes significance at 10% level.
** denotes significance at 5% level.
† denotes significance at 1% level.

Beyond what we have reported here, we did a number of checks for robustness. First, we experimented with other instrument sets. Using area, construction cost, and rent, rather than the predicted probabilities formed with them, resulted in negative but even more imprecisely estimated coefficients. We also estimated these equations with and without area, and these results confirm those reported previously.

Table 9-7
Omitting Case Mix Controls

Sample	Naive	OLS	IV2
pooled	+52	+23	−5
government	+65	+16	−13
private	+45	+27	16

As a final examination of the effects of case mix and endogeneity on our results, we run all the analyses described previously without using emergency room, cancer, neurology, or orthopedics in any of our regressions. By dropping these, we have worse control for case mix than we have done so far. If the endogeneity of the MR variable gets "worse," we take this as evidence that unobserved case mix is indeed important in explaining our results and in mediating the endogeneity of MR. Table 9-7 reports these results. Our intuition is borne out by the findings. In each case, government, private, and pooled, the OLS coefficient on MR rises when the other case mix variables are omitted. Furthermore, the coefficient in each of these regressions becomes negative or insignificant when the correction for endogeneity is made.

Conclusions

In this chapter, we investigate the relationship between the adoption of MRI by hospitals and the level of CT scanning they do. If we make no correction for the endogeneity of the MRI adoption decision, then a hospital adopting MRI appears to perform more CT scans than it would have done without adoption. However, once the endogeneity of MRI acquisition is accounted for, hospitals seem to substitute away from CT scanning when they adopt MRI. In our preferred specification, a government hospital adopting MRI performs, on average, 30 fewer CT scans per week. A private hospital adopting MRI performs, on average, two fewer CT scans per week. This means that a government hospital forgoes about 1537 CT scans a year when adopting MRI, and a private hospital performs about 90 fewer. This is a cost savings of approximately ¥18 million for government and ¥104,000 for private hospital adoption (assuming 1,150 points per CT scan). These savings are noticeable, but they are a fraction of the annual cost of an MRI unit.

Notes

[1] These figures are the reimbursement rates for a body CT scan and an MRI study from the April 1990 fee schedule.

[2] Notice that a utility-maximizing rather than profit-maximizing hospital may adopt even if the net present value of adoption is negative. However, as long as the hospital values MRI positively in its utility function and values positive revenue flows positively, the threshold adoption model will be correct.

[3] There is an extensive discussion of the subsidies received by Japanese teaching hospitals in Chapter 5. Other Japanese public hospitals also receive such subsidies.

[4] The coefficients on the instruments in the selection "probit" part of the Type II Tobit are jointly very highly significant in all models, however. The likelihood ratio test rejects the hypothesis of all being zero at significance far beyond 1%.

10

Functional Differentiation and Competition

In a market with price competition, competitive pressures are likely to enhance the degree of product differentiation. However, without price competition, the relationship between differentiation and competition is unclear. As discussed in Chapter 1, the Japanese uniform fee schedule, coupled with a closed physician employment system that creates few incentives to promote referrals among medical facilities, has engendered an environment in which hospitals of various sizes and ownership types compete for the same pool of patients without a clear division of specialization.[1] In this chapter, we measure the degree of functional differentiation among Japanese hospitals by using the entropy index[2] and conduct a regression analysis in order to explore the factors associated with the level of functional differentiation.[3]

We measure specialization using the entropy of distribution. Introduced by Shannon (1948) as a measure of information in communication theory, entropy was first utilized in economic analysis by Theil (1971). Recently, many authors have used entropy to represent the flatness of distribution, particularly in the case of income inequality (Maasoumi and Zandvakili, 1990). In Japanese health research, Ishihara (1995) reports that entropy is used to measure the complexities of the Japanese reimbursement system. The entropy index is occasionally referred to as the information theory index (ITI).

Farley (1989) introduced the entropy index to health economics and examined the nature of the ITI by analyzing case mix special-

This chapter is based upon: Aoki, K., Bhattacharya, J., Vogt, W.B., Yoshikawa, A., and Nakahara, T. 1995. "The Relationship between Functional Differentiation and Competition: Existence and Interpretation," *mimeo*. Asia/Pacific Research Center, Stanford University.

ization in hospitals.[4] He reports that specialization could lower a hospital's operational costs. Similarly, Farley and Hogan (1990) demonstrate that specialization can indeed lower hospital costs and that the degree of specialization in competitive markets is large. They find that, in a competitive hospital market, hospitals tend to specialize in patients by diagnosis-related group (DRG). Dayhoff and Cromwell (1993) also find a positive correlation between competition and the degree of specialization.

Competition and Functional Differentiation

The relationship between competition and product differentiation is important because product differentiation affects resource allocation and welfare.[5] Two theories explain why competitive pressures enhance the degree of product differentiation.

First, the producer's cost-reducing incentive provides that if one producer can produce the goods at a lower cost than competitors, that producer can lower prices and obtain a greater market share. Thus, if specialization reduces costs, producers in price-competitive markets will specialize. Panzar and Willig (1981) show that specialization becomes the equilibrating factor in a competitive market if there are diseconomies of scope with respect to the partition of products. Shaked and Sutton (1990) reparametrize the condition where the fragmented equilibrium becomes the outcome in an oligopoly model. According to their definition, when few firms offer many products each, the equilibrium is concentrated. Conversely, when many firms offer one product each, the equilibrium is fragmented. By following their method, one can easily show that the equilibrium becomes fragmented when there are diseconomies of scope.

Second, the producer has an incentive to relax price competition in an oligopolistic market. Because diversification segments the market, prices above marginal cost are sustainable in an oligopoly. Many studies show that producers differentiate their products in order to avoid price competition (Bonnano, 1987; Economides, 1986; Gabszewicz and Thisse, 1979; Shaked and Sutton, 1982). In sum, each producer differentiates as the market tends toward greater competition.

In each of these situations, price competition is the link between competition and differentiation. However, the Japanese uniform fee schedule virtually eliminates price competition in the Japanese hospital market. Without price competition, do hospitals have an incentive to specialize?

If there are diseconomies of scope among different medical services, a hospital may attempt to specialize in order to reduce costs. However, absent price competition, the relationship between competition and specialization is unclear because producers can benefit from specialization independent of competitive pressure in the marketplace. Furthermore, because price competition is inoperative, Japanese hospitals have no incentive to differentiate their products to ameliorate the nonexistent price competition.

Hence, whether nonprice competition enhances differentiation in the Japanese hospital market is unclear. We investigate this relationship with the following model.

Model

In this section, we explore the conditions under which a more competitive market evinces greater differentiation than a less competitive one. Specifically, we explore conditions under which duopoly hospitals specialize, while monopoly hospitals do not.

We make three assumptions: (1) There are two types of patients, internal medicine and surgical, and there are N patients of each type. (2) The medical services provided by hospitals are differentiated into two types, internal medicine and surgical services, i and s, respectively. (3) Service i (or s) can treat only internal medicine (or surgical) patients.

In deciding which services to provide, hospitals have four choices: no service, i service only, s service only, or both i and s services. These behaviors are denoted by 00, 10, 01, and 11, respectively. Hospitals are functionally differentiated when they provide only one service (i.e., 10 or 01). Because each hospital has four choices, there are 16 possible combinations of actions. Figure 10-1 shows the combinations of hospitals' actions. The combinations marked x denote functional differentiation, while the combinations marked o denote a lack of functional differentiation.

When a hospital can and does provide i service for X persons and s service for Y persons, the cost of providing the service is denoted by $C_2(X, Y)$. When a hospital can and does provide only one service for Z persons, the cost is denoted by $C_1(Z, 0)$ or $C_1(0, Z)$. The subscript denotes the potential number of services that hospitals can provide with their equipment. We assume that the prices, P, of both

	00	01	10	11
00				
01			×	
10		×		
11				○

00: hospital provides no service
01: hospital provides type s service
10: hospital provides type i service
11: hospital provides both services

× indicates "specialization"
○ indicates "non-specialization"

Figure 10-1
Hospital Services

services are equal, determined by policymakers (as is the case in Japan). In this setting, the situation in which a monopoly hospital will provide both services is given by $2PN - C_2(N,N) > PN - C_1(N,0) = PN - C_1(0,N)$. This condition means that the profit a hospital earns by providing both types of service is larger than the profit earned when a hospital provides only one type of service. When a hospital provides two services, it receives twice the revenue. Thus, unless there are strong diseconomies of scope or strong diseconomies of scale, this condition is not restrictive.

In order for one hospital's action 01 (10) to be the best response to its rival's action 10 (01), the profit made by providing both services must be less than the profit earned by providing a service different from its rival. Assuming a simple demand-rationing rule, each hospital equally shares the market when two hospitals provide the same service. Under this rationing rule, the condition under which the combination of actions, x, becomes the Nash equilibrium can be written as $PN - C_1(N,0) > 3PN/2 - C_2(N,N/2)$. This condition is sustainable under the existence of strong diseconomies of scope or diseconomies of scale and is not itself restrictive.

If this condition and the previously presented one are satisfied simultaneously, competition promotes functional differentiation. However, it is hard to satisfy both conditions simultaneously, namely that $2PN - C_2(N,N) > PN - C_1(N,0) > 3PN/2 - C_2(N,N/2)$. There is a conflict between the two conditions because a lack of strong diseconomies of scope or scale is required to satisfy the first half, while strong diseconomies of scope or scale are required to satisfy the second half. Thus, the cost factor alone is unlikely to promote functional differentiation.

The demand-rationing rule states that each hospital must have an equal market share, $N/2$, when two hospitals provide the same services to the market. We adopt this rule in our model. This rationing rule is simple and neutral to patient preferences. However, the main cause of this conflict seems to be this rationing rule. We can easily avoid this conflict by changing the demand-rationing rule. If patients prefer a specialized hospital to a nonspecialized hospital, then when one hospital provides both i and s and another hospital provides service s only, every surgical patient will go to the second hospital. Therefore, when the rival hospital provides s only, a hospital can earn more profit by providing i only rather than providing both services. This is written as $PN - C_1(N, 0) > PN - C_2(N, 0)$. It is natural to think that the fixed cost for providing one service is less than the fixed cost for providing two services. Thus, this condition is not restrictive.

The condition that a hospital provides both services when there is one hospital in the market is written as $2PN - C_2(N, N) > PN - C_1(N, 0)$. Even if patients prefer the specialized hospital, they must go to the nonspecialized hospital because there is no alternative. This condition is natural for the same reason as was the previous condition. Moreover, there is no conflict between the two conditions: $2PN - C_2(N, N) > PN - C_1(N, 0) > PN - C_2(N, 0)$.

When we use the demand-rationing rule, based upon the neutrality of patient preference for specialization, there is a conflict in the cost structure when explaining the phenomenon that competition promotes functional differentiation. However, when we assume that patients prefer a specialized hospital to a nonspecialized one, we can explain that phenomenon in a natural way.

These are not the only possible explanations for competition promoting functional differentiation. For example, differentiation may permit a relaxation of some nonprice competition in the same way that it relaxes price competition in the models discussed earlier.

Empirical Analysis

Method

In order to test whether competition enhances specialization, we employ individual hospitals as the unit of analysis and regress the degree of specialization on hospital and market characteristics. The entropy of various distributions measures the degree of specialization. We include in the model inpatient distribution across length of stay, hospital department, and diagnostic category.

Let p_{hi} represent the proportion of cases that fall into category i in hospital h. In this case, hospital h's entropy of distribution on categories is defined by

$$E_h = \sum_i p_{hi} \log\left(\frac{1}{p_{hi}}\right)$$

$$p_{hi} = \log\left(\frac{1}{p_{hi}}\right) \equiv 0, \quad \text{if } p_{hi} = 0.$$

E_h takes the greatest value when cases are uniformly distributed in each category. The entropy of distribution decreases when hospital h concentrates on a particular category and assumes the value zero when h specializes in one category. We utilize the entropy of distribution as the measure of specialization.

Entropy has the useful property of taking the same value for a distribution that has the same degree of concentration, even in different categories. When we compare the degree of functional specialization, we need not distinguish between the services in which each hospital specializes. For example, the entropy measure takes the value zero when the distribution concentrates on one category, but this value does not depend upon the specific category.

The entropy measure also has a negative property. Farley (1989) points out that there is a systematic bias in entropy measure caused by the implicit assumption that the distribution is continuous when the actual distribution is discrete. However, Farley and Hogan (1990) later show that this measure has an intuitively correct relationship with the factor that affects the degree of specialization. For example, specialization is negatively related to hospital size, and selective contracting organizations, such as health management organizations (HMOs) and preferred provider organizations (PPOs), are more specialized.

For this study, we define entropies for the distributions of three different variables. First, we define entropy for inpatient length of stay (LOS). Recently, *Koseisho* has tried to separate hospitals into acute care and long-term care facilities. LOS is one factor used to separate hospitals into these two types. We divide LOS into ten intervals, each representing ten percentile points defined on the overall LOS distribution in Japan. Hospital h's LOS entropy is defined by

$$E_h = \sum_{i=1}^{10} p_{hi} \log\left(\frac{1}{p_{hi}}\right),$$

where p_{hi} is the ratio of inpatients who belong to LOS category i at hospital h. If hospitals have the same distribution as the overall distribution, entropy assumes the maximum value. Therefore, if a hospital has the same distribution as the overall distribution, then that hospital is not specialized according to our definition. A hospital with a distribution different from the overall distribution is specialized.

Second, we define entropy for the distribution of the number of inpatients across several medical departments (internal medicine, respiratory, etc.). The types of departments a hospital has characterizes its function and its variety of output. We construct the degree of specialization measure from the inpatients' distribution over medical departments. In the Facility Survey, medical departments are partitioned into 32 departments. We define the departmental entropy for inpatient distribution over all 32 departments by

$$E_h = \sum_{i=1}^{32} p_{hi} \log\left(\frac{1}{p_{hi}}\right),$$

where p_{hi} is the ratio of inpatients admitted to i department in hospital h.

Finally, we define entropy based upon disease categories. (For ICD-9 codes see the appendix to Chapter 3.) We characterize the output of a hospital based upon the disease types of its inpatients. If a hospital provides medical care for inpatients in one ICD category only, while another hospital treats inpatients from various ICD codes, the former is more specialized than the latter. We then measure the degree of specialization by calculating the entropy for the inpatients' distribution over ICD-9 categories. In the discharge section of the Patient Survey, diagnostic data are coded by a system based upon the ICD-9 CM code book, with rarer diseases grouped in categories. For the purposes of this study, we use information on major ICD-9 codes only, defining the entropy for the inpatient distribution over 17 major ICD-9 codes:

$$E_h = \sum_{i=1}^{17} p_{hi} \log\left(\frac{1}{p_{hi}}\right),$$

where p_{hi} is the ratio of inpatients who receive care for i ICD in hospital h.

We pay special attention to the relationship between competitive pressure and the degree of differentiation by conducting regression analyses in which the three types of entropy measure are the dependent variables. We adopt independent variables that depict features of the hospital and the market conditions. The number of beds, ownership, and teaching affiliation are hospital characteristic variables. Population density, proportion of patients over 65, and the Herfindahl index[6] depict market conditions. Regional dummies defined at the prefecture level are added to control for the regional features that the other variables cannot explain.

Data

Data for each hospital are derived from the Facility Survey. We observe (1) the ownership type of each hospital (public vs. private), (2) whether it is affiliated with a medical school, (3) number of beds, (4) number of inpatients treated in a day in each department, and (5) location.

We match patient-specific data with hospital-specific data by using the Patient Survey. The Patient Survey was conducted during three days in September 1990. Data are collected from a randomly chosen third of the hospitals on each day, each hospital being surveyed on one day only. Information on all patients who visit the institution during the survey period, as well as on all inpatients already enrolled there, is included in the data set. We focus on the discharge portion of the survey. From the Patient Survey, we observe the LOS and ICD code for each patient. We derive other data from public sources. We obtain data on population and age structure from the Management and the Coordination Agency (1990).

Because our primary objective is to measure the entropy index among ordinary Japanese hospitals, we eliminate hospitals that treat specific groups of patients only, such as leprosy patients. We also eliminate psychiatric, contagious disease, and tuberculosis hospitals, by removing those which devote more than half of their beds to these specialties; this reduces our sample for the department study to 8,593. The hospital sample size is further reduced to 2,587 in the LOS and ICD studies because both facility and patient information are needed, and the Patient Survey includes only a random third of all hospitals.

Results

Figures 10-2, 10-3, and 10-4 show the average entropy by ownership and size. These figures show that size plays an important role in

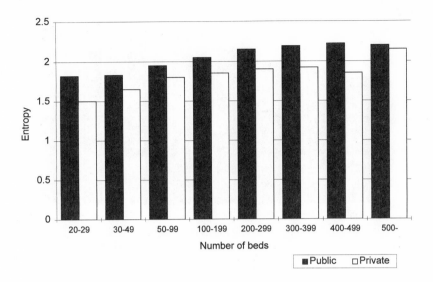

Figure 10-2
Length of Stay

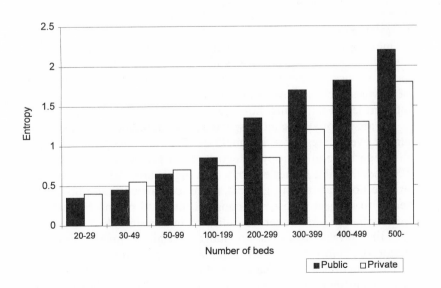

Figure 10-3
Department

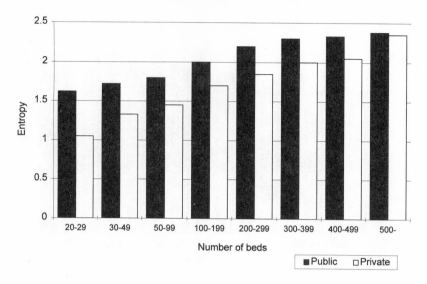

Figure 10-4
ICD Code

determining the level of product diversification as measured by the entropy index. For all three entropy definitions, entropy takes a greater value when hospital size increases. Thus, larger hospitals provide more diversified services than smaller ones. In general, hospitals must incur additional fixed costs in order to provide supplemental services. Thus, if small hospitals offer a full range of medical services, they face low volume and high costs for each individual service. In contrast, larger hospitals may offer a wider range of services because they can operate the individual services at more efficient levels than small hospitals.

Private hospitals are more specialized than public hospitals across almost every category of hospital size. The only exception is that, in the departmental entropy category, small private hospitals (under 100 beds) exhibit higher entropy than public hospitals. The fact that private hospitals are, in general, more specialized than public ones seems to suggest a cost reduction incentive to promote functional differentiation.[7] However, as indicated in our simplified model, the fact that private hospitals are more specialized may reflect their greater flexibility in terms of responding to patient preferences.

These figures also indicate that the LOS entropy is less sensitive than departmental entropy to size and ownership. With universal health insurance and the patient's freedom to choose a hospital without regard to price, hospitals cannot explicitly select patients in Japan. However, by making certain departments available, hospitals can influence patients. If a hospital is not capable of providing a specific service (e.g., radiation therapy), patients who need the service will choose another hospital. Separating patient types with respect to LOS is more difficult for a hospital.

Table 10-1 presents the results of five regression models for each of the three definitions of entropy. Each column shows a different selection of independent variables.

The ownership dummy, OWN, which equals one if the hospital is owned by the public sector, has a positive and statistically significant coefficient. As already shown, other things being equal, private hospitals are more specialized than public ones.

Table 10-1
Regression Result

Length of Stay

	CASE 1	CASE 2	CASE 3	CASE 4	CASE 5
Intercept	1.809†	1.680†	1.599†	1.618†	1.609†
TEACH	0.139**	0.038	0.039	0.044	0.034
OWN	0.288†	0.170†	0.173†	0.168†	0.169†
BED		1.22×10^{-3}	$1.22 \times 10^{-3\dagger}$	$1.23 \times 10^{-3\dagger}$	$1.29 \times 10^{-3\dagger}$
BED2		$-8.77 \times 10^{-7\dagger}$	$-8.86 \times 10^{-7\dagger}$	$-8.92 \times 10^{-7\dagger}$	$-8.95 \times 10^{-7\dagger}$
DENSITY			7.98×10^{-6}	9.18×10^{-6}	9.24×10^{-6}
OVER65			-0.040	-0.420	-0.422
H				0.339	0.496*
BED*H					-1.04×10^{-3}
Adjusted R^2	0.084	0.119	0.120	0.120	0.120

Department

	CASE 1	CASE 2	CASE 3	CASE 4	CASE 5
Intercept	0.761†	0.397†	0.199†	0.211†	0.220†
TEACH	0.683†	0.129†	0.132†	0.135†	0.141†
OWN	0.596†	0.226†	0.220†	0.216†	0.215†
BED		$3.17 \times 10^{-3\dagger}$	$3.19 \times 10^{-3\dagger}$	$3.20 \times 10^{-3\dagger}$	$3.13 \times 10^{-3\dagger}$
BED2		$-1.44 \times 10^{-6\dagger}$	$-1.46 \times 10^{-6\dagger}$	$-1.46 \times 10^{-6\dagger}$	$-1.45 \times 10^{-6\dagger}$
DENSITY			$9.70 \times 10^{-6\dagger}$	$1.07 \times 10^{-5\dagger}$	$1.06 \times 10^{-5\dagger}$
OVER65			0.779†	0.499*	0.524*
H				0.284**	0.346**
BED*H					1.34×10^{-4}
Adjusted R^2	0.177	0.375	0.377	0.377	0.377

Table 10-1 (continued)

ICD

	CASE 1	CASE 2	CASE 3	CASE 4	CASE 5
Intercept	1.608†	1.304†	1.097†	1.135†	1.110†
TEACH	0.198**	0.070	−0.063	−0.053	−0.078
OWN	0.602†	0.320†	0.308†	0.298†	0.300†
BED		2.84×10^{-3}†	2.89×10^{-3}†	2.91×10^{-3}†	3.07×10^{-3}†
BED2		-1.95×10^{-6}†	-2.00×10^{-6}†	-2.01×10^{-6}†	-2.02×10^{-6}†
DENSITY			7.41×10^{-6}	9.81×10^{-6}	9.99×10^{-6}
OVER65			1.137**	0.373	0.367
H				0.681†	1.109†
BED*H					2.83×10^{-3}†
Adjusted R^2	0.190	0.306	0.307	0.309	0.310

46 prefecture dummies are included in regression analysis.
* denotes significance at the 10% level.
** denotes significance at the 5% level.
† denotes significance at the 1% level.

Variable   **Definition**
Intercept-constant term
TEACH   1 if the hospital is teaching hospital
OWN   1 if the hospital is publicly owned
BED   number of beds
BED2   squared number of beds
DENSITY   population density in medical zone
OVER65   fraction of patients aged over 65
H   Herfindahl index defined in medical zone

The teaching dummy, TEACH, which equals 1 if the hospital is affiliated with a medical school, also has a positive and statistically significant coefficient for the departmental entropy. The results are less convincing for the LOS and ICD entropies. Nonetheless, in both cases, we find that teaching hospitals are less specialized. Given the wide range of services offered by teaching hospitals for educational purposes, this result is expected.

Hospital size has positive and significant coefficients, and its square value has negative, significant coefficients. The curve is upward-sloping to 690, 1,093, and 723 beds in the LOS, department, and ICD cases, respectively. Nearly all (98.2%) hospitals have fewer than 700 beds in our LOS and ICD studies, and 99.7% of hospitals have fewer than 1,090 beds in our department study. Thus, there is a positive but concave relationship between entropy and number of beds in our sample.

In order to isolate the relationship between competitive pressures and specialization, we introduce the Herfindahl Index, defined by the market share of beds in each medical zone. The coefficients of the Herfindahl Index are positive and statistically significant. The Herfindahl Index takes a smaller value as the market becomes more competitive; a positive coefficient means that each hospital is more specialized as the market becomes more competitive. As discussed earlier, absent price competition in the Japanese hospital market, this result may evince that patients prefer specialized hospitals over nonspecialized hospitals and that hospitals are strategically responding to these preferences.

Why do patients prefer specialized hospitals? One possible explanation is that patients perceive a positive correlation between quality and specialization. Some authors have shown that patient volume is positively associated with quality for certain types of service (Flood et al., 1984; Hughes et al., 1987; Kelly and Hellinger, 1987; Luft et al., 1987; Showstack et al., 1987) Controlling for hospital size and other variables, this indicates that hospitals facing a higher volume of similar patients may be able to provide higher quality services.

An interesting interaction may exist between hospital size, competition, and specialization. In order to examine this, we conduct the fifth regression, which includes the independent variables and the number of beds multiplied by the Herfindahl index. The negative coefficients on Bed*H mean that smaller hospitals are more sensitive to changes in market competition. With respect to ICD, the coefficient of Bed*H is negative and statistically significant, but the others are not statistically significant. Thus, in the ICD case, when the market becomes more competitive, small hospitals respond more acutely by becoming more specialized than do larger hospitals.

Our results support the theory that hospitals in competitive markets specialize in order to attract patients. Such "niche marketing" or "market segmentation" involves the producers' segmenting potential consumers in the market into subgroups, each of which has a similar response to a particular marketing strategy. Niche marketing focuses on a few market segments and drives the producer to make finer adjustments of products and services in order to match the consumer desires. Absent price competition, as the market becomes more competitive, producers segment the market in order to increase their market share.

We conduct a second type of regression to test the niche market-

Table 10-2
Entropy Quartile Regression

Length of Stay

	25 percentile	50 percentile	75 percentile
Intercept	1.406[†]	2.032[†]	2.192[†]
H	2.439**	1.180**	0.475*
DENSITY	2.67×10^{-5}*	1.33×10^{-5}	2.85×10^{-6}
OVER65	−1.989	−1.579	−0.437
Adjusted R^2	0.094	0.201	0.155

Department

	25 percentile	50 percentile	75 percentile
Intercept	−0.163	0.572[†]	1.836[†]
H	0.997[†]	0.524**	0.208
DENSITY	2.81×10^{-5}**	2.11×10^{-5}*	1.92×10^{-5}*
OVER65	0.827	−0.219	−1.852[†]
Adjusted R^2	0.178	0.211	0.235

ICD

	25 percentile	50 percentile	75 percentile
Intercept	1.134[†]	1.677[†]	1.990[†]
H	4.806[†]	2.860[†]	1.583[†]
DENSITY	1.97×10^{-5}	2.06×10^{-5}*	9.51×10^{-6}
OVER65	−1.562	−0.889	0.637
Adjusted R^2	0.054	0.198	0.287

46 prefecture dummies are included in regression analysis.
* denotes significance at the 10% level.
** denotes significance at the 5% level.
[†] denotes significance at the 1% level.

ing theory. With niche marketing, as the market becomes more competitive, consumer demand is more finely segmented. We expect that more highly specialized producers exhibit greater sensitivity toward competition than do less specialized producers.

To test this theory, we define the 25, 50, and 75 percentile value of entropy in each medical zone and conduct the regression of entropy quartiles on regressors, Herfindahl Index, population density, fraction of population over 65, and regional dummies. In this regression, a lower quartile point translates into a relatively speci-

Table 10-3
Medical Zone Level Regression

	Length of Stay	Department	ICD
Intercept	2.369[†]	2.010[†]	2.638[†]
H	−0.568[†]	−0.744[†]	−1.256[†]
DENSITY	2.83×10^{-6}	4.58×10^{-5}[†]	1.34×10^{-5}
OVER65	−1.171**	−4.740[†]	−2.173[†]
Adjusted R^2	0.118	0.223	0.376

46 prefecture dummies are included in regression analysis.
* denotes significance at the 10% level.
** denotes significance at the 5% level.
[†] denotes significance at the 1% level.

alized hospital in the market. Therefore, we expect the coefficient of the Herfindahl index to be larger for the lower quartile.

Table 10-2 presents the results of the regressions. The smallest percentiles have the steepest upward sloping curve with respect to the Herfindahl Index for every definition of entropy. This result shows that a highly specialized hospital attempts to become even more specialized as the market becomes more competitive.[8]

Finally, we check that our results are not caused by market differences (e.g., regional concentration of a specific group of patients) but by hospital differences by defining the entropy for the overall market at the medical zone level and using this entropy as the dependent variable in a regression analysis. A positive relationship between Herfindahl and entropy may indicate that our previous results are due to market differences.

Table 10-3 presents the results of this regression. The coefficient on the Herfindahl Index in a medical zone is negative. We therefore conclude that the positive relationship between competition and specialization is due to hospital differences rather than to market differences.

Conclusions

By utilizing the entropy of distribution as the index, we measure the relationship between functional differentiation and competition and run regressions in order to determine the factors associated with functional differentiation. With respect to department and ICD, as the market becomes more competitive, hospitals become more differentiated. This result does not arise from cost factors, but rather suggests that patients prefer specialized to nonspecialized hospitals. In response to consumer preferences, hospitals strategically specialize in order to attract patients.

We also find that the most important factor that determines the degree of functional differentiation is hospital size. Large hospitals provide relatively diversified services compared with small hospitals. If small hospitals were to offer a full range of medical services, they would face low volume and high costs for each individual service. Large hospitals have the option of offering a wider range of services because they can operate the individual services at more efficient levels than small hospitals. By analyzing the relationship between ownership and functional differentiation, we also find that private hospitals are more differentiated than public hospitals. This is probably because private hospitals are more flexible in terms of responding to patient preferences, in part because they rely exclusively on patient fees for revenues, whereas public hospitals also receive government subsidies.

Entropy of LOS is less sensitive to hospital features and market conditions than is entropy of department and ICD. This reflects the fact that hospitals can indirectly select patients by choosing to provide certain services with respect to department and ICD, but not to LOS.

Notes

[1] *Koseisho*, by manipulating the fee schedule, recently attempted to promote division of labor by encouraging referrals through special referral fees. For example, the 1992 fee schedule revisions attempted to codify the distinction between hospitals as providers of inpatient care and clinics as providers of outpatient care by adopting a different pricing system for the two facilities. The 1992 revisions also distinguished in pricing between acute and long-term care. The 1994 fee schedule revision provided incentives for small hospitals to specialize in primary care.

[2] Few studies treat functional differentiation in the Japanese medical care market. Some authors classify the function of hospitals by the services they provide. For example, Takimura et al. (1994) and Urushibara (1985) attempt to classify the function of hospitals by utilizing principal component analysis, specifically, by finding key components of a hospital to represent its function.

[3] Because hospitals specialize when functional differentiation exists, we use the terms "differentiation" and "specialization" interchangeably.

[4] Farley (1989) notes that the ITI has statistical bias when computed from discrete data.

[5] Some authors show that there is an equilibrium where the player uses the differentiation strategy and an excess variety of products is supplied in comparison to the social optimum (Bonnano, 1987; Dixit and Stiglitz, 1977; Economides, 1986; Salop, 1979; Shaked and Sutton, 1982; Spence, 1976).

[6] Herfindahl index is defined in each medical zone.

$$\text{Herfindahl index of } i \text{ medical zone} = \sum_{j \in M_i} \left(\frac{\#\,beds_j}{\sum_{k \in M_i} \#\,beds_k} \right)^2$$

where $\#\,beds_j$ is the number of beds of hospitals j and M_i is the set of hospital indices that belongs to i medical zone.

[7] Public hospitals that receive large subsidies may not have the same incentive that private hospitals have to reduce costs.

[8] Highly specialized hospitals also include small hospitals. This result may be caused by the fact that small hospitals are more sensitive to competition. As we mentioned earlier, the result of ICD reflects an interaction between hospital size and competition.

Part IV

Supply of and Demand for Doctors

Nearly all theoretical economic models fall into the optimization-equilibrium paradigm. In this paradigm, economic agents (firms, individuals, government agencies, etc.) are assumed to choose among actions available to them in order best to meet some objective; they are said to be maximizing an objective function. Achievement of an agent's objectives often depends upon both the agent's own actions and those of others. In this case, an agent may wish to take different actions, depending upon which actions others take. Clearly, there must be some mechanism coordinating the various agents' actions. In a market with flexible prices, price is the equilibrating mechanism; that is, prices adjust so that the demand for a good equals its supply.

As an example of this paradigm, consider a hypothetical labor market. In this market, a number of firms are considering hiring workers and a number of individuals are considering going to work. At any given wage, w, a certain number of workers, say $S(w)$, would choose to seek employment. $S(w)$ embodies the aggregation of the labor supply decision of the individual workers. Workers choose their level of labor supply in light of their preferences and other opportunities. Conversely, at any given wage, w, firms would choose to hire $D(w)$ workers in the process of pursuing their goals (usually taken to be profit maximization). We are left with the question of how wages are determined. Wages move to balance workers' desire to work and firms' desire to hire labor. Thus, at the equilibrium wage, $S(w) = D(w)$—that is, the number of people choosing to work equals the demand for workers in the market.

A typical strategy in an empirical study is to measure the influences on $D(w)$ and particularly to quantify the slope of $D(w)$. We pursued this strategy in Chapter 6, "A Utility-Maximizing Model of Input Demand." One of the most important aspects of $D(w)$ is its

223

slope. The slope of D measures the sensitivity of labor demand to a change in the wage. Other objects of interest are the effects on $D(w)$ of wages of other types of labor, of the output price, and of non-labor prices (e.g., capital). Aside from purely scientific interest, these quantities can be useful in assessing some effects of policy. For example, $D(w)$ can be used to predict the quantity of labor that would be demanded if the government were to impose a minimum wage or a wage cap.

An empirical study may also measure $S(w)$. Again, the focus is typically on the nonwage determinants of S and the slope of S with respect to w. These quantities may provide insight into policy in this case as well because they allow us to determine the effect of other changes in the economy on the supply of labor. As in the previous case of D, we could determine the amount of labor that would be supplied under a minimum wage.

However, if we want to forecast the effects of a government policy or a change elsewhere in the economy on the equilibrium in the labor market, we need to know both $S(w)$ and $D(w)$. For example, in order to know exactly how much unemployment would be caused by a minimum wage, we would have to calculate how much labor would be supplied and demanded at the minimum wage. Similarly, suppose that the demand for the good produced in this industry increases. This would increase the demand for labor by firms in this industry so that $D(w)$ would rise at any given wage. In order to calculate the new wage and new supply of labor, we would have to know both the demand for and the supply of labor in the industry. The task of Chapter 11 is to measure the parameters of an equilibrium model of the labor market for physicians in Japan.

11

Equilibrium Wages of Hospital-Based Doctors

This chapter analyzes the market for hospital physician services in Japan in a partial equilibrium framework. Geographical variation in physician wages and population can best be explained in the context of a model that specifically recognizes the unique determinants of the supply and demand for doctors. Here we simultaneously develop and estimate a physician location choice model and a medical zone level factor demand model.

It is important to understand the difference between U.S. and Japanese hospitals and their relationship with community physicians. Doctors in the U.S. traditionally have admitting privileges at community hospitals while simultaneously maintaining private offices where they provide primary care. Essentially, in this "open" system, doctors and hospitals act as firms contracting with one another, but usually without direct cash payment. In Japan, there are virtually no open hospitals (Yoshikawa, 1993). Japanese clinic-based doctors do not have admitting privileges at hospitals. In Japan's closed system, only doctors who are employees of the hospital have privileges there.

Because of this inherent difference in the two countries' hospital systems, the analytical framework for our study of Japanese hospital-based doctors is different from that of other studies analyzing the distribution of doctors in the U.S. We use a traditional labor market approach, modelling labor supply and demand functions of hospital-based doctors and simultaneously estimating them. The demand function models the hospitals' decision to employ doctors in a

This chapter is based upon: Nakayama, N., Bhattacharya, J., Vogt, W.B., Yoshikawa, A., and Nakahara, T. 1995. "Equilibrium Wages of Hospital-Based Doctors," *mimeo*. Asia/Pacific Research Center, Stanford University.

region, and the supply function models doctors' choice of region in which to seek employment.

Once estimated, this model affords an opportunity to conduct comparative statics exercises for policies and demographic trends that impact the physician services market. We describe two such experiments here. Japanese health officials often allege that there is an excess supply of doctors, even though there is no unemployment problem for doctors in Japan. In 1986, the Ministry of Health and Welfare estimated that Japan will have a 10% excess supply of doctors until 2025.[1] Using the estimated demand and supply functions of hospital-based doctors in Japan, we conduct an experiment that hypothetically reduces the number of doctors and measures the impact of such a supply shock. Another important feature of Japanese demographics has been a rapidly aging population. In the second experiment, we assess the impact of an aging society on the geographical location of hospital-based doctors (*kinmu-i*). The percentage of people over 65 is expected to increase to almost 26% by 2025 (Ministry of Health and Welfare Institute of Population Problems, 1992). This aging will likely affect the demand for medical care in Japan, because elderly people are high utilizers. This increased demand will affect the demand for physicians, potentially changing their wages and geographical distribution.

Previous Studies

Even though there are few empirical Japanese health economics studies on this topic, due largely to the lack of available microdata, a number of related studies have been conducted in the U.S. Benham, Maurizi, and Reder (1968) estimate the parameters of a simple structural model that determines the location of doctors. Utilizing a logit model, Newhouse et al. (1982) analyze the geographical distribution of doctors with data from 23 U.S. states. They measure the impact of population and region on the supply of specialists. Dionne, Langlois, and Lemire (1987), by including additional independent variables, such as the distance to central city areas and the average income, expand the Newhouse study and obtain similar results. Other related studies include those by Morrisey, Kletke, and Marder (1991), Feldman (1979), and Frank (1985). Morrisey, Kletke, and Marder (1991) analyze the effect of the presence of community hospital beds on the number of doctors practicing in rural counties and estimate the impact of hospital closures on the net flow of doctors into rural counties. They find that closures and hospital bed reductions do not affect the availability of doctors. Instead, population changes and the number of existing doctors in the county determine the majority of doctor entry and exits. Feldman (1979) examines factors influencing the distribution of hospital beds, interns, and residents across geographical region, and finds that the location of interns and residents depends on training opportunities, demand factors, and anticipated future income. Using a simultaneous equation model, Frank (1985) analyzes pricing and location of psychiatric service, and concludes that psychiatrists choose location based on noneconomic factors, such as per capita income of a state (quality of life) and number of medical schools per 1,000 people.

As mentioned, under the Japanese closed hospital system without visiting privileges, all hospital-based doctors are employed by hospitals. Hence, we consider the labor market of hospital-based doctors. Under such conditions, simultaneously modelling and estimating the supply and demand functions of hospital-based doctors is appropriate. In modelling physicians' choices of where to practice, it is important to consider the characteristics of both the market chosen and markets rejected. Unlike the location-theoretic models used elsewhere, we treat the equilibrating influence of doctors' wages and regional variables in our analysis.

Model

We model the distribution of hospital-based doctors, determined by the labor market, with a structural model. Our empirical specification follows Berry (1994). We specify doctor i's utility for medical zone j, U_{ij}, as depending upon observed characteristics of the medical zone[2] (including wage) X_j and unobserved characteristics μ_j:

$$U_{ij} = X_j\beta + \mu_j + \varepsilon_{ij}, \qquad (11\text{-}1)$$

where ε_{ij} is a choice and individual specific error, and is independent of X_j and μ_j; ε_{ij} has a type I extreme value distribution. μ_j is an error term that incorporates unobserved medical zone-specific variables that impact location choice. β is the parameter to be estimated. Doctors choose particular medical zones by multinominal logit probabilities:

$$P_j = \frac{\exp(X_j\beta + \mu_j)}{1 + \sum_{k=1}^{302} \exp(X_k\beta + \mu_k)}, \qquad (11\text{-}2)$$

where P_j is the probability of choosing medical zone j. P_0 is the probability of the outside alternative, which in this case is assumed to be the choice of becoming a clinic doctor:

$$P_0 = \frac{1}{1 + \sum_{k=1}^{302} \exp(X_k\beta + \mu_k)}. \tag{11-3}$$

The number of hospital-based doctors in medical zone j is denoted by

$$\#\text{HDOC}_j = N\frac{\exp(X_j\beta + \mu_j)}{1 + \sum_{k=1}^{302} \exp(X_k\beta + \mu_k)}, \tag{11-4}$$

where N is the total number of doctors in Japan. This is the medical zone level supply equation of hospital-based doctors. To estimate β, rewrite Equation 11-4 as follows:

$$\ln(\#\text{HDOC}_j) = \ln N + \ln P_j$$

$$= \ln NP_0 + \ln\left(\frac{P_j}{P_0}\right)$$

$$= \ln NP_0 + X_j\beta + \mu_j. \tag{11-5}$$

Equation 11-5 is specified as follows, with the j subscript dropped for convenience:

$$\ln \#\text{HDOC} = \ln NP_0 + \beta_0 + \beta_1 \ln ¥\text{HDOC} + \beta_2 \ln \text{INFLOW}$$

$$+ \beta_3 \ln \text{SERVICE} + \beta_4 \ln \text{POP} + \mu \tag{11-6}$$

where $\#\text{HDOC}$ is number of hospital-based doctors in a medical zone, $¥\text{HDOC}$ is the wage of a hospital-based doctor in a medical zone, INFLOW is the ratio of the number of 23-year-olds in 1990 to the number of 18-year-olds in 1985 in a medical zone, SERVICE is the ratio of the number of workers in the service sector to the number of all workers in a medical zone, POP is the population in a medical zone, and NP_0 is the number of clinic-based doctors.

Because β is interpreted as a coefficient of doctors' utility functions, we expect the following signs. $¥\text{HDOC}$ is expected to have a positive sign. INFLOW, SERVICE, and POP are all included as proxies for nonpecuniary benefits of location in the market. IN-FLOW indicates the extent to which young people remain in the market. Because young people in Japan tend to move away from areas with few amenities, a high INFLOW rate indicates a high desirability of living in the market. SERVICE, the ratio of workers employed in the service sectors (e.g., restaurants, entertainment, and hotels), can also be regarded as a proxy for living amenities.

The short-run demand for doctors is the derived demand of producing services in hospitals. We model the hospitals' short-run production function as

$$f(\#\text{HDOC}, \#\text{RN}, \#\text{PN}, K, \#\text{INPAT}, \#\text{OUTPAT}) = 0$$

$$(11\text{-}7)$$

where $\#\text{HDOC}$ is the number of doctors, $\#\text{RN}$ is the number of registered nurses, $\#\text{PN}$ is the number of practical nurses, $\#\text{INPAT}$ is the number of inpatients, and $\#\text{OUTPAT}$ is the number of outpatients. $\#\text{INPAT}$ and $\#\text{OUTPAT}$ are outputs of the hospital. K is the flow of services based on capital. Cost minimization requires

$$\frac{\text{¥HDOC}}{\text{¥RN}} = \frac{f_{\#\text{HDOC}}}{f_{\#\text{RN}}} \tag{11-8}$$

$$\frac{\text{¥HDOC}}{\text{¥PN}} = \frac{f_{\#\text{HDOC}}}{f_{\#\text{PN}}} \tag{11-9}$$

$$\frac{\text{¥RN}}{\text{¥PN}} = \frac{f_{\#\text{RN}}}{f_{\#\text{PN}}} \tag{11-10}$$

where ¥RN is the real wage of hospital-based RNs, ¥PN is the real wage of hospital-based PNs, and the subscript on f indicates partial differentiation. We solve Equations 11-8, 11-9, and 11-10 for K, and substitute each of the derived values in Equation 11-7. These three equations can be solved for $\#\text{HDOC}$, $\#\text{RN}$, and $\#\text{PN}$. The conditional factor demand equation of hospital doctors is then expressed as

$$\#\text{HDOC} = g(\text{¥HDOC}, \text{¥RN}, \text{¥PN}, \#\text{INPAT}, \#\text{OUTPAT}). \tag{11-11}$$

In order to investigate distribution of hospital-based doctors, we aggregate the demand equation to the medical zone level. To simplify the analysis, we specify the demand equation of hospital-based doctors at the medical zone level as follows:

$$\#\text{HDOC} = \gamma_0 + \gamma_1 \ln \text{¥HDOC} + \gamma_2 \ln \text{¥RN} + \gamma_3 \ln \text{¥PN}$$

$$+ \gamma_4 \ln \#\text{INPAT} + \gamma_5 \ln \#\text{OUTPAT} + \delta, \tag{11-12}$$

where γ_i are the coefficients to be estimated, δ is an error term representing unobserved factors that determine the demand for doctors, #HDOC is number of hospital-based doctors in a medical zone, ¥HDOC is wage of hospital-based doctors in a medical zone, ¥RN is wage of registered nurses in a medical zone, ¥PN is wage of practical nurses in a medical zone, #INPAT is the number of inpatients in a medical zone, and #OUTPAT is the number of outpatients in a medical zone.

We expect γ_1, the coefficient associated with ¥HDOC, to have a negative coefficient. The signs of the coefficients of ¥RN and ¥PN are determined by the productive relationships among the inputs. Positive signs indicate that the inputs are substitutes for hospital-based doctors, and negative signs indicate a complementary relationship.

Data and Variables

The data used in estimating supply and demand equations are a cross-section of data from 1990 obtained from several sources, including the Facility Survey. In order to investigate the distribution of hospital-based doctors, we aggregate the microdata to the level of medical zones. In Japan, there are 345 medical zones. Due to a restriction in the wage data (described later in this section), we use data from 302 of the 345 medical zones to estimate the supply and demand equations.

The data for number of hospital-based doctors (#HDOC), number of inpatients (#INPAT), and number of outpatients per day (#OUTPAT) are from the 1990 *Iryo Shisetsu Chosa* (Facility Survey). Because of the nature of our data set, we are unable to separate doctors who own hospitals (*kaigyo-i*) from those who are employed in hospitals (*kinmu-i*). However, only a small number of hospital-based doctors in our sample are *kaigyo-i*, so we use the terms "hospital-based doctors" and "*kinmu-i*" interchangeably and proceed as if all hospital-based doctors are *kinmu-i*.

We obtain the wages of hospital-based doctors (¥HDOC) and nurses (¥RN and ¥PN) from Chiho Koeikigyo Keiei Kenkyukai (1994). Because this report collects only public hospital data, the wage data are for public hospitals. With those data, we calculate average monthly wages for each of the 302 available medical zones. We deflate nominal wages by the GDP deflator, obtained from the Economic Planning Agency (1990). Surprisingly, our data reveal that the wages of registered nurses, ¥RN, are less than those of practical nurses, ¥PN, despite the longer training period of RNs.

Table 11-1
Descriptive Statistics

Variable	Mean	Standard Deviation
ln#HDOC	5.165	1.203
ln¥HDOC	9.276	0.235
ln¥RN	8.225	0.182
ln¥PN	8.342	0.217
ln#INPAT	7.806	1.108
ln#OUTPAT	8.112	1.012
lnINFLOW	−0.162	0.158
lnSERVICE	−0.622	0.166
lnPOP	12.339	0.967

One likely reason for this is that the average age of RNs is less than that of PNs.

We calculate INFLOW, the mobility of young populations toward a specific medical zone, from the Population Census in 1985 and 1990. We also obtain the numbers of 19-year-olds and 25-year-olds for each medical zone. From the 1990 Population Census, we obtain the number of workers of all types and the number of workers in the service sector and calculate the ratio of number of workers in the service sector to the number of all workers in each medical zone. Descriptive statistics are shown in Table 11-1.

Estimation, Identification, and Empirical Results

We estimate the supply equation and demand equation of hospital-based doctors at the medical zone level by 3SLS. We use INFLOW, SERVICE, POP, #INPAT, and #OUTPAT as instrumental variables, and identify by natural exclusion the restrictions implied by our theoretical model. In particular, variables such as INFLOW, SERVICE, and POP do not enter any particular hospital's production function and thus cannot be included in the medical zone level aggregate conditional factor demand equation we postulate. Furthermore, because the physician demand location choice does not depend directly on the number of inpatients and outpatients in a particular medical zone, we identify the supply equation. This restriction is justified by the fact that although physicians may care about the number of patients they have, the total number of patients in a medical zone is unlikely to enter a particular doctor's utility function. The institutional fact that hospital-based doctors obtain their whole income from a salary and not on a per-patient

Table 11-2
Estimated Results of Distributon of Hospital-based Doctors

Variable	Supply Equation	Demand Equation
constant	−63.940[†]	−29.033
ln¥HDOC	4.554[†]	−1.914**
ln¥RN		6.805
ln¥PN		−1.359
ln#INPAT		0.527
ln#OUTPAT		0.396
lnINFLOW	0.340	
lnSERVICE	1.469[†]	
lnPOP	1.343[†]	

* denotes significance at the 10% level.
** denotes significance at the 5% level.
[†] denotes significance at the 1% level.

basis further buttresses this assertion. 3SLS is an appropriate estimation technique because of the possibility of correlation between μ and δ in the presence of endogenous variables in both estimating equations. The results are shown in Table 11-2.

First we examine the supply equation. The coefficient of ¥HDOC is positive and significant, as expected. The wage elasticity of supply, 4.6 at the sample mean, is very high.[3] (A 1.0% wage increase will raise the supply of hospital-based doctors by 4.6%.) The coefficient of INFLOW is positive but not significant, with an implied elasticity of 0.34. INFLOW is a proxy for amenities in the medical zone. In the high-amenity medical zones, the supply of hospital-based doctors is larger; thus, the sign is consistent with expectation.

If ¥HDOC increases and INFLOW decreases, their impact on the dependent variable will be in opposite directions. Regarding INFLOW as a proxy for desirability of living in the area, will doctors accept a lower wage? Suppose INFLOW increases by one standard deviation (0.134). To keep the utility level the same, the wage of hospital-based doctors must fall by ¥11,697.[4] The standard deviation of wages is ¥233,479. The wage decrease, in response to the inflow increase, is smaller than the standard deviation of wages.

The coefficient of SERVICE is positive and significant. Doctors prefer to be employed in an area with a greater ratio of workers in the service sector, such as the restaurant, hotel, and entertainment industries. Similar to the tradeoff relationship between wages and SERVICE, we also see a tradeoff between ¥HDOC and SERVICE. Suppose SERVICE goes up by one standard deviation (0.092). To keep the utility level the same, the wage of hospital-based doctors must fall by ¥5,988. This decrease is smaller than the decrease after INFLOW increases by one standard deviation.

The coefficient of POP is positive and significant, meaning that the larger the population in a region, the more attractive that region is to hospital-based doctors. Similar to the previous examples, suppose POP goes up by one standard deviation (about 450,000). To keep the utility level the same, the wage of hospital-based doctors falls by ¥388,461. This is the biggest decrease of all three.

In the factor demand equation, the coefficient of ¥HDOC is negative and significant. The higher the wage, the smaller is the demand for medical doctors. The wage elasticity of demand is −1.9. If the wage of hospital-based doctors increases by 1%, the number of hospital-based doctors decreases by 1.9%. The decision concerning the number of hospital-based doctors to employ is very sensitive to the wages of doctors in the medical zone. The coefficient of ¥RN is positive but not significant, and that of ¥PN is negative but not significant. For doctors and registered nurses, the cross-wage elasticity of demand is 6.8. This indicates that MDs and RNs are substitutes in production.[5] For doctors and practical nurses, the cross-wage elasticity is −1.4.

The coefficients of #INPAT and #OUTPAT are positive but not significant. *Ceteris paribus*, when the number of patients increases, demand for hospital-based doctors increases.

Policy Experiments

We conduct two experiments by introducing exogenous shocks. In the first experiment, we measure the effect of decreasing the number of doctors; in the second, we assess the effect of an aging society. Utilizing our estimated simultaneous model, we solve supply and demand functions in order to obtain the wage and number of hospital-based doctors in each of 302 medical zones. The supply and demand functions are as follows:

$$\#\mathrm{HDOC}_j^s = N\frac{\exp(\beta_1 \ln \text{¥HDOC}_j + X_j\beta_{-1} + \mu_j)}{1 + \sum\limits_{k=1}^{302} \exp(\beta_1 \ln \text{¥HDOC}_k + X_k\beta_{-1} + \mu_k)} \quad (11\text{-}13)$$

$$\#\mathrm{HDOC}_j^d = \exp(\gamma_1 \ln \text{¥HDOC}_j + Z_j\gamma_{-1} + \delta_j). \quad (11\text{-}14)$$

234   SUPPLY OF AND DEMAND FOR DOCTORS

We define:

$$A_j \equiv \exp(X_j\beta_{-1} + \mu_j) \tag{11-15}$$

$$B_j \equiv \exp(Z_j\gamma_{-1} + \delta_j). \tag{11-16}$$

The equilibrium condition is

$$\#\mathrm{HDOC}_j^s = \#\mathrm{HDOC}_j^d. \tag{11-17}$$

From Equations 11-13, 11-14, 11-15, 11-16, and 11-17, we derive Equation 11-18:

$$\ln \yen\mathrm{HDOC}_j = \frac{1}{\beta_1 + \gamma_1}\left(\ln\frac{B_j}{NA_j} + \ln\left(1 + \sum_{k=1}^{302} \exp(\beta_1 \ln \yen\mathrm{HDOC}_k \right.\right.$$

$$\left.\left. + X_k\beta_{-1} + \mu_k) \right)\right) \tag{11-18}$$

which can be expressed as follows:

$$\ln \yen\mathrm{HDOC}_{t+1} = f(\ln \yen\mathrm{HDOC}_t). \tag{11-19}$$

Using the Gauss-Seidel method, we iterate on Equation 11-19 until $\yen\mathrm{HDOC}_t$ equals $\yen\mathrm{HDOC}_{t+1}$. The initial value ($\yen\mathrm{HDOC}_0$) is the observed value. We then substitute the calculated wage into Equations 11-13 or 11-14 to obtain the number of hospital-based doctors.

The Effect of Decreasing the Number of Doctors

Health care policymakers often claim there is an excess supply of doctors in Japan. The government has recently attempted to cut the number of medical school graduates by reducing the number admitted. The government can attempt to decrease the number of doctors by, for example, raising the passing score on the National Examination for Medical Practitioners, reducing the acceptance rate of medical schools, or even closing a few schools. Assuming that these policies are successful, we can use our model to estimate what impact they will have on the distribution of physicians and on their wages. We consider 5, 10, 15, 20, 25, and 30% reductions in *N*, the total number of doctors in Japan. Table 11-3 shows the experimental results.

Figure 11-1 shows the change in the number and wage of hospital-based doctors. The wage of hospital-based doctors and the number of

Table 11-3
Simulation: Restricting the Supply of Physicians

% Decrease in Total Physicians	% Decrease in Hospital Physicians	% Increase in Hospital Physician Wages
5	2.6	1.4
10	5.3	2.9
15	8.1	4.5
20	11.1	6.4
25	14.3	8.4
30	17.6	11.1

doctors are inversely related. A 30% reduction in the number of doctors increases the wage by 10.6%. This same decrease would lead to only a 17.6% decrease in the number of hospital-based doctors, with clinic doctors switching to fill the gap.

The Effect of an Aging Society

In Japan, a rapidly aging society is one of the main concerns of policymakers. There will be dramatic demographic changes in the future as the ratio of those over 65 years old to those under 65 increases from 11.0% in 1990 to 25.8% in 2025 (Institute of Population Problems, 1992). The two major reasons for the rapidly aging society are that people are living longer, indexed by Japan's ever-increasing life expectancy, and that there is a lower birth rate. Life expectancy jumped from 68 years in 1965 to 76 years in 1990 (Ministry of Health and Welfare, 1992, *Seimei Hyo*; Ministry of Health and Welfare, 1994, *Kani Seimei Hyo*), while the birth rate dropped from 2.14% in 1965 to 1.54% in 1990 (Ministry of Health and Welfare, 1990, *Jinko Dotai Chosa*). If the birth rate remains lower than 2.0%, the population is expected to decrease after 2015.

An aging society affects both the supply and demand functions for hospital-based doctors. The increasing percentage of the geriatric population shifts the demand function to the right. Increasing population shifts the supply curve to the right, and decreasing population shifts the supply curve to the left. Therefore, the net effect of an aging society on hospital-based doctors is ambiguous based on theoretical considerations alone. Whether the demand or supply effect dominates is an empirical question that we answer with our model.

To perform this simulation, we estimate population, number of

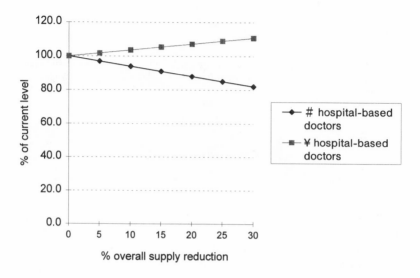

Figure 11-1
Effects of Supply Reduction

inpatients, and number of outpatients after 15 years (in 2005) in each medical zone. First, we estimate the population structure using five age categories (0–14, 15–29, 30–44, 45–64, over 65). Then we assume that the death rate is constant in each age structure (calculated from Ministry of Health and Welfare, 1990) and that the ratio of population in the 0–14 and 15–44 categories is constant in each medical zone. Using the former assumption, we can estimate the 15–29, 30–44, 45–64, and over-65 populations, and using the latter, we can estimate the 0–14 population. Figure 11-2 shows the age structure in 1990 and the predicted age structure in 2005 under these assumptions. Figure 11-3 shows the percentage of the population in each age category in 1990 and 2005.

Next we estimate the numbers of inpatients and outpatients. We assume that the utilization rates of medical services by age in each prefecture will remain constant at 1990 levels and calculate them using data from the patient survey. That is, we assume that the utilization rate in 1990 will be the same in 2005 within each age and prefecture bracket. Figure 11-4 shows the numbers of inpatients and outpatients in 1990 and 2005.

We estimate the number of hospital-based doctors and their wages in each medical zone in 2005 using Equation 11-18. The number of

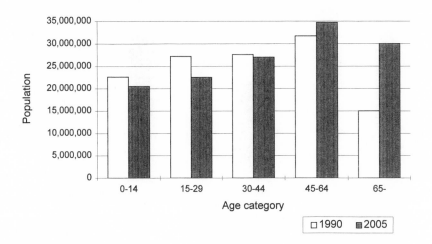

Figure 11-2
Age Structure

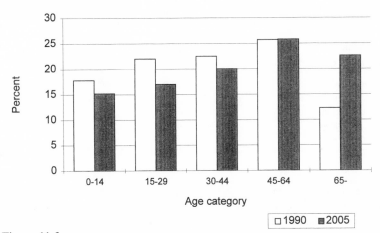

Figure 11-3
Population Age Distribution

hospital-based doctors increases in all but five medical zones, and their wages increase in all medical zones. Table 11-4 shows the values of the change in number of physicians and in physician wages for percentiles of the distribution (across medical zones) of change in number of physicians. On average, the number of hospital-based doctors will increase by 43% in response to the aging of the population, while their wages will increase 25% in real terms.

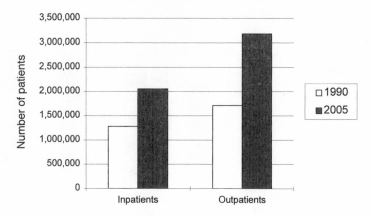

Figure 11-4
Health Care Use Projections
* The number of patients is the total from 302 medical zones.

Table 11-4
Percent Change in the Number of Hospital-based Doctors and Their Wages

Percentiles of % change of #HDOC	#HDOC	¥HDOC
5th percentile	90.33	31.75
10th percentile	73.99	30.68
median	37.26	24.02
90th percentile	14.97	19.78
95th percentile	9.27	18.47

We report average percent change in #HDOC and ¥HDOC within each decile of the distribution of percent change in #HDOC by medical zone. These figures are shown in Table 11-5 in addition to the average value of SERVICE within each of these percentile groupings. SERVICE is a proxy for the non-pecuniary benefits of the location.

Conclusions

By simultaneously estimating the supply and demand equations of hospital-based doctors, we analyze the distribution of hospital *kinmu-i* in Japan. In the supply function, the coefficients of wage and of proxies for desirability of location in the market are positive.

Table 11-5
Relation between the Percent Change in the Number of Hospital-based
Doctors and Their Wages and SERVICE

Percentiles	#HDOC	¥HDOC	SERVICE (percent)
min–10th percentile	214.53	135.95	0.51
11th–20th percentile	164.04	128.94	0.52
21st–30th percentile	153.31	126.92	0.54
31st–40th percentile	145.34	126.02	0.53
41st–median	139.91	124.81	0.53
51st–60th percentile	133.99	123.31	0.56
61st–70th percentile	128.69	122.65	0.54
71st–80th percentile	124.38	121.76	0.56
81st–90th percentile	118.13	120.40	0.56
91st–max	106.85	118.18	0.59

In the demand function, the coefficient of wages is negative and the coefficients of outputs are positive.

When we consider a policy experiment of globally restricting the total number of doctors using the estimated supply and demand equations, we find that the wage of hospital-based doctors increases as their number is decreased. A 10% reduction in the number of doctors decreases the number of hospital-based doctors from 110,068 to 104,227 and increases their monthly wage from ¥1,093,200 to ¥1,124,800. In another simulation, we find that under a hypothesis of an aging society, the number of hospital-based doctors increases in most medical zones. The wage of hospital-based doctors increases in all medical zones.

In our model, we have assumed that the wages of nurses do not respond to the exogenous changes we introduce via the experiments. This amounts to an assumption that nursing labor is supplied perfectly elastically. Since this assumption is questionable, it would be desirable to incorporate simultaneous equilibrium changes in the markets for nursing and physician labor in future work in order to improve our estimates.

Notes

[1] This figure is quoted by the Ministry of Health and Welfare (1990). See also *Shukan Shakai Hosho* (1994). The definition of "optimal" number of physicians in a community is problematic in both sources.

[2] The medical zone is a geographical area used by the Ministry of Health and Welfare to delineate market areas for hospital care. In Japan, there are 345 medical

zones. However, as described in "Data and Variables" later in this Chapter, due to a restriction in the wage data, we use data from 302 of the 345 medical zones.
[3] We can calculate elasticity using

$$\# \text{HDOC}_j = N \frac{\exp(X_j \beta + \mu_j)}{1 + \sum_{k=1}^{302} \exp(X_k \beta + \mu_k)}$$

$$\frac{\partial \# \text{HDOC}_j}{\partial \yen \text{HDOC}_j} = N \frac{\exp(X_j \beta + \mu_j)}{1 + \sum_{k=1}^{302} \exp(X_k \beta + \mu_k)} \left(1 - \frac{\exp(X_j \beta + \mu_j)}{1 + \sum_{k=1}^{302} \exp(X_k \beta + \mu_k)} \right) \frac{\beta_1}{\yen \text{HDOC}_j}$$

$$\frac{\partial \text{HDOC}_j}{\partial \yen \text{HDOC}_j} \frac{\yen \text{HDOC}_j}{\# \text{HDOC}_j} = \left(1 - \frac{\exp(X_j \beta + \mu_j)}{1 + \sum_{k=1}^{302} \exp(X_k \beta + \mu_k)} \right) \beta_1$$

Other independent variables follow the same calculation.
[4] We can calculate this effect as follows:

$$\# \text{HDOC}_j = N \frac{\exp(X_j \beta + \mu_j)}{1 + \sum_{k=1}^{302} \exp(X_k \beta + \mu_k)}$$

$$d \# \text{HDOC}_j = \left(\frac{\beta_1}{\yen \text{HDOC}_j} d \yen \text{HDOC}_j + \frac{\beta_2}{\text{INFLOW}} d \text{INFLOW} \right)$$
$$\times \frac{N \exp(X_j \beta + \mu_j)}{\left(1 + \sum_{k=1}^{302} \exp(X_k \beta + \mu_k) \right)^2}$$

When the number of doctors does not change,

$$\frac{\beta_1}{\yen \text{HDOC}_j} d \yen \text{HDOC}_j + \frac{\beta_2}{\text{INFLOW}} d \text{INFLOW} = 0.$$

Therefore,

$$\frac{d \ln \yen \text{HDOC}_j}{d \ln \text{INFLOW}} \times \frac{\text{S.D. of INFLOW}}{\text{INFLOW}} \times \frac{\yen \text{HDOC}_j}{100} = -\frac{\beta_2}{\beta_1} \frac{\text{S.D. of INFLOW}}{\text{INFLOW}} \frac{\yen \text{HDOC}_j}{100}$$

S.D. of INFLOW is the standard deviation of INFLOW. $\overline{\text{INFLOW}}$ is the mean of INFLOW.
[5] As in Chapter 6, we mean substitutes in production in the technical economic sense here; this does not imply that MDs and RNs literally substitute for one another in the same tasks at the hospital.

Part V

Cost, Quality, and Length of Stay

Because the goal of any health care system is to provide high-quality care at an affordable cost, the interrelationship between health care institutions, cost, and quality is of paramount importance. For example, in an environment of centrally fixed fees, cost containment cannot be expected to occur via the price mechanism, as it does in other markets. Such cost containment may have to be achieved through manipulating the economic institutions that provide the services. Similarly, mechanisms for maintaining high-quality care are institution-dependent.

In a fixed-price setting, incentives for quality maintenance may favor either private or government providers. If quality is an important instrument of competition among providers, private institutions' profit-seeking activities will lead them to provide quality care. Conversely, if the provision of quality is costly and bestows no competitive advantage, only nonprofit and government institutions may have the proper incentives.

Similarly, the fixed-price setting may provide either good or bad incentives vis-à-vis cost reductions to the private firm. If prices are set too high relative to equilibrium price, providers may be encouraged to engage in wasteful competition, leading to an unnecessary increase in costs. Government institutions, lacking a profit motive, have poor incentives to seek low-cost methods, regardless of their market setting.

It well behooves policymakers to know which of these regimes is extant so they can either encourage institutional arrangements appropriate to the market circumstance or modify the market circumstance to conform to that best suited to the existing mix of institutional arrangements. In this section, we explore the prevailing relationship between cost, quality, and institutional arrangements in the Japanese hospital market.

243

12

In-Hospital Mortality

There is a general consensus among policymakers in many industrialized countries that hospitals should be regulated so that at least a minimum quality level can be guaranteed to patients. Although such regulation has historically involved process certification, in the past decade, there has been in the United States a move toward examining outcomes as a measure of hospital quality. Process certification has traditionally involved assessing patient care procedures or evaluating structural aspects of hospital organization, such as personnel mix and material resources. Outcomes measurement has focused on case mix or severity-adjusted mortality rates.

The main argument against process measures is that the link between process and hospital quality is not one-to-one; in particular, the processes followed by one high-quality hospital may not yield such good results if followed by another hospital in different circumstances. Arguments of this nature are quite persuasive and have led to the adoption of outcomes measures in the United States, most notably by the Health Care Financing Administration (HCFA), which administers the Medicare program.

Outcomes measures have not escaped criticism. For example, some have argued, quite reasonably, that mortality rates do not tell the whole story; patient morbidity and quality-of-life improvements are important as well. However, the main attack on mortality-based outcomes measures has focused on shortfalls in the statistical methods used to implement them (e.g. Blumberg, 1986). Although many early statistical shortcomings have been fixed, there is continued criticism that such studies use inadequate controls of severity and

This chapter is based upon: Bhattacharya, J., Vogt, W.B., Yoshikawa, A., and Nakahara, T. 1995. "In-Hospital Mortality," *mimeo*, Asia/Pacific Research Center, Stanford University.

case mix. Almost invariably, hospitals that perform poorly according to outcomes measures claim that they attract patients who are sicker than average and that the severity corrections used in the measures do not adequately control for this effect.[1]

One important aspect of these mortality regressions that has not received much attention is the functional form assumptions made about the relationship between various covariates and mortality. For example, the most popular model used in estimating mortality curves is the logistic regression, which is, in a fundamental sense, linear in the covariates. Such functional forms have been used largely for computational convenience and for lack of theoretical specifications restricting the form of the relationship to be estimated.

The main purpose of this chapter is to identify the significant correlates of hospital mortality in Japan, including hospital type, using a large, nationally representative, patient-specific data set. This is the first published report of these relationships for Japanese hospitals; in the past, such databases were unavailable to researchers. Further, we examine the sensitivity of our estimates to functional form assumptions in our statistical methods.

Literature Review and Background

The American literature on estimating the correlates of hospital mortality is extensive. Rather than attempting a comprehensive review of all the work that has been done in this area, we identify three important strands in the literature and present some representative articles from them. More comprehensive literature reviews are available elsewhere (e.g. Fink, Yano, and Brook, 1989). This chapter falls in the first strand in its estimation technique, though it has implications for the methodology used in the second strand.

Papers in the first strand of this literature are concerned with estimating mortality regressions that include both patient and hospital characteristics. From these regressions, the statistical relationship between mortality and hospital characteristics, controlling for observed case mix, can be inferred. For example, Hartz et al. (1989) ask the following question: What hospital characteristics are associated with variations in observed mortality rates, adjusting for observed patient characteristics and case mix? They find that private, for-profit hospitals have a higher mortality rate than nonprofit hospitals and that teaching hospitals have a lower adjusted mortality rate. Luft and Hunt (1986) used discharge abstracts to find that, for hospitals that offer cardiac catheterization services, those with a higher volume have lower mortality rates. Manheim et al. (1992) measure regional variation in hospital mortality rates and observe that the variation does not disappear after adjusting for case mix and severity. Al-Haider and Wan (1991) dispute Luft and Hunt's findings. They find that hospital size and degree of specialization are unrelated to predicted mortality, but service intensity is positively correlated with it.

In the second strand, mortality regressions are run using only patient-specific variables in order to identify outlier hospitals with observed mortalities that significantly exceed expected mortality. Blumberg (1986), in response to a HCFA study which uses this methodology, provides an early critique and a set of recommendations to increase its reliability. The HCFA adopted many of his suggestions in constructing subsequent analyses. DuBois et al. (1987) examine medical chart information from outlier hospitals identified by the statistical approach and conclude that, although high-mortality outlier hospitals see a sicker set of patients, they also have a larger number of preventable deaths. Iezzoni et al. (1994) criticize the approach because it typically does not account for chronic disease conditions when estimating expected mortality. One part of this strand, exemplified by studies like Flanders et al. (1994), concerns itself with identifying outlier hospitals when the risk of death is small. In this case, p-values calculated from typical asymptotic approximations can be misleading.

The third strand differs from the first two in that it uses data not usually available in large administrative databases, such as patient-specific physiological data, to estimate the patient's prognosis. Typically, these systems are sold commercially to hospitals interested in predicting how patients are likely to fare. Two prominent examples of these systems are APACHE (e.g., Knaus et al., 1986) and MedisGroups (e.g., Steen et al., 1993).

In addition to the large American literature, there are articles focused on a similar set of questions in international settings, though not Japan. For example, Incalzi et al. (1992) use mortality regressions to identify the predictors of in-hospital mortality of geriatric patients in an acute-care hospital in Italy. They find that the use of six or more pharmaceutical products, a low activities of daily living score, and an abnormal Mini-Mental Status Exam correlate with high mortality. Kind (1990) measures surgical mortality rates in England.

In Japan, however, because large, nationally representative data sets have not previously been available to researchers, outcomes research has seldom been performed. Most clinics and hospitals resist releasing mortality information (Okimoto and Yoshikawa, 1993, p. 76). Powell and Anesaki (1990, p. 234) point out that "Japanese hospitals lack formal systems for evaluating the nature and quality of the services they provide, government requirements for routine admissions and patient data being limited in scope and utilization."

The Ministry of Health and Welfare (*Koseisho*)'s efforts to regulate hospital quality has instead consisted of instituting nursing standard regulation. The aim of such regulation is to increase the number of nurses per bed by increasing the reimbursement rate per patient for hospitals that adopt a higher standard. The presumption by *Koseisho* is that a hospital with a high nurse:bed ratio will provide high-quality service for its patients, though such an assertion has never been tested in the Japanese health services literature.

Data

To conduct our study, we use data from the discharge portion of the 1990 Patient Survey (*Kanja Chosa*). This portion of the Patient Survey is similar to large discharge databases that are used for outcomes analysis in the United States. We observe information on all inpatient discharges that took place in a three-day period in September 1990 from a one-third random sample of hospitals and clinics in Japan. In particular, for each discharge, we observe whether the patient was alive on discharge, age, sex, primary diagnosis, whether surgery was performed during the stay, and length of hospital stay (LOS). We code diagnosis using a scheme described in the Appendix to Chapter 3. Here we use diagnostic information disaggregated to the lowest level available in the data set. Finally, for each patient, we observe from which facility the discharge took place.

Using this last piece of information, we link the patient record to hospital- or clinic-specific information from the 1990 Facility Survey (*Iryo Shisetsu Chosa*) data set. Specifically, we obtain for each facility information on its number of beds, registered nurses (RNs), practical nurses (PNs), nurse aides (NAs), doctors (MDs), and residents. Further, we are able to classify each hospital by teaching status and ownership class. In particular, we observe whether it is a privately owned nonprofit, privately owned for-profit, insurance society-owned, or publicly owned institution. Table 12-1 contains a

Table 12-1
Variable Descriptions

Variable	Definition
DEAD	1 if the patient died in the hospital, otherwise 0
GERIAT	1 if the hospital is a designated geriatric hospital, otherwise 0
TEACH	1 if the hospital is a designated teaching hospital, otherwise 0
NEWDOC	Number of newly licensed doctors and residents as a fraction of total number of doctors
CRITCARE	Number of critical care beds as a fraction of total number of beds
OCCUP	Number of occupied beds at the time of the survey as a fraction of total number of beds
PHYS	Number of physicians per bed
RN	Number of registered nurses
PNPLUS NA	Number of practical nurses plus number of nurse aides per bed
INSURER	1 if the hospital is insurer owned, otherwise 0
PRIVATE	1 if the hospital is privately owned and for-profit, otherwise 0
NPO	1 if the hospital is privately owned and nonprofit, otherwise 0
MALE	1 if the patient is male, otherwise 0
IN PREF	1 if the patient is visiting a hospital within his home prefecture, otherwise 0
DEPEND	1 if the patient is a dependent, 0 if the patient is head of household
BED	Number of hospital beds
AGE	Age of the patient
LOS	Length, in days, of the hospital stay

list of variable definitions. Because we are concerned with in-hospital mortality and because many clinics do not have inpatient beds, we exclude clinics from our analysis.

Method

Model Specification

In order to control as much as possible for patient diagnostic heterogeneity, we break up the patient population into groups based on the finest-level diagnostic information available in the data set. There are 320 different diagnostic categories in the data set, many of which have a small sample size, so we restrict our attention to 7 epidemiologically important categories: acute myocardial infarction (AMI), breast cancer, lung cancer, pneumonia, stomach cancer, colon cancer, and a broader category of all gastrointestinal (GI) disease.

We select these categories because of their large sample sizes and important contribution to in-hospital mortality rates. Our selections

Table 12-2
Descriptive Statistics: Means and Standard Deviations

Variables	AMI	Breast Cancer	GI Diseases	Colon Cancer	Stomach Cancer	Lung Cancer	Pneumonia
DEAD	0.13	0.09	0.24	0.17	0.22	0.33	0.09
	(0.34)	(0.29)	(0.43)	(0.37)	(0.41)	(0.47)	(0.28)
GERIAT	0.008	0.00	0.009	0.008	0.007	0.009	0.007
	(0.03)	(0.00)	(0.02)	(0.01)	(0.03)	(0.03)	(0.03)
TEACH	0.09	0.14	0.11	0.09	0.08	0.11	0.03
	(0.28)	(0.35)	(0.32)	(0.29)	(0.28)	(0.31)	(0.16)
NEWDOC	0.15	0.21	0.19	0.14	0.13	0.16	0.08
	(0.26)	(0.32)	(1.48)	(0.24)	(0.23)	(0.27)	(0.17)
CRITCARE	0.02	0.01	0.01	0.01	0.01	0.01	0.01
	(0.03)	(0.02)	(0.02)	(0.02)	(0.02)	(0.01)	(0.02)
OCCUP	0.80	0.82	0.82	0.81	0.82	0.82	0.80
	(0.14)	(0.11)	(0.12)	(0.13)	(0.12)	(0.11)	(0.13)
PHYS	0.14	0.16	0.15	0.14	0.14	0.14	0.10
	(0.11)	(0.13)	(0.13)	(0.11)	(0.11)	(0.12)	(0.06)
RN	161.58	207.10	167.88	153.04	156.25	181.40	104.45
	(154.86)	(149.17)	(146.05)	(142.38)	(137.86)	(142.12)	(110.39)
PNPLUSNA	0.20	0.15	0.18	0.19	0.19	0.17	0.22
	(0.12)	(0.10)	(0.11)	(0.12)	•(0.11)	(0.10)	(0.12)

INSURER	0.02	0.03	0.04	0.04	0.04	0.02
	(0.15)	(0.18)	(0.19)	(0.19)	(0.18)	(0.15)
PRIVATE	0.38	0.29	0.32	0.29	0.23	0.43
	(0.49)	(0.45)	(0.47)	(0.45)	(0.42)	(0.49)
NPO	0.23	0.22	0.20	0.23	0.22	0.21
	(0.42)	(0.42)	(0.40)	(0.42)	(0.41)	(0.41)
MALE	0.69	0.64	0.54	0.55	0.72	0.57
	(0.46)	(0.48)	(0.50)	(0.48)	(0.45)	(0.49)
IN PREF	0.95	0.94	0.93	0.95	0.94	0.97
	(0.24)	(0.25)	(0.27)	(0.23)	(0.26)	(0.19)
DEPEND	0.26	0.30	0.30	0.30	0.27	0.45
	(0.44)	(0.46)	(0.46)	(0.46)	(0.44)	(0.50)
BED	391.79	406.23	379.25	383.93	441.00	298.92
	(283.94)	(273.09)	(267.67)	(258.61)	(267.72)	(230.91)
AGE	65.98	65.26	65.96	65.11	67.39	48.36
	(12.48)	(12.39)	(12.84)	(12.76)	(11.02)	(32.09)
LOS	38.66	55.62	47.38	54.42	59.77	29.41
	(82.59)	(114.15)	(75.44)	(69.65)	(83.74)	(70.58)
N	1811	10,526	1746	4275	2256	4793

are guided further by a desire to include both acute and chronic diagnoses in the analysis. For each category, we estimate a separate mortality regression that includes as independent variables information on both patient and hospital characteristics.[2] Table 12-2 provides summary statistics on these variables by disease category.

Linear Logit vs. Overlap Polynomials

In order to estimate the effect of the various previously described covariates on in-hospital mortality, we estimate, by maximum likelihood methods, the logit probability of death conditional on the covariates, using individual patients as the unit of observation. The logit is a popular way to model the mortality risk, with the probability of in-hospital death given by:

$$p[\text{death}] = \frac{\exp(f(X_i, \beta))}{1 + \exp(f(X_i, \beta))} \tag{12-1}$$

where X_i is a vector of patient i's covariates, b is a vector of parameters to be estimated, and f is a function specified before the estimation.

We first specify f as follows: $f(X_i, b) = X_i'b$. We estimate mortality regressions for all diagnostic groups using this linear logit. This is overwhelmingly the most common specification of the functional form for f. It is especially attractive when the sample size is small because there is only one parameter to be estimated per covariate. However, this linear specification imposes significant restrictions on the shape of the graph of $p[\text{death}]$ vs. one of the covariates, say X_{ik}, where k indexes over covariates. For example, if b_k is positive, negative, or zero, the graph is, over its range, monotonically upward-sloping, downward-sloping, or flat, respectively, holding all other covariates constant. Hereafter, we drop the index over patients and set without loss of generality $X_j = 0 \ \forall j \neq k$ to simplify the notation.

One common method used to generalize the specification for f is to include polynomial terms in X_k, for example, $f(X_k, b) = b_{k1}X_k + b_{k2}X_k^2 + \cdots + b_{kp}X_k^p$, where now there are p parameters for the single covariate X_k. Unfortunately, increasing the number of terms in the polynomial does not necessarily improve the accuracy of the approximation.[3] The result arises because polynomials are inflexible approximating functions, and has important implications for proper functional form specifications.

A more flexible alternative is to use splines to approximate f. In this approach, one partitions the range over which a dependent variable spans. For example, if $X_k \in [a, b]$, then a partition of the space into n contiguous intervals is $[a_1, a_2), [a_2, a_3), \ldots [a_n, a_{n+1}]$, where $a = a_1 < a_2 < \cdots < a_{n+1} = b$. Over each of these intervals, a separate polynomial is fit while imposing continuity restrictions at the edges of each interval, called knots. These continuity restrictions might include restrictions on the continuity of derivatives of the polynomials as well. One can vary the level of flexibility of the approximation by changing the number of knots, the degree of the polynomial used, or the continuity requirements.

We use a variation on the spline approach known as an overlap polynomial approximation.[4] As before, we partition the X_k space and fit a separate polynomial in each partition. We allow the influence of each polynomial to extend past its native interval into surrounding intervals. Intuitively, the approximation is therefore made up of a linear combination of polynomial estimates, each weighted by its distance from its native interval. One advantage of this approach over traditional splines is that there is no need to impose continuity restrictions at the knots. The advantage over the linear specification is that overlap polynomials allow the $p[\text{death}]$ vs. X_k curve to be nonmonotonic. Figure 12-1 displays this possibility. The linear logit must be everywhere upward-sloping, downward-sloping, or flat, but the overlap polynomial can have upward, downward, and flat regions within the same graph.

Formally, let X_k be partitioned as previously, and let $p_i(x; \beta_i)$ be a polynomial of arbitrary degree corresponding to interval i, where $i = 1 \ldots n$. Further, let $\Phi_i(x)$, $i = 1 \ldots n + 1$ be the cumulative distribution function of a normal random variable with mean a_i, and variance σ_i^2. Then the overlap polynomial approximation of f is given by

$$f(X_k; \beta) = \sum_{i=1}^{n} [\Phi_i(X_k) - \Phi_{i+1}(X_k)] p_i(X_k; \beta_i) \qquad (12\text{-}2)$$

where β is the parameter vector to be estimated. The number of parameters to be estimated per dependent variable treated this way depends on the degree of $p_i(x)$ and on the number of knots. For example, if quadratic polynomials are used with n intervals, there will be $2n$ parameters to estimate for X_k.

Figure 12-2, which graphs the weighting function in the ith interval, $\Phi_{i+1}(x) - \Phi_i(x)$, clearly shows that most of the weight falls on the interval $[a_i, a_{i+1}]$ and falls off rapidly outside of it. A corollary to this fact is that, for any given value of $x \in [a_i, a_{i+1}]$, the polynomial $p_i(x)$ will have the greatest influence on the approximation to $f(k)$,

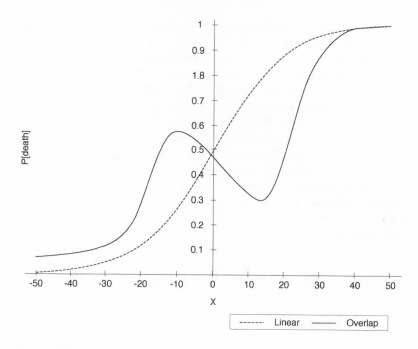

Figure 12-1
Linear Logit vs. Overlap Polynomial

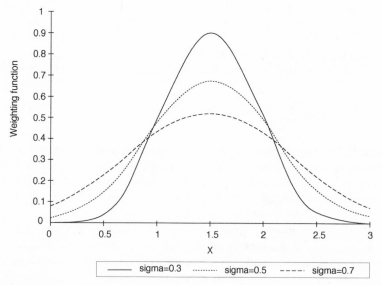

Figure 12-2
Weighting Function

and polynomials native to intervals farther away will have progressively less influence on it. The rate at which the weight diminishes outside the native interval depends on the value of σ chosen; smaller values of σ result in a more rapid drop in the weight outside the interval. Thus, σ can be viewed as a smoothing parameter that influences the extent to which polynomials outside the interval impact the approximation within the interval.[5]

In order to limit the number of parameters and because we are concerned with the possibility of a nonmonotonic effect on mortality in the case of only a few covariates, in the actual regression, we specify only three covariates with overlap polynomials: age, number of beds, and LOS. There are five knots in the age, bed, and LOS polynomials. We use a quadratic specification for the bed and LOS polynomials in every interval, and fit a linear polynomial for age within each interval. For the remaining covariates, we use a standard linear logit specification.

Results and Discussion

For each diagnostic group, Table 12-3 shows the parameter estimates with the linear logit model. Table 12-4 shows the parameter estimates for the linear covariates within the overlap polynomial model. Few patient-specific empirical regularities persist across all disease categories. Such a result is not surprising given that different diseases have different care requirements and varying natural histories. The most important point is that the sign on many of the variables is different for the two models, even within a given diagnostic category. This change in sign induced by introducing a more flexible model indicates that the linear model, which is the typical one in the literature, is misspecified. This is especially true given that the overlap polynomial model nests the linear model.

Hospital Characteristics
The most consistent result across the two models and across diagnostic categories is that hospitals with a larger number of new doctors and residents, relative to the total number of doctors, tend to have a lower in-hospital mortality rate. This result is consistent with Garber, Fuchs, and Silverman (1984), who report a similar finding in the context of a single teaching hospital with faculty and non-faculty services. Following them, we interpret this result to mean that new doctors and physicians in training are more aggressive than older doctors in keeping patients alive inside the hospital. They find, however, that patients on the nonfaculty service have the same six-

Table 12-3
Coefficient Estimates for the Linear Logit Model

Coefficient	AMI	Breast Cancer	Lung Cancer	Pneumonia	GI Diseases	Stomach Cancer	Colon Cancer
C	-6.55**	-4.31**	-1.51**	-7.28**	-1.88**	-1.47**	-2.97**
GERIAT	1.96	N/A	-0.560	1.70	2.63**	1.09	7.60**
TEACH	0.937	-0.239	-0.648*	0.366	0.257	0.219	-0.387
NEWDOC	-0.353	-0.659	-0.207	-0.397	-0.458**	-0.366	-1.23**
CRITCAR	-6.51*	4.99	0.516	-6.01**	-1.05	-4.24*	1.11
OCCUP	-0.377	-0.0335	-1.08**	0.372	-0.209	-0.764**	-0.224
PHYS	-1.59	-0.557	0.370	-0.212	-2.12	-2.36**	-0.0887
RN	0.00143	-0.000006	0.000725	-0.00204	0.000286	0.000809	-0.000622
PNPLUSNA	1.07	-0.495	0.803	0.902	0.312	0.534	0.0676
INSURER	0.0278	0.400	0.113	-0.181	-0.223	-0.264	-0.270
PRIVATE	-0.198	0.544*	0.0213	0.122	0.117*	0.142	0.365*
NPO	-0.252	0.243	-0.265**	0.144	-0.0182	0.456×10^{-2}	0.186
MALE	0.336**	N/A	-0.226**	-0.347**	-0.0199	0.107	0.0344
IN PREF	-0.0435	0.412	0.0529	-0.394	-0.0924	0.122	-0.671**
DEPEND	0.174	0.634**	0.0929	-0.463*	0.0128	-0.0474	0.0701
BED	-0.00129	0.000349	-0.000464	0.00147**	0.000109	-0.000175	0.00121*
AGE	0.0708**	0.0194**	0.0284**	0.0753**	0.0183**	0.0113**	0.0268**
LOS	$-.658 \times 10^{-4}$	0.135×10^{-4}	-0.985×10^{-6}	-0.353×10^{-6}	-0.995×10^{-6}	-0.982×10^{-5}	0.874×10^{-5}

* 10% significance level.
** 5% significance level.

Table 12-4
Coefficient Estimates for the Overlap Polynomial Model

Coefficient	AMI	Breast Cancer	Lung Cancer	Pneumonia	GI Diseases	Stomach Cancer	Colon Cancer
C	-6.61×10^{-4}**	-6.33×10^{-4}**	-4.33×10^{-4}*	-1.06×10^{-4}	4.767	-2.79×10^{-4}	-5.64×10^{-3}
GERIAT	0.905	N/A	-0.680	1.32	2.67**	0.617	9.53**
TEACH	0.436	-0.116	-1.14**	-0.315	0.110	0.258	-0.388
NEWDOC	0.0263	-0.455	-0.126	-0.144	-0.489**	-0.429	-1.35**
CRITCAR	-4.18	4.87	-0.350	-5.44	-1.51	-4.45*	-1.71
OCCUP	0.388	0.240	-1.41**	-0.0914	-0.396*	-0.943**	-0.947
PHYS	-1.41	-0.416	0.939	0.919	-1.49**	-1.87**	1.13
RN	0.156×10^{-2}	0.138×10^{-2}	0.196×10^{-2}*	0.503×10^{-3}	0.112×10^{-2}	0.198×10^{-2}*	0.181×10^{-2}
PNPLUSNA	0.251	-0.213	1.31*	1.48**	0.571*	0.908*	0.490
INSURER	0.121	0.445	0.184	-0.253	-0.201	-0.167	-0.299
PRIVATE	-0.220	0.229	0.0654	0.218	0.0666	0.0241	0.333
NPO	-0.389	0.195	-0.361**	0.131	0.0119	-0.0209	0.221
MALE	0.408**	N/A	-0.319**	-0.399**	-0.0723	0.0260	-0.825×10^{-2}
IN PREF	0.0919	0.257	0.0284	-0.425	-0.0506	0.149	-0.727**
DEPEND	0.101	0.476*	0.107	-0.361	0.0439	-0.0230	0.0715

* 10% significance level.
** 5% significance level.

month mortality rate as those on the faculty service. Given the cross-sectional nature of our data set, we cannot examine this phenomenon here. However, teaching hospital status has mixed results on predicted mortality.

Hospitals with larger numbers of PNs and NAs per bed, relative to RNs per bed, have a higher predicted mortality rate in most of the diagnostic categories we examine. This is consistent with the hypothesis that higher skill mixes lead to increased hospital quality, though this relationship does not hold true for breast cancer.

Private hospitals have a higher in-hospital mortality than public hospitals, holding all observables constant, in all categories except acute myocardial infarctions, although none of these results are statistically significant. Although this may be a consequence of a quality difference across these hospital types, one should be careful in drawing this conclusion. In particular, important elements of unobserved patient-specific severity may drive this result. Such a case may arise, for example, if patients who are more severely ill choose preferentially to be admitted to private hospitals rather than public hospitals. The other two types of hospitals, nonprofit and insurer-owned, have mixed results relative to public hospitals; they are better in some diagnostic categories, worse in others. Additionally, geriatric hospitals have higher mortality rates than nongeriatric, general hospitals in every category except lung cancer.

There is some evidence here for a volume-outcome relationship, though the previously noted selection problem prevents a concrete test of a causal hypothesis. For example, hospitals that maintain a high ratio of patients to beds tend to have a lower mortality rate, though this is not true in the case of breast cancer. Large hospitals do not categorically fare better than small ones in terms of predicted mortality. Of course, number of beds is a crude measure of the number of cases of a particular disease seen at a given hospital. Table 12-5 shows the mean predicted mortality rate given various hospital sizes. The main lesson to be learned from this table is that the relationship between hospital size and predicted mortality is likely to be nonmonotonic, unlike the prediction generated by the linear logit.

Finally, in the overlap polynomial specification, we find that hospitals with critical care units (CCUs) have lower predicted mortality than those without one for all disease categories except breast cancer. This negative relationship is not as pervasively apparent if one were to examine only the linear logit results. Although this result may seem odd at first, it is consistent with scope economies in the

Table 12-5
Mean Predicted Mortality vs. Number of Beds

	Number of Beds	20	100	200	350	500	650
AMI	linear logit	0.182	0.169	0.153	0.132	0.113	0.0961
	overlap polynomial	0.0799	0.135	0.182	0.145	0.103	0.0664
Breast Cancer	linear logit	0.0815	0.0836	0.0863	0.0904	0.0947	0.0992
	overlap polynomial	0.226	0.139	0.135	0.0895	0.0742	0.0865
Lung Cancer	linear logit	0.376	0.367	0.357	0.342	0.327	0.312
	overlap polynomial	0.115	0.474	0.372	0.329	0.295	0.265
Pneumonia	linear logit	0.0650	0.0714	0.0802	0.0949	0.111	0.129
	overlap polynomial	0.0344	0.0748	0.110	0.0938	0.122	0.0992
GI Disease	linear logit	0.237	0.238	0.240	0.243	0.246	0.249
	overlap polynomial	0.197	0.265	0.238	0.256	0.256	0.220
Stomach Cancer	linear logit	0.228	0.226	0.223	0.218	0.214	0.209
	overlap polynomial	0.0194	0.232	0.244	0.241	0.257	0.174
Colon Cancer	linear logit	0.121	0.132	0.146	0.168	0.194	0.222
	overlap polynomial	0.192	0.145	0.155	0.172	0.174	0.214

provision of hospital care. Hospitals with CCUs are better at keeping even their noncritically ill patients alive. Selection effects cannot explain this result because one would expect such concerns to drive the coefficient estimate toward a positive relationship between the presence of a CCU and predicted mortality.

Patient Characteristics
The sign of the correlation between most patient-specific characteristics, such as sex, and predicted mortality depends largely on the disease category. This is as one might expect, because diseases vary in their severity by sex. As in the case of other variables, whether or not the hospital stay took place within the patient's home prefecture and the patient's dependency status have a variable effect on predicted mortality.

The importance of using a flexible functional form is again apparent in Table 12-6, which presents mean predicted mortality for different diagnoses by LOS for the linear-logit and the overlap polynomial models. LOS never predicts severity of illness for any disease category in the linear model. But with the more flexible model, one detects the nonlinear dependence of predicted mortality on LOS. For example, in the case of acute myocardial infarction, the overlap polynomial predicts a large spike in mortality on the first day of the hospital stay. This is consistent with intuition and medical fact, but is missed by the linear model.

The strongest relationship between a patient-specific variable and predicted mortality is found in the case of patient age. Table 12-7 shows mean predicted mortality for patients of selected ages by diagnosis category. For both the overlap polynomial model and the linear model, predicted mortality is generally increasing with age. However, the overlap polynomial model reveals that this dependence is not monotonic. For example, Figure 12-3 shows a plot of predicted mortality vs. age for gastrointestinal diseases. The observed differences between the overlap polynomial model and the linear model may arise from important physiological factors in the disease process that determine its natural history and thus the age dependence of predicted mortality. There is no *a priori* reason to believe that this complicated relationship should be monotonic.

One implication of Figure 12-3 is that one should be very careful in identifying hospitals that are predicted mortality outliers using the typical linear methods. For example, notice that the overlap polynomial is above the linear logit for ages 80–100, and below it for ages 60–80. This means that if residuals from the linear logit

Table 12-6
Mean Predicted Mortality vs. LOS

	Length of Stay	1	10	20	40	100	200
AMI	linear logit	0.132	0.132	0.132	0.131	0.131	0.130
	overlap polynomial	0.416	0.00065	0.00021	0.0109	0.0608	0.106
Breast Cancer	linear logit	0.0923	0.0924	0.0924	0.0924	0.0925	0.0926
	overlap polynomial	0.150	0.00	0.0888	0.117	0.271	0.341
Lung Cancer	linear logit	0.334	0.334	0.334	0.334	0.334	0.334
	overlap polynomial	0.247	0.254	0.225	0.446	0.432	0.633
Pneumonia	linear logit	0.0840	0.0840	0.0840	0.0840	0.0840	0.0840
	overlap polynomial	0.276	0.0746	0.0932	0.0346	0.115	0.173
GI Disease	linear logit	0.244	0.244	0.244	0.244	0.244	0.244
	overlap polynomial	0.194	0.0216	0.0295	0.156	0.353	0.581
Stomach Cancer	linear logit	0.219	0.219	0.218	0.218	0.218	0.218
	overlap polynomial	0.270	0.00184	0.0362	0.146	0.344	0.613
Colon Cancer	linear logit	0.167	0.167	0.167	0.167	0.167	0.167
	overlap polynomial	0.0822	0.00032	0.00083	0.0562	0.395	0.541

Table 12-7
Mean Predicted Mortality vs. Age

AMI						
Age	51	60	69	78	87	96
linear logit	0.0381	0.0694	0.122	0.207	0.326	0.472
overlap polynomial	0.0349	0.0729	0.118	0.228	0.305	0.332
Breast Cancer						
Age	21	33	45	57	69	81
linear logit	0.0504	0.0626	0.0776	0.0956	0.117	0.143
overlap polynomial	0.00	0.0296	0.0824	0.117	0.0862	0.0989
Lung Cancer						
Age	24	36	48	60	72	84
linear logit	0.127	0.169	0.222	0.285	0.358	0.438
overlap polynomial	0.00	0.178	0.255	0.258	0.329	0.483
Pneumonia						
Age	6	30	54	69	84	93
linear logit	0.000763	0.00462	0.0274	0.0797	0.207	0.336
overlap polynomial	0.0816	0.0466	0.0426	0.0972	0.288	0.321
GI Disease						
Age	3	21	39	54	66	87
linear logit	0.0928	0.124	0.164	0.205	0.243	0.319
overlap polynomial	0.0943	0.132	0.208	0.229	0.236	0.342
Stomach Cancer						
Age	30	42	54	66	78	90
linear logit	0.157	0.175	0.195	0.217	0.241	0.266
overlap polynomial	0.0287	0.00114	0.0262	0.0493	0.149	0.230
Colon Cancer						
Age	27	39	51	63	75	87
linear logit	0.0649	0.0871	0.115	0.152	0.197	0.214
overlap polynomial	0.000886	0.109	0.0897	0.154	0.197	0.185

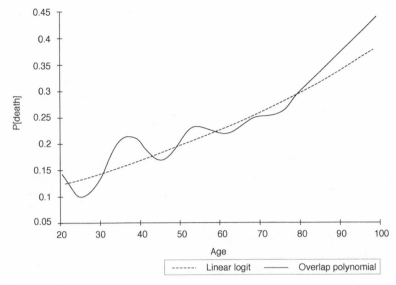

Figure 12-3
Predicted Probability of Mortality—GI Diseases

were used to identify hospitals with unusually high mortality rates, those hospitals with a large number of 80- to 100-year-olds would appear to do worse than they should, but those with many 60- to 80-year-olds would appear to do better than they should.

Conclusions

Although some may criticize predicted mortality as an insufficient measure of hospital quality, it seems clear that decreasing it while holding constant case mix and patient severity should at least be viewed as a necessary step in improving hospital quality. As a public policy tool, the analysis of hospital mortality can provide regulators with some guidance about where to focus their efforts, though of course it does not provide all the answers.

Especially in the context of the Japanese health care system, where such work has not previously been done, such an exercise can be useful. For example, the fact that private hospitals do not differ significantly from public ones in adjusted mortality rates means that the subsidies public hospitals receive from the government are not necessary to achieve quality in this dimension. There are a variety of possible policy interventions, including modifying or eliminating the fee system or eliminating public hospital subsidies.

Other factors need to be considered in identifying the correct response.

Future work on this topic should focus on adjusting the estimation of mortality regressions for sample selection bias. This shortcoming in the usual method has not been adequately addressed in the literature. Although this chapter shows that some conclusions reached from these regressions can be quite sensitive to statistical assumptions, further sensitivity testing is appropriate. For example, it would be interesting to know how the conclusions change when causality issues are addressed. In particular, if patients choose hospitals based on their anticipated mortality rates, then the patient-specific variables in the regression are endogenous and, unless properly instrumented, lead to biased estimates. The issue of scope economies in the provision of quality also needs to be examined further. Are hospitals that do well in treating one diagnosis more likely to do well in other diagnostic categories? Finally, for the Japanese context, it would make sense to estimate these models for other diagnostic categories.

Notes

[1] For evidence that this is the prototypical response by hospitals one need merely skim the letters generated by the publication of Health Care Financing Administration outcome rankings. (HCFA, 1989).

[2] It is appropriate to include both classes of variables here because we are attempting to determine the correlates of hospital quality. If the purpose instead were to find predictors of patient mortality, which can then in turn be used to evaluate hospital quality, including hospital characteristics would not be appropriate.

[3] For example, suppose $g(x) = (1 + x^2)^{-1}$ is to be estimated by $f_p(x) = b_0 + b_1 x + b_2 x^2 + \ldots b_p x^p$ in $x \in [-1, 1]$, where b is determined by fitting $f_p(x)$ exactly to $p + 1$ equally spaced points between $x = -1$ and $x = 1$. It can be shown that at $x = -1$ and $x = 1$:

$$\lim_{p \to \infty} |g(x) - f_p(x)| = \infty.$$

See Shumaker (1981).

[4] This technique is introduced into health economics by Garber and MacCurdy (1993) in the context of estimating length of stay survival curves for nursing home patients.

[5] Although it is in principle possible to use the data to estimate σ, we do not do so in our estimation due to computational complexity.

13

Hospital Utilization among the Elderly

As the populations of Japan and the United States age, questions surrounding the costs of care for the elderly are increasingly coming to the forefront. Increased cost of caring for the elderly is often cited as an important determinant of the growth in costs in the medical systems of industrialized countries, and the population of many industrialized countries is aging. This "graying" of the population has led to fears that health care costs will increase as older people increasingly utilize the health care system in the future.

An additional feature of the health care systems of industrialized countries is the variety in the providers of services. Hospitals differ widely in such attributes as size and ownership arrangements. The number and mix of hospitals change over time. For example, in the U.S., there has been a major shakeup in the hospital sector since the early 1980s, and in Japan, there has been a continuing movement of physicians out of clinics and into hospitals.

Policymakers need to forecast the effects of changes in the demographics of populations and in the number and composition of health care institutions if they are to anticipate changes in health care costs. Toward this end, it is useful to examine the differences in expenditures between different age groups, regions, and types of hospital. In this chapter, we explore a few of these issues in the context of expenditures on Japan's elderly. We seek to answer four research questions: How are cost, length of stay (LOS), and cost per day related to a patient's age and sex? How are these variables related to the characteristics—including ownership and size—of the hospital at which the patient seeks care? To what extent is geo-

This chapter is based upon: Vogt, W.B., Bhattacharya, J., Yoshikawa, A., and Nanbu, T. 1995. "Hospital Utilization among the Elderly," *mimeo*, Asia/Pacific Research Center, Stanford University.

graphical variation in costs important? Does geographical variation take the form primarily of differences in length of stay or of cost per day?

Data

The data we use in this chapter come from a different source than those used elsewhere in this book. They are based upon claims data for a sample of elderly patients in Japan. The patients in the data set are people over the age of 70 and disabled people over the age of 65, similar to the *Roken* group described in Table 1-1. The claims were collected in the month of September 1990.

Originally collected in paper form, the claims were very detailed. Each contained a variety of demographic, diagnostic, and procedural data. There were line items for each billable item, and some of the forms went on for tens of pages.

The data set used in this chapter contains information on approximately 60,000 inpatients. For each, age, sex, primary and secondary diagnoses, length of stay during the month, total charges during the month, and charges broken out by revenue center are reported. Primary and secondary diagnoses are not recorded *per se* on the claims forms, so the research group included a committee of physicians who reviewed the paper claims and assigned primary and secondary diagnoses based upon their findings. Also reported is whether or not the patient died, had surgery, or had a CT scan, MRI scan, or X-ray during the month. There is also information on the hospital and the ward in which the patient received service. The type of hospital (ordinary, mental, geriatric, etc.), ownership of the hospital, size of the hospital (in beds), and distribution of beds (by ordinary, geriatric, etc.) are reported.

Although these data do not constitute a random sample of elderly patients in Japan, they are fairly representative of the population of Japanese elderly inpatients. According to the 1990 Point Survey (*Shakai Iryo Shinryo Koibetsu Chosa Hokoku*), the average points per case and length of stay for elderly patients were 31,414 and 22.6, respectively. The corresponding averages in our data are 33,812 and 23.2. The distribution of points among categories is also quite similar between our data and national averages. For example, 52.7% of points are allocated to room and board in the national data, and 53.7% are allocated for this purpose in our data set. Similarly, the geographical distribution of patients in our data is similar to that of elderly patients in Japan as a whole.

One variable in the data set deserves special attention. Our length-of-stay variable is the length of stay of a particular patient in a particular hospital in a particular month. This variable may be either longer or shorter than the discharge length of stay used in other research. If a patient has more than one hospitalization in a single month, then her length of stay for the month will be greater than her length of stay for any particular hospitalization in the month. Conversely, if the patient was already in the hospital at the start of the month, her length of stay will be understated by our measure.

Method

Our primary research questions focus on the effects upon charges, LOS, and charge per day of age and sex of the patient, size of the hospital, ownership of the hospital, and geographical area. We are interested in addressing these questions with as flexible a statistical form as we can manage given our data. To address these questions, we develop the following model. Consider the identity:

Charge = LOS * charge/day

$$\log(\text{Cost}) = \log(\text{LOS}) + \log(\text{charge/day}) \quad (13\text{-}1)$$

Because the data set contains information on both cost and length of stay, we may estimate two separate equations:

$$\log(\text{LOS}) = \sum_{i=1}^{47} \text{pref}_{i,t}\pi_{1,i} + \sum_{j=70}^{99} \text{age}_{j,t}\alpha_{1,j}$$

$$+ \sum_{k=1}^{7} \text{owner}_{k,t}\delta_{1,k} + \sum_{l=1}^{10} \text{size}_{l,t}\sigma_{1,l} + \varepsilon_1.$$

$$(13\text{-}2)$$

$$\log(\text{Charge/Day}) = \sum_{i=1}^{47} \text{pref}_{i,t}\pi_{2,i} + \sum_{j=70}^{99} \text{age}_{j,t}\alpha_{2,j}$$

$$+ \sum_{k=1}^{7} \text{owner}_{k,t}\delta_{2,k} + \sum_{l=1}^{10} \text{size}_{l,t}\sigma_{2,l} + \varepsilon_2.$$

$$(13\text{-}3)$$

In these equations, $\text{pref}_{i,t}$, $\text{age}_{j,t}$, $\text{owner}_{k,t}$, and $\text{size}_{l,t}$ are dummy variables; for example, $\text{pref}_{i,t}$ takes a value of one if patient t is from prefecture 1 and zero otherwise. t indexes the patients, and it runs from one to T, the total number of records. The total charge equation may be consistently estimated using this framework:

$$\log(\text{Charge}) = \sum_{i=1}^{47} \text{pref}_{i,t}(\pi_{1,i} + \pi_{2,i}) + \sum_{j=70}^{99} \text{age}_{j,t}(\alpha_{1,j} + \alpha_{2,j})$$

$$+ \sum_{k=1}^{7} \text{owner}_{k,t}(o_{1,k}o_{2,k}) + \sum_{l=1}^{10} \text{size}_{l,t}(\sigma_{1,l} + \sigma_{2,l})$$

$$+ (\varepsilon_{1,t}\varepsilon_{2,t}) \tag{13-4}$$

With these estimates in hand, we may calculate the average charges, average length of stay, and average charge per day for various values of the variables of interest, controlling for the influences of the others.

We obtain estimates $\pi, \alpha, \delta, \sigma$ via ordinary least squares regression applied to Equations 13-2 through 13-4. We run the regressions separately for men and women, and run them both for the sample as a whole and only for disease category 5, cardiovascular diseases of the brain, the most prevalent disease category. The graphs in the "Results" section are generated with these estimates. These graphs may be interpreted as giving the effect of, for example, age on length of stay, holding the size, ownership, and geographical area of the hospital constant.

Before we perform our analyses, we must choose a relatively homogeneous sample for estimation. The full inpatient data set has 58,914 observations. This includes observations that come from geriatric and mental hospitals, as well as clinics. Some of the data come from mental or geriatric wards of hospitals. Furthermore, the data contain observations with missing values for ICD codes, ownership categories for the hospital, and other variables. We remove all observations from mental or geriatric hospitals or wards and observations with missing values. Finally, all those observations associated with patients under the age of 70 or over the age of 99 are selected out. After all the selections, there are 46,234 observations remaining, 12,195 of which correspond to male patients and 34,039 to female. The most common disease in the sample is cardiovascular diseases of the brain (15,697 of the 46,234 observations or 34.00%). The second most common disease category is cardiovascular disease of the heart (3,600 observations, or 7.79% of the sample). Sample means for the data set appear in Table 13-1.

Table 13-1
Sample Means

Variable	Male	Female
Number	12,195	34,039
Points	36,144	32,613
Length of stay	21.11	23.25
% having CT	19.89	16.50
% having MRI	3.05	1.61
% having surgery	82.24	85.31
Average bed size	307.42	269.13

Results

Before we present our main results, there are a few interesting aspects of the table of sample means to discuss. There are a number of interesting differences in the table between men and women. Women, on average, are 11% less costly than men; they experience a 10% longer length of stay, and they are less likely to receive CT and surgery. They also, on average, seek care at smaller hospitals than do men. An interesting question arises: Are women less costly because they seek care at (less costly) smaller hospitals, or would they be less costly even were they to seek care at larger ones?

The main results of our analyses are reported in a series of graphs. In the first group of graphs, Figures 13-1 through 13-3, we examine the relationship between charges, length of stay, and age. Figure 13-1 graphs total charges (in points) against age and sex. Each point represents the expected cost of a patient, conditional upon age and sex, evaluating prefecture, ownership, and size at their means. In Figure 13-1, we see several important features of the data. The most striking thing about the figure is the flatness of the distribution of charges by age. Except at very high ages, older people do not seem to be any more expensive to treat than younger patients. At the high ages, sample sizes are small (there are only 33 patients who are 99 years old), and the results are consequently less reliable. Similarly, the much smaller sample size for males seems to contribute to the more variable behavior of the males' curve. It is also interesting to note in Figure 13-1 that men and women cost approximately the same amount to treat (per month) given that they have received care. This is true after controlling for the size, ownership, and geographical location of the hospital. So, it appears that women cost less than men, on average, because they seek care

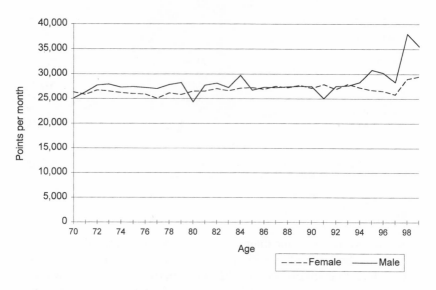

Figure 13-1
Adjusted Points by Age and Sex

at different hospitals. The two stories of Figure 13-1 are that older people do not, on average, cost more to treat per month once they have sought care and that men and women cost approximately the same amount to treat, given that they have sought care.

Figure 13-2 plots the relationship between age and length of stay. In this figure, we can see that men tend to stay in the hospital for a briefer period of time than do women and that older people tend to stay in the hospital longer than younger people. Again in this graph we see the greater instability of the estimates at the extremely high ages and for men, due to the smaller sample size in those groups. Figure 13-3 shows the relationship between age and points expended per day in the month. In this graph, we can see that the intensity of medical care (at least as measured by expenditures) decreases by the age of the patient and is greater for men than for women. Figures 13-2 and 13-3 tell us that, although older patients cost approximately the same amount to treat as younger patients, the treatment patterns for the two groups are not exactly the same. Older patients tend to spend a long time in the hospital and tend to consume fewer resources per day than do younger.

In our analyses to this point, we have been making no use of the

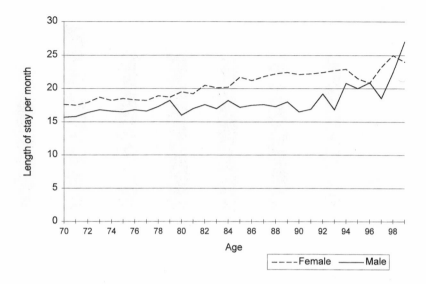

Figure 13-2
Adjusted LOS by Age and Sex

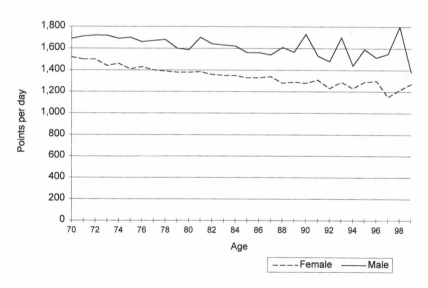

Figure 13-3
Adjusted Points per Day by Age and Sex

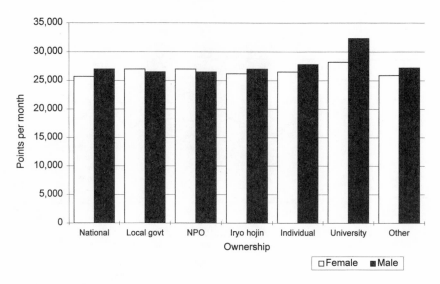

Figure 13-4
Adjusted Points by Ownership

diagnosis information in the data. We were concerned that the failure to control for differences in diagnosis might tend to bias our results, so we checked that these results were robust to a more careful control of case mix. We reran the previously described analysis using only those patients in disease category 5, cardiovascular diseases of the brain. None of the results changed when we performed this control for case mix.

In the next set of graphs, we explore the relationships between hospital ownership and cost, cost per day, and length of stay of the elderly patients. Figure 13-4 depicts the adjusted points per month by the various ownership categories. The point totals for each ownership category are similar, after controlling for patient age and hospital location and size. With the exception of university hospitals, all of the ownership categories cluster around 25,000 points. University hospitals create higher expenditures, likely because their caseload is more complex. Also evident in this graph again is the similarity in charges between men and women after age, hospital size, and location are taken into account.

Figures 13-5 and 13-6 explore the composition of charges among the different ownership classes. Here we see substantial differences among the different kinds of hospitals. In Figure 13-5, it appears

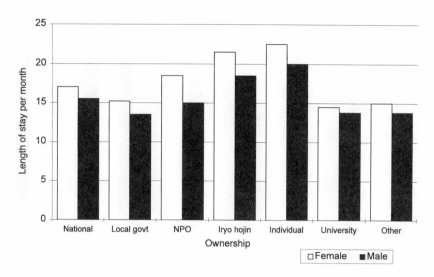

Figure 13-5
Adjusted LOS by Ownership

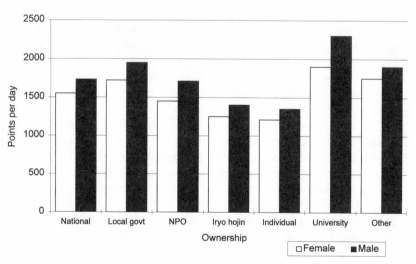

Figure 13-6
Adjusted Points per Day by Ownership

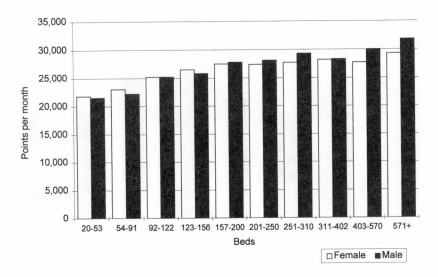

Figure 13-7
Adjusted Points by Size

that the private, nonprofit (*iryo-hojin*) and individually owned hospitals have substantially longer lengths of stay than do the government, nonprofit organization or university hospitals. By contrast, *iryo-hojin* and individual hospitals have substantially lower points per day than do university or government hospitals. These differences in length of stay and points per day exist after controlling for hospital size and patient characteristics.

The next set of graphs allows us to examine how hospital size affects costs, length of stay, and points per day for elderly patients. Figure 13-7 shows an increasing relationship between the hospital size and the cost of a case. This relationship is largely as one would expect because more complex and difficult cases tend to go to larger hospitals. Interestingly, the effect appears to be stronger for women than for men because women treated at small hospitals are less expensive than are men, but women treated at large hospitals are more expensive than their male counterparts.

Figures 13-8 and 13-9 reveal a complex relationship among size, length of stay, and cost. Figure 13-7 demonstrates an increasing relationship between size and cost. This relationship could be due to increasing length of stay at larger hospitals or to increasing cost per day. For small to medium-sized hospitals (less than 200 beds),

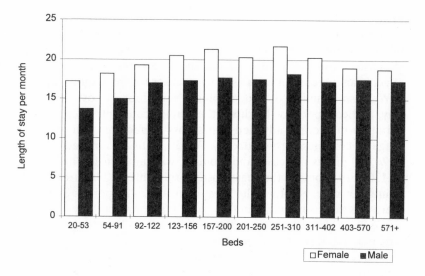

Figure 13-8
Adjusted LOS by Size

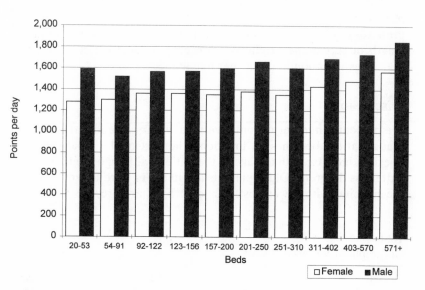

Figure 13-9
Adjusted Points per Day by Size

Figures 13-8 and 13-9 reveal that rising costs in size are due to increasing lengths of stay and flat charges per day. For large hospitals (over 300 beds), there is a decrease in length of stay as size increases; however, points per day increase so rapidly that the net effect is an increase in costs as size increases for the larger hospitals.

We also examine the geographical variations in cost, length of stay, and cost per day, holding other things constant. There is wide variation in average adjusted cost across prefectures. For men, the range of costliness is bounded by Tottori, with an adjusted average of 20,949 points per case, and Aomori, with an adjusted average of 37,170. For women, the least costly prefecture is Fukui at 22,855 points per case. Kyoto is the most dear at 32,425 points. Similarly, there are ranges in both length of stay and points per day.

We were curious as to whether differences in length of stay or in cost per day were the more important drivers of the geographical cost differences. To examine this question, we consider what the standard deviation in average costs (across prefectures) would be if all prefectures were to have the overall mean value for length of stay but their points per day varied as they do now. Similarly, we examine how costs would vary if all prefectures had the same cost per day but points per case varied as they do now. Our findings are presented in Table 13-2. For both males and females, variation in length of stay alone produces more geographical variation in cost than does variation in points per day alone.

Discussion

We present a number of tentative results. First, we find that, given that a patient becomes an inpatient, the cost of the inpatient stay does not increase with the age of the patient, although the treatment pattern is different. Older patients are likely to have longer stays in the hospital with lower costs per day. Furthermore, we find that,

Table 13-2
Geographical Variance of Cost

Variable	Male	Female
Cost per case	2146	2890
Costs with LOS fixed	2201	2361
Costs with points per day fixed	2436	3376

after controlling for hospital characteristics, women and men cost the same amount to treat; however, they too show some significant differences in treatment patterns because men tend to have shorter stays with higher cost per day.

It is not possible to conclude from these two results that the total costs of an elderly person do not increase with age. It could be that older people seek care more frequently than do younger people, running up higher costs even if the per-case costs are the same. Our data do not allow us to address this question, because they contain only observations on those people who did seek care in the month of September 1990. Furthermore, older people may tend to seek care more than once in a month and to seek care at different hospitals. Because our data cannot follow a particular person from one hospital to another, we cannot ensure that this is not occurring. Despite all of this, however, the finding that people of different ages do not cost different amounts when they seek care is surprising in and of itself.

Similarly, we cannot conclude that there are no differences between the costs of males and females from the analysis we have presented. Again, it may be that males or females seek care more often, or that either males or females are more likely to spread their care among different hospitals. However, the differences in length of stay and intensity of care are interesting. As a general rule, females are more likely to provide home caregiving to males than are males to provide it to females. Because males are more likely to have a female caregiver at home, they may be more willing to go home from the hospital earlier than are females. This effect could then explain the differences between length of stay and intensity of care revealed by our analysis.

Surprisingly, we found that neither ownership nor hospital size had any large effect on the cost per case. In fact, hospital size seems to have little effect on any of the variables we examine. Hospital ownership, however, has a substantial impact on the composition of the services hospitals provide. Patients in our sample receiving care at private hospitals tend to stay longer and to cost less per day than their counterparts in government and university hospitals. One of the problems often mentioned in the context of Japan's health care system is the use of Japanese hospitals essentially as nursing homes, and our analyses suggests that the private hospitals are providing more nursing home type care than are their government counterparts.

Conclusions

In this chapter, we provide a preliminary exploration of a number of issues surrounding health expenditures on the elderly. Our primary finding is that, given that a patient seeks inpatient health care, the amount of monthly health care expenditures does not rise with the patient's age. However, older patients do seem to receive a different type of care, if not more expensive care. Older patients tend to stay in the hospital longer and tend to spend less per day in the hospital.

There are secondary findings as well. The characteristics of the hospital at which a patient seeks care do not seem to have an important impact on expenditures. However, they do have an impact on the type of care a patient receives. Policies that focus on influencing a patient's choice of hospital may not be an effective method of achieving savings and may instead lead patients to styles of care they do not want.

Part VI

Surgery

The preceding chapters have focused on Japan, presenting studies relying on Japanese data and engineered to address economic issues central to the evaluation of the Japanese health care system. In this section, we expand the scope of our analysis to present an international comparative case study. We focus our attention upon issues related to surgeries. Chapter 14 is a study to set the stage for Chapter 15. The purpose of Chapter 14 is to analyze the factors which lead to differential rates of surgery across prefectures in Japan. We find that teaching hospitals and publicly owned hospitals tend to provide more surgery than do private hospitals.

In Chapter 14, we focus on surgical interventions in order to complement the wide body of medical literature on the existence of and explanation for area variation in surgical rates, both within and between various countries (Escarce, 1993; Halliday and LeRiche, 1987; Nattinger et al., 1992; Vayda, Mindell, and Rutkow, 1982). Such area variation of surgical intervention has many implications for health care policymakers, including challenges to the efficient delivery of care.

The structure of the Japanese medical care system makes it uniquely suited to investigate some of the causes of the area variation of surgical intervention, because the Japanese point system eliminates the differences in financial remuneration to providers for a given surgery. Although we have demonstrated that patient demand is price-sensitive, Japanese patients are unlikely to be swayed by price factors in choosing among alternative hospitals, as prices are uniform and set by the government. This situation contrasts with the multiple-payer U.S. system, in which a patient enrolled in a managed care program may face a higher cost of care for choosing a particular provider.

Japanese providers do not discriminate between patients on the

281

basis of their personal income levels or insurance affiliations because of the uniform fee schedule. Again, this situation is different from that in the U.S., where hospitals may compete for traditional indemnity insurance patients while attempting to channel indigent and uninsured patients to public, county hospitals. Hence, by eliminating the income effects on both the patient and provider sides of the equation, the Japanese data allow us to focus on patient and provider characteristics other than income.

The case study in Chapter 15 examines the volume of and length of stay for surgical operations at the Stanford University and the University of Tokyo hospitals and begins to uncover the reasons for the significantly higher surgical rate at Stanford and in the U.S. in general, relative to Japan. We decompose the steps in the operating procedure in order to determine whether relative efficiencies in the two hospitals explain the surgical rate differences. By following patients from the time they enter the surgical ward until they leave for recovery, we find that the bulk of the operation time difference between Stanford and Tokyo is explained by the amount of time spent on the surgery itself, from incision to closure. Although Tokyo requires slightly more time than Stanford to accomplish some of the pre- and postoperative procedures, narrowing these differentials would not decrease significantly the total amount of the aggregate time differential.

Our decision to compare Stanford and the University of Tokyo hospitals is a deliberate one. In addition to the fact that the University of Tokyo surgical rates in relation to those at Stanford parallel aggregate international differences, we choose these two hospitals to minimize the confounding variables inherent in any cross-cultural comparison. The utility of the comparison is helpful only to the extent that we are able to isolate two relatively similar products. Our task is to compare a Japanese hospital to an American one. Examining two premier teaching hospitals accomplishes this goal.

14

Differential Surgical Rates

Many of the important technical advances in health care over the last few decades have taken the form of new surgical techniques. For example, coronary artery bypass grafting was developed in the 1960s and by the 1990s had become both very prevalent and an important contributor to the cost of health care. Another example which has been important in Japan has been stomach resection for the treatment of gastric cancer. One of the approaches taken to the analysis of surgery in the context of the U.S. is area variations. In this chapter, we analyze rates of surgery in Japan to shed light on the causes for variation.

We compare surgical performance primarily because of the stark differences in surgical rates between the two countries: Japanese surgical rates per capita are roughly one-fourth those in the U.S., though the Japanese inpatient admission rate is one-half that of the U.S. Given that some have suggested that one factor responsible for increasing American health care costs has been the substitution of surgical for medical intervention, understanding the root of this differential may go a long way toward explaining the lower overall medical care expenditures in Japan (Showstack et al., 1985).

Several theories have been posited to explain the area variation across geographically dispersed providers in the U.S. First, it has been suggested that physician-induced demand is at least partly responsible for differential surgical rates (Fuchs, 1978; Lewis, 1969). More recent results have not consistently supported this explanation (Escarce, 1993; Halliday and LeRiche, 1987; Javitt et al., 1995). Second, the economic factors of the fee-for-service reimbursement system, particularly in the multiple-payer insurance context, may influence area variation (Bunker and Brown, 1974). Finally, many attribute differences in the observed patterns of use to decisions made by providers (Blumberg, 1986; Wennberg, 1985,

283

1987). These variations in the use of medical care may occur because a lack of professional consensus about the benefits of alternative treatments leads each physician to adopt different personal
practice styles. Thus, rates of use vary among areas because the
mix of physicians favoring different treatments also varies. Socioeconomic factors have also been found to be significant determinants of medical practice differences in small area variation
analysis.[1] Paul-Shaheen, Clerk, and Williams (1987) provide an
excellent summary of the research to date on medical practice
variations.

A number of factors influence the decision to perform surgery;
both the characteristics of the patient and of the provider have been
found to be important. Nattinger et al. (1992), studying variations
in the relative rates of radical mastectomy vs. breast-conserving
surgery for breast cancer, find that the latter is used more in urban
than in rural areas, in teaching hospitals more than in nonteaching
hospitals, and in large hospitals more than in small hospitals. Halliday and LeRiche (1987) report that a hospital's teaching status
dwarfs nearly all other factors that may contribute to variations in
Canadian surgical rates. Escarce (1993) finds that the variation in
patient care-seeking behavior for cataract surgery, a factor that
contributes to the area variation of cataract surgical rates, is influenced by economic and socioeconomic variables.[2] Using data
from Medicare beneficiaries, Javitt et al. (1995) report that latitude,
race, age, gender, allowed charges, and the concentration of opto-
metrists are each strongly associated with an individual's probability
of undergoing cataract surgery.

Since our interest focuses on the contributions of both patient and
provider to surgery rates, we model the decision to perform surgery
as a function of characteristics of both. The dependent variable in
the analysis is a dummy variable equaling 1 if the patient underwent
surgery and 0 otherwise. The model is estimated via logit maximum
likelihood.[3]

We include the following explanatory variables. Hospital characteristics are (1) an ownership dummy (OWN) taking the value of 1
if a hospital is owned by the government, (2) a teaching hospital
dummy (TEACH), assuming the value of 1 for teaching hospitals,
and (3) the number of beds (#BED). The hospital-specific data are
collected from the Facility Survey.

There are three patient characteristics included. The sex dummy
(SEX) assumes a value of 1 if the patient is female. The patient's
age (AGE) is reported in years, while the death dummy (DEATH)

equals 1 if the reason for discharge was death. We collect these patient-specific data, as well as the dependent variable, from the Patient Survey and link them to the Facility Survey data.

The socioeconomic data we include are intended to model the effects of the costs of physician labor, the effects of quality competition, and the characteristics of the hospital market. Specifically, we include the wage of medical doctors (¥MD), the Herfindahl index (HI) for medical zones, and the ratio of service sector workers to all workers (SERV) to control for differences in population health status related to employment.[4]

Table 14-1 presents the regression results by disease category. The regression can be viewed as a reduced form analysis of equilibrium surgical rates.

For most cancer diagnoses, the coefficients on both OWN and TEACH are positive, indicating that the probability of performing surgery is higher at government hospitals and at teaching hospitals, holding constant patient characteristics and other provider characteristics. Number of beds similarly correlates positively with the probability of performing surgery.[5] For noncancer diagnoses, results are similar. These differences may arise from a variety of causes. First of all, different types of hospitals may have different propensities to operate on a given patient. Secondly, there may be unobserved differences in case mix among the different hospital types. Large hospitals, government hospitals, and teaching hospitals may attract a population of more severely ill patients. These differences in case mix may arise from referral patterns which direct patients needing surgery toward larger, specialty hospitals. Another potential cause of the differences in case mix lies in the geographical distribution of hospitals. Rural areas tend to have smaller hospitals, and are less likely to have teaching hospitals. Since rural residents tend to use health services less, the differences in surgery rates among hospital types may be due to these rural/urban differences combined with the different distributions of hospital types.

Turning now to patient characteristics, for cancer diagnoses, AGE and DEATH correlate negatively with the decision to operate. This is probably due to the fact that physicians are hesitant to operate on patients who are older and sicker and, thus, more likely to die. This decision may result from the greater likelihood of complications and the decreased health benefits relative to the costs of surgery. The results are similar for other diagnoses.

The Herfindahl index, a measure of competition in the market, yields a negative coefficient in all of the cancer diagnoses, indicating

Table 14-1
Predictors of Surgery: Logit Model

Variable	All Neoplasms	Stomach Cancer	Intestinal Cancer	Trachea, Bronchus, and Lung Cancer	Breast Cancer	Uterine Cancer	Cataract	Appendicitis	Cholelithiasis
Constant	1.141†	1.760†	0.358	−0.045	1.196	1.362†	2.844**	3.252†	0.153
OWN	0.075†	0.113	0.077	0.500†	0.182	0.047	−0.489**	0.022	0.273†
TEACH	0.181†	0.796†	0.673†	0.788†	−0.371	0.426†	0.232	0.642**	0.116
#BED	0.257×10^{-3}†	0.758×10^{-3}†	0.725×10^{-3}†	0.386×10^{-2}†	0.922×10^{-3}†	-0.295×10^{-3}	-0.336×10^{-3}	-0.466×10^{-3}***	0.105×10^{-3}
AGE	−0.016†	−0.024†	−0.350	−0.023†	−0.138	−0.023†	−0.011	−0.190	-0.999×10^{-2}†
SEX	0.421†	−0.079	−0.075	−0.243*			−0.036	−0.256†	0.172**
DEATH	−1.493†	−1.488†	−1.324†	−0.985†	−2.487†	−0.781			
¥MD	0.160	0.725	0.354	0.731	−0.150	0.564	0.389	−0.444	0.750
HI	−0.435**	−0.543	−1.076**	−3.748†	−0.529	−0.440	−0.666	−1.828†	0.193
SERV	−0.604†	−0.210	−0.277	0.187	−0.457	−0.796	0.023**	−0.011**	0.246

* denotes significance at the 10% level.
** denotes significance at the 5% level.
† denotes significance at the 1% level.

that, in a competitive hospital market, the probability of surgery will be higher. In three of the four noncancer diagnoses, Herfindahl also produces a negative coefficient. For cancer-related surgeries, the service-sector variable obtains a negative parameter estimate; the probability of surgery is greater in areas with few service employees. For surgeries performed on noncancer patients, the results are mixed.

These data provide a rough overview of the factors affecting the probability of performing surgery based upon Japanese patient, hospital, and socioeconomic factors. In general, surgery is more likely to be performed on patients who show a greater prospect of reaping the benefits of surgery and who present themselves at government-owned hospitals, large hospitals, and teaching hospitals.

Notes

[1] McLaughlin et al. (1989) report that socioeconomic variables influence the variation in hospital discharge rates.

[2] In Bombardier et al. (1977), there are relationships between operation rate and socioeconomic variables. Roos and Roos (1982) assess the contribution of population characteristics to unexplained variations in surgical rates.

[3] The logit model is

$$y^* = \beta'x + \varepsilon$$

where y^* is an index function representing the propensity to perform surgery on a particular patient with characteristics x, β is an unknown parameter vector to be estimated, and ε is an error term distributed with a logistic distribution.

[4] See Anderson (1991) and Callthorpe (1989) for a discussion of employment groups and health.

[5] The fact that this result is insignificant may result from the high level of correlation between teaching hospital status and number of beds ($p = 0.529$).

15

Surgical Volume and Operating Room Efficiency

One of the most persistent and important questions in international comparisons of health systems pertains to the wide divergence in costs among countries. Japan, despite having a fee-for-service reimbursement system and universal coverage, has significantly lower per capita health care costs than the U.S. This is particularly surprising in view of Japan's aggressive purchase and utilization of equipment-embodied medical technologies (Yoshikawa, Shirouzu, and Holt, 1991). One important factor in the increase in American health care costs has been the substitution of surgical intervention for medical treatment (Showstack, Stone, and Schroeder, 1985). This leads us to consider differential rates of surgery as a potential explanation for the divergent cost performance. Indeed, although Japan has one-half the inpatient admission rate of the U.S., it has only one-quarter the surgery rate per capita (Ikegami, 1991).

In order to understand more completely the reasons for the differences in surgical rates between the U.S. and Japan, we present a case study comparing data derived from the University of Tokyo and Stanford University hospitals' information systems. Our primary purpose in undertaking this research is to investigate the volume and length of surgical operations at the two hospitals, to decompose these differences into their component parts, and eventually to apply this information toward explaining them in terms of social, economic, and practice style differences between the two countries.

This chapter is based upon: Bhattacharya, J., Kupor, S., Vogt, W.B., Woo, A., Slezak, L., Christ, D., Hopkins, D.S.P., Middleton, B., Nishimura, M.Y., Yoshikawa, A., Du, H.L., Ishikawa, K.B., Yamada, Y., Kaihara, S., Kobayashi, H., and Saito, H. 1996. "Surgical Volumes and Operating Room Efficiency in Stanford and Tokyo University Hospitals." *Occasional Paper Series*, Asia/Pacific Research Center, Stanford University. We are grateful for the support of Akira Furuse and Toshiko Nagase.

289

There are a number of important differences in the health care delivery systems between Japan and the U.S. that potentially confound the results of comparative studies. These factors include the substitution of acute hospital care for nursing home care in Japan, variations in hospital ownership structure and financing arrangements, and dissimilarities in disease prevalence (Okimoto and Yoshikawa, 1993). We focus on teaching hospitals in order to control for the effects of some possible confounding influences. Stanford University and the University of Tokyo hospitals occupy similar positions in their respective countries—technology-intensive, tertiary care teaching institutions with reputations for quality medical care delivery and research. Thus, by choosing hospitals that have similar delivery systems and missions, we hope to control for these influences in our results.

In this case study, we analyze case mix-adjusted durations for surgeries in the two hospitals, utilizing patient-specific data. We analyze surgical operations by preoperative time (hereafter preop), operative time, postoperative time (hereafter post-op), and idle time. By looking at the time allocations for similar procedures and across similar patients, we hope to pinpoint the sources of the volume differentials between the two hospitals.

Because in-depth studies of Tokyo and Stanford have been reported elsewhere (Holt, 1993; Holt et al., 1993; Ishikawa et al., 1993), we provide only a brief summary of relevant hospital characteristics. Stanford operating rooms (hereafter OR) can be divided into two categories: There are 20 rooms in the main OR and 8 in the ambulatory surgery center (ASC). As the names suggest, the main ORs serve primarily hospital inpatients, and the ASC serves primarily hospital outpatients, providing same-day surgeries. Tokyo does not perform outpatient surgery in its 13 OR suites and has no significant number of outpatient surgeries elsewhere in the hospital.

Data and Methods

The data utilized in this study are derived from surgical patients at Tokyo and Stanford between January 1, 1993, and June 30, 1993. The data contain descriptions of the room used, the procedures performed, the times that the patient entered and left the OR, the times of the incision and closure, and demographic information for each patient. There were a total of 8,769 patients at Stanford and 2,318 at Tokyo. We compare pre-op, post-op, and operating times at Stanford and Tokyo while adjusting for observed case mix differences.

In 1993, Stanford used an in-house coding system based loosely upon the American Medical Association's CPT codes; Tokyo used the World Health Organization's International Classification of Procedures in Medicine (ICPM) codes. Because the two hospitals use different classification systems to categorize operations and there is no mapping program available from Stanford's in-house system to ICPM codes, we created a unified coding scheme to match procedures between the two institutions. This scheme consists of major subheadings from the ICPM code book, a plan largely organized by organ systems. The unified scheme classifies procedures into considerably fewer detailed categories than do its parent schemes used by the hospitals.

The advantage of this approach is that any given procedure, regardless of how the hospitals record it, will be mapped to the same place in the more aggregated unified scheme. Attempting to define a direct map would have created more distortions because the parent schemes differ along various dimensions of detail in ways that do not naturally nest. The drawback of aggregation is that it ignores details that often contain potentially important information regarding the difficulty of a procedure. However, the aggregated unified scheme maintains the feature of distinguishing broad case mix distinctions.

An important difference between the two hospitals is that Stanford has both ambulatory and main OR facilities. Of the 8,769 Stanford operations, 2,725 (31.1%) were conducted in the ambulatory rooms; Tokyo does not perform ambulatory surgery. Because there is no way to determine which of Tokyo's patients would have been operated on in an outpatient setting at Stanford, we have no way of separating Tokyo's data into categories corresponding to Stanford's main and ambulatory categories. It would not be appropriate to exclude Stanford's ambulatory patients because the corresponding patients are operated upon in an inpatient setting in Tokyo. For example, at Stanford, most cataract surgery is performed in the ASC on an outpatient basis; at Tokyo, such surgery is always performed on an inpatient basis. To exclude Stanford's outpatient cataract surgery from the analysis would likely bias the Stanford figures toward longer operations because more severely ill patients would be included.

In the Stanford main OR, 6,045 procedures were performed from

January to June 1993 (302 operations per room). Over the same period, 2,724 operations were performed in the ASC (341 operations per room). In Tokyo, 2,318 procedures were performed in 12 rooms in the same amount of time (193 operations per room). That Tokyo's surgical volume is just over one-fourth that of Stanford parallels the aggregate difference in volume between the two countries. The Tokyo figures may overstate the number of operations per room, however, because one of its rooms has two operating tables. A comparison of number of patients per table reveals that Stanford performs 313 operations per table, nearly twice Tokyo's 178 operations per table.

The Stanford data are also divided into faculty-performed and community physician-performed operations. Because Stanford gives surgical privileges to nonfaculty practitioners, not all operations involve a large teaching component. In fact, 47% of all Stanford surgeries are performed by nonfaculty practitioners, although only 37% of the main OR operations are performed by nonfaculty. To maintain comparability of the data, we exclude surgeries performed by nonfaculty. After this restriction, there remain 4,612 cases at Stanford to analyze. This division of the Stanford data is justified by reports of important case mix and severity differences between teaching and nonteaching hospitals in general and faculty and nonfaculty practitioners in particular.[1] We need not make this distinction for Tokyo because the closed medical staff system there ensures that only faculty physicians perform operations.

The Tokyo data are partitioned into type I, II, and III patients. Types I and II are both surgeries utilizing general anesthesia, but type I patients are moved from the operating theater to the recovery area within the center. These patients are subsequently moved either to a general ward or the surgical ICU as necessary. In contrast, type II patients remain in the OR and then are moved to the surgical ICU. Type III patients receive local anesthesia only. This distinction is relevant largely for descriptive purposes.

We match data from Stanford and Tokyo by the department that performed the operation. In most cases, it is obvious how departments map from one institution to another. We combine surgical departments to maintain a consistent definition of departments across institutions. In doing so, we guarantee that similar operations will be assigned to the same department regardless of where the surgery takes place.

The principal objects of interest in the study are pre-op, operation, post-op, and idle times. Pre-op time is the time between patient entry into the room and the incision. Operative time measures the interval between incision and closure. Post-op time is the period between closure and patient exit from the OR, to either the recovery room or the ICU. Idle time begins at patient exit from the room and concludes with the entry of the next patient.

In addition to providing evidence about differences in surgical volumes and operation lengths between Japan and the United States, these quantities are of independent interest. For example, such information aids in planning the optimal number of operating rooms in a hospital surgical suite (Hopkins et al., 1982) and in devising an optimal scheduling algorithm (Charnetski, 1984; Weiss, 1990). Furthermore, these quantities can be used to calculate common measures of operating room efficiency (Bridenbaugh, 1979; Hejna and Gutmann, 1984; McQuarrie, 1981).

We report age-, sex-, and case mix-adjusted pre-op, post-op, and operation times for Tokyo and Stanford. Case mix is standardized by age category, gender, and primary procedure. Additionally, three sets of case mix weighting are developed: One constructs weights using only Stanford data, one does so using only Tokyo data, and one combines the two. For each of these alternatives, the full complement of operations is partitioned into age–sex–case cells. The age categories are newborn (one week or less), older than one week but less than 6 years, 6–20 years, 21–40 years, 41–60 years, and older than 60 years. The operations that fall into each cell are counted and divided by the total number of operations. These fractions are then used as weights in calculating the age-, sex-, and case mix-adjusted weighted averages, which are reported in the Results section. Though we calculate these weighted means using all possible permutations of weights, we use the combined weights for overall comparison in the discussion. The absolute value of the time differentials across the different weighting systems is small.

Finally, in order to evaluate the impact of unobserved factors that determine the timing of the sequence of operations, we estimate a joint model of pre-op, post-op, operation, and idle times. Within any given room, the sequence of events that takes place every day is, from the point of view of process analysis, fairly stylized. As shown in Figure 15-1, the sequence consists of a patient entering the room, the surgery and anesthesiology teams preparing for work, the incision, the surgery, the close, and the post-op period, after which the patient is removed from the room. The room is then cleaned and is ready for another patient to enter.

Because the state of the room at the end of the cycle is exactly the

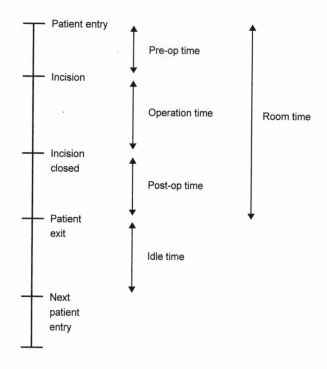

Figure 15-1
Flow Chart of Time Variation

same as it was at the beginning, clean and ready for surgery, it is natural to model the state of the room as a Markov process. We measure the impact of important covariates on the state variables in this process—pre-op, post-op, operation, and idle times—by estimating the following set of simultaneous equations:

$$pre\text{-}op = X_1'\beta_2 + \mu_1 \tag{15-1}$$

$$operation = X_2'\beta_2 + \mu_2 \tag{15-2}$$

$$post\text{-}op = X_3'\beta_3 + \mu_3 \tag{15-3}$$

$$idle = X_4'\beta_4 + \mu_4 \tag{15-4}$$

where μ is i.i.d. with zero mean and variance-covariance matrix $\Sigma, X_1 \dots X_4$ are covariate vectors, and β is a parameter vector to be estimated. Although X_1, X_2, and X_3 contain both patient-specific variables, like age and sex, and sequence-specific variables, such as

Table 15-1
Raw OR Times, Stanford Faculty vs. Tokyo (minutes)

Hospital		Cases	Pre-op (SD)	Operation (SD)	Post-op (SD)
Stanford	All	4612	40.2 (25.8)	122.3 (108.0)	12.6 (30.5)
	Main	3834	42.8 (27.1)	132.1 (113.6)	13.4 (33.3)
	Ambulatory	778	27.3 (11.9)	73.7 (51.4)	8.4 (7.0)
Tokyo	All	2318	52.8 (27.2)	164.5 (161.5)	20.6 (17.1)
	Type I	1369	50.6 (27.4)	170.5 (131.2)	19.9 (14.2)
	Type II	544	60.2 (30.4)	284.8 (245.4)	34.5 (23.3)
	Type III	405	52.7 (23.1)	59.7 (35.0)	11.9 (10.5)

an indicator for first surgery of the day, X_4 contains sequence-specific variables only, because idle time is not associated with any patient in particular. We estimate this system separately for Stanford and Tokyo hospitals using seemingly unrelated regressions. For Stanford, we include both faculty and nonfaculty physician-performed surgeries in the analysis, but we include controls for teaching status of the surgeon in the covariate vector X_2.

Results

Raw OR times for Stanford faculty physicians and all Tokyo physicians are presented in Table 15-1. Average operation time is 122 minutes at Stanford and 165 minutes at Tokyo ($p < 0.001$). Mean nonoperation in-room time is 53 minutes at Stanford and 73 minutes at Tokyo ($p < 0.001$). Raw pre-op and post-op times differ by 13 ($p < 0.001$) and 8 ($p < 0.001$) minutes respectively between the two institutions. Our principal purpose in the remainder of the chapter is to determine the contributions of case mix, patient demographics, and scheduling in explaining these differences.

Figure 15-2 presents summary demographic data showing that Tokyo has an older patient population than does Stanford. The proportion of men and women also differs between the two hospitals. Stanford's patients are 46.8% men, and Tokyo has 53.9% men. These differences notwithstanding, our ability to analyze the data at the level of the individual patient allows us to control for the case mix differentials.

In Figure 15-3, we highlight variations in the number of procedures performed per operative session between Stanford and Tokyo. As the figure demonstrates, Stanford physicians perform substantially more procedures per operation. Stanford does not record more than four procedures, so the actual difference in the

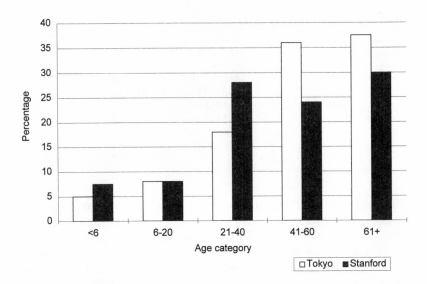

Figure 15-2
Age Structure

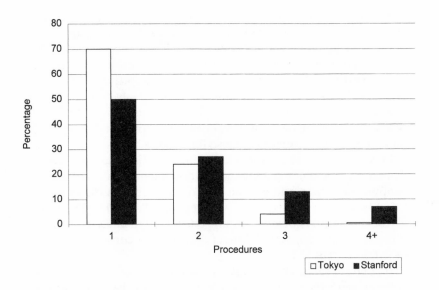

Figure 15-3
Procedures per Operative Session

Table 15-2
Twenty Most Frequently Performed Procedures

Stanford Main	Cases	Tokyo	Cases
Exploration of bowel	299	Insertion of prosthetic lens	229
Cytoscopy	255	Other cataract extraction	202
Inguinal hernia repair	181	Facilitation of intraocular	
Open skull exploration	175	circulation	113
Insertion of vein catheter	136	Craniotomy	74
Laminectomy	124	Myringoplasty	60
Diagnostic pelvic laparoscopy	119	Repair of inguinofemoral hernia	52
CABG, single vein	114	Cholecystectomy	52
Total hip procedure	114	Other retina repair operations	46
Removal of orthopedic hardware	114	Other free skin grafts	44
Breast biopsy incisional	114	Other scleral buckling	44
Discectomy	112	Scleroplasty	44
Appendectomy	111	Partial gastrectomy	40
Pelvic lymphadenectomy	105	Vitreous operations	36
Skin tissue procedure	102	Classical cesarean section	35
Diagnostic bronchoscopy	99	Other larynx and trachea	
Radical prostatectomy	96	operations	33
Endoscopic cholecystectomy	96	Extracapsular extraction of lens	33
Abdominal surgery, unspecified	95	Replacement of heart valve	32
Laser prostatectomy	93	Other nasal sinus operations	32
		Partial excision of large intestine	30
		Regional lymph node excision	28

number of procedures is even greater than the one we present. Our subsequent results present time per operative session, not by procedure, because procedure time is not recorded. Clearly, operation time per session overstates Stanford's time per procedure more so than does it Tokyo's.

Table 15-2 lists the 20 most frequently performed procedures at Tokyo and in the Stanford main OR. The top three Tokyo procedures are cataract-related, and eight of the top 20 operations are ophthalmic. Cataract surgeries are performed, for the most part, at Stanford's ASC, on an outpatient basis.

We present pre-op, post-op, and operation times by department for the main center and the ambulatory surgery center in Table 15-3. The table shows that the operations performed in the ambulatory surgical suites are without exception shorter, on average, than their main OR counterparts. In addition, the pre-op and post-op times are considerably shorter in the ASC. This pattern reflects the case mix differences between the two centers, with the ASC specializing in shorter, outpatient surgeries.

Table 15-3
Stanford Faculty OR Times, Main and Ambulatory (minutes)

Department	Main			Ambulatory		
	Pre-op	Operation	Post-op	Pre-op	Operation	Post-op
General	34.1	131.7	10.8	21.9	63.8	6.9
Neurosurgery	60.4	163.8	15.2	N/A	N/A	N/A
Cardiac/thoracic	58.4	163.3	12.7	N/A	N/A	N/A
Orthopedic	45.6	136.6	17.4	28.0	83.9	9.7
Ob/gyn	37.1	139.6	12.6	26.6	78.8	8.8
Ophthalmic	29.4	103.3	8.9	25.4	56.3	6.2
Urology	33.9	111.9	10.5	24.5	57.4	5.6
Ear/nose/throat	30.0	136.0	18.8	19.6	58.2	12.4
Plastic/reconstructive	38.9	112.2	12.9	32.2	84.5	8.4
Gen. pediatric surgery	31.5	67.7	13.3	N/A	N/A	N/A
Others	35.1	69.0	10.4	31.5	94.1	8.5

Table 15-4
Tokyo OR Times (minutes)

Department	Pre-op	Operation	Post-op
General	54.4	222.1	25.2
Neurosurgery	61.5	252.6	32.9
Cardiac/thoracic	77.3	355.8	30.4
Orthopedic	70.9	224.8	27.9
Ob/gyn	49.0	135.1	20.1
Ophthalmic	54.8	68.0	12.0
Urology	59.3	156.8	25.8
Ear/nose/throat	37.3	132.8	16.5
Plastic/reconstructive	45.2	188.8	19.1
Pediatric	32.3	85.5	16.2
Oral	38.3	170.5	16.4
Others	66.7	141.6	20.7

In Table 15-4, pre-op, post-op, and operation times are presented for Tokyo by department. For most of the departments, Stanford surgeries have shorter times, even if one focuses only upon the Stanford main OR. For example, operative time for general surgery at Stanford is 131.7 minutes; at Tokyo, it is 222 minutes ($p < 0.001$). However, Tokyo is speedier in some departments, such as ophthalmic surgery. Stanford physicians complete an average operation in 103.3 minutes, and Tokyo physicians take 68 minutes ($p < 0.001$).

Table 15-5
Stanford Faculty Case-mix Adjusted Averages (minutes)

Patients	Pre-op (SD)	Operative (SD)	Post-op (SD)
All	34.3 (26.7)	100.8 (91.2)	10.7 (25.3)
Main	36.0 (27.9)	114.8 (92.5)	12.0 (30.6)
Ambulatory	21.8 (11.1)	52.0 (38.1)	6.4 (5.6)

Table 15-6
Tokyo Case-mix Adjusted Averages (minutes)

Patients	Pre-op (SD)	Operative (SD)	Post-op (SD)
All	46.1 (22.1)	142.4 (102.3)	19.7 (16.9)
Type I	43.3 (20.1)	175.1 (120.1)	21.0 (14.8)
Type II	53.2 (26.8)	280.3 (190.2)	35.4 (22.4)
Type III	41.7 (19.9)	50.3 (22.6)	11.2 (9.9)

These patterns hold for the pre- and postoperative times as well and are likely to reflect case mix differences.

The two institutions are similar in the distribution of times within the operative episode. Stanford spends 27.5% of the total in-room time on pre-op, 63.3% on the operation, and 9.2% on post-op. Similarly, Tokyo spends 29.0% ($p < 0.001$), 60.6% ($p < 0.001$), and 10.4% ($p < 0.001$), respectively. Although these differences are significant, their magnitudes are small. These similarities show that the time differences between Stanford and Tokyo are not concentrated in any particular part of the in-room time, but are rather diffused through all three of the relevant intervals.

In Tables 15-5 and 15-6, the case mix-adjusted times are shown for Stanford and Tokyo. These tables report utilization time adjusted for procedure, gender, and age. After these adjustments, the differences in pre-op, post-op, and operation times remain. Tokyo utilizes 11.8 ($p < 0.001$), 9.0 ($p < 0.001$), and 41.6 ($p < 0.001$) more minutes in pre-op, post-op, and operation times per operative session. From these tables, we can see that crude case mix cannot account for all the differences we observed earlier in operative times.

In Table 15-7, we present operative session times for a number of frequently performed procedures coded by the unified scheme at the two institutions. These figures further bear out the differences

Table 15-7
Stanford Faculty, Tokyo Procedure Results (minutes)

Procedure	Stanford			Tokyo		
	Pre-op	Operative	Post-op	Pre-op	Operative	Post-op
Endoscopy	29.29	76.09	10.02	43.35	92.95	18.05
Brain, nerve, and skull	52.80	162.55	15.06	61.36	266.36	31.77
Endocrine operations	33.40	125.50	10.58	44.09	221.09	21.26
Eye operations	26.82	70.54	7.20	54.66	65.02	11.88
Ear operations	24.14	90.98	28.15	41.03	147.39	14.03
Nose, mouth, and pharynx	29.11	87.41	11.86	41.04	128.13	15.73
Respiratory system	45.27	152.82	14.14	34.61	146.33	22.76
Cardiovascular system	60.94	175.41	13.31	71.01	316.68	26.16
Digestive tract	29.89	96.62	10.17	49.57	203.60	23.95
Urinary tract	37.26	138.02	11.06	58.87	169.02	29.44
Male genital organ	34.84	128.05	11.17	48.78	90.80	15.15
Female genital organ	37.26	105.02	10.44	53.15	151.34	20.75
Musculoskeletal	37.30	96.01	10.98	66.44	221.91	26.13
Breast operations	30.21	139.68	13.34	47.24	190.41	21.41
Skin and subcutaneous	34.98	99.13	11.78	51.97	163.85	19.06

Note: A procedure is included if both Tokyo and Stanford perform at least 20.

noted previously. In most cases, Stanford exhibits shorter times during an operative session than does Tokyo, and these differences are diffused throughout the operative session.

Tables 15-8 and 15-9 report the distribution of idle times and room utilization by day of the week at Stanford and Tokyo. In Table 15-8, it is apparent that Stanford has greater average idle time between patients. This phenomenon is explained by two factors, both related to scheduling. First, there are many more cancellations at Stanford, approximately 2-4 per day; there are only 50 cancellations over the entire sample period at Tokyo. Second, physicians at Stanford are able to reserve specific times and rooms for their patients, and the OR department must schedule around these "physician demand times." This causes rigidity in the schedule, especially when the demanded times are incompatible with normal scheduling.

The utilization figures in Table 15-9 are based upon a 24-hour day because no objective measure of hours of operation could be developed for purposes of comparison. Utilization figures are remarkably consistent across the two institutions, with both Stanford and Tokyo using their ORs on average 23% of the day on weekdays, though Stanford has a slightly higher utilization rate.

Table 15-8
Stanford, Tokyo Idle Time (minutes)

Day	Stanford (SD)	Tokyo (SD)
Monday	54.75 (6.77)	52.50 (36.56)
Tuesday	57.38 (4.55)	28.17 (11.85)
Wednesday	52.01 (4.40)	46.49 (27.68)
Thursday	49.12 (3.06)	47.48 (27.77)
Friday	63.31 (6.26)	26.18 (8.88)

Note: This excludes the time from the last patient of the day until the first patient the next morning.

Table 15-9
Stanford, Tokyo Room Utilization

Day	Stanford %24 hours (SD)	Tokyo %24 hours (SD)
Monday	20.18% (0.058)	25.49% (0.061)
Tuesday	25.92% (0.031)	24.95% (0.047)
Wednesday	25.10% (0.027)	24.24% (0.067)
Thursday	25.15% (0.033)	17.51% (0.055)
Friday	21.02% (0.048)	24.00% (0.070)
Weekday total	23.45% (0.047)	23.28% (0.066)

This difference is not significant ($p = 0.815$). Also interesting is the pattern over the days of the week. At Stanford, Monday and Friday show lower utilization, probably explained by the incidence of both official and personal holidays adjacent to weekends. In Japan, official holidays do not fall preferentially on Mondays and Fridays.

Table 15-10 reports the parameter estimates for the joint model of pre-op, operation, post-op, and idle time equations for both Stanford and Tokyo. A positive coefficient in particular implies that an increase in the associated variable increases the predicted time for that equation. An interesting result, which is true for both Stanford and Tokyo, is that the first and last case of the day, holding all else constant, tend to have longer pre-op, post-op, and operation times. One possible explanation for this is that difficult cases are scheduled for the beginning and end of the day. For Tokyo, operation times are increasing with patient age, at the mean value of that variable; the opposite is true at Stanford, though no age coefficient

Table 15-10
Parameter Estimates

Equation	Variable	Tokyo Estimate	Stanford Estimate
Pre-op	Constant	37.60†	18.16†
	Age	−0.045	0.087**
	Age^2	0.002	−5.2 × 10$^{-5\dagger}$
	Female	−0.38	2.10†
	Emergency	−1.92	−2.36**
	First Case of Day	17.28†	9.23†
	Last Case of Day	14.82†	4.55†
	Only Case of Day	0.94	4.51†
	Faculty Operation	N/A	11.36†
	Type I	−6.55	N/A
	Type II	9.89**	N/A
Operation	Constant	163.69†	6.32†
	Age	2.85†	0.023
	Age^2	−0.029†	−1.1 × 10^{-4}
	Female	−15.47†	−0.27
	Emergency	−104.25†	1.25
	First Case of Day	22.77†	0.92
	Last Case of Day	49.26†	0.80
	Only Case of Day	107.91†	2.18*
	Faculty Operation	N/A	3.22†
	Type I	−86.39†	N/A
	Type II	−148.79†	N/A
	Department Indicators	Yes	Yes
Post-op	Constant	15.71**	8.72**
	Age	0.12	1.54†
	Age^2	−0.0004	−0.013†
	Female	−3.83	6.91†
	Emergency	16.27†	−0.12
	First Case of Day	4.54	35.16†
	Last Case of Day	11.11†	26.75†
	Only Case of Day	0.58	58.04†
	Faculty Operation	N/A	44.32†
	Type I	−7.13*	N/A
	Type II	−7.53	N/A
Idle time	Constant	84.79*	61.95†
	Last Case of Day	2241.64†	1661.03†
	Only Case of Day	−324.91†	99.68**
	Weekend	16.98	−7.50
	Friday	−109.35	−59.30

* denotes significance at the 10% level.
** denotes significance at the 5% level.
† denotes significance at the 1% level.

Table 15-11
Residual Covariance Matrices, Tokyo and Stanford

Equation	Pre-op Time	Operation Time	Post-op Time	Idle Time
Tokyo				
Pre-op time	1	—	—	—
Operation time	0.037	1	—	—
Post-op time	0.364	0.056	1	—
Idle time	−0.048	−0.008	−0.057	1
Stanford				
Pre-op time	1	—	—	—
Operation time	0.092	1	—	—
Post-op time	0.906	−0.055	1	—
Idle time	−0.026	−0.089	−0.013	1

attains statistical significance. At Stanford, faculty-performed operations take longer than those performed by nonfaculty.

Perhaps even more interesting is the estimate of Σ, the correlation of the error terms, ε, across the four equations, shown in Table 15-11. Because ε consists of patient-specific and room-specific unobserved factors that influence pre-op, operation, post-op, and idle times, we can glean some information about the influence of, for example, unobserved severity on the previous results. As might be expected, the errors in the pre-op, post-op, and operation time equations are all positively correlated. This is consistent with our interpretation of these errors; a patient who, for some unobserved reason, has a high pre-op time is also likely to have a high post-op and operation time. Furthermore, a patient who spends a long total time in the operating room is likely to be followed with a quick room turnaround time. These conclusions hold for both Tokyo and Stanford.

Discussion

When case mix is adjusted for, Tokyo's total in-room times are 142.8% those of Stanford. The time differential is driven largely by the operating time, accounting for 67% of the 62.4-minute difference in total in-room time. Furthermore, our data underestimate the procedure-specific time differential because Stanford patients more often undergo multiple procedures per operative episode. That is, because nearly one-half of the Stanford patients undergo more than one procedure in a single operative session (compared with one-fourth of the Tokyo patients), the surgical time difference per procedure is greater than our analysis reveals.

Given that the operation time differential explains a large part of the total in-room time difference, the pre- and post-op differences become less important. For example, suppose that Tokyo's case mix-adjusted average pre-op and post-op times could be instantly reduced to Stanford levels while maintaining the same average operation time as before. In this hypothetical scenario, Tokyo's total in-room time would decrease by only 10%. Operative times constitute the largest component of the overall difference in in-room times between Tokyo and Stanford because of their large contribution to the level of in-room time in both places.

Tokyo's smaller recovery area may contribute to the higher in-room time by increasing the post-op time. With an adjusted differential of 9 minutes post-op time, relative to the total in-room time differential of 62.4 minutes, a 9-minute change in post-op time would decrease the case mix-adjusted differential by 14.4%.

One of Tokyo's strengths is its shorter idle time. On average, there are about 55 minutes of idle time between operations at Stanford, compared to only about 40 minutes at Tokyo. This difference is likely due to the variations in scheduling environment between the two institutions. Stanford's experience of more cancellations and more scheduling rigidity likely leads to greater idle time. The fact that unobserved determinants of idle time are negatively correlated with the total in-room time of the previous patient is also explained by scheduling regimes. For example, if a patient's surgery overruns the time allotted to it, the idle time until the next patient is brought into the room is likely to be lower than average if the scheduling system makes changing the operating room difficult.

Conclusions

By comparing surgical time differentials at Stanford and Tokyo aggregated by both procedure and surgical department, we find that the average Tokyo total in-room time exceeds that at Stanford by nearly one hour per case. The major driving force behind the time differential appears to be the operation time, with pre-op and post-op times contributing 33% of the difference. Finding that case mix, staffing inputs, and scheduling are not the most significant causes of the time gap, we conclude that the difference in volume is due to lower room utilization rates and longer in-room times. The longer times could be due to practice style differences, unobserved case mix differences, or differences in teaching technique. Our data do not provide the opportunity to pinpoint specifically what the various practice patterns are; future research at the level of procedure-specific case studies, however, should be aimed at exploring the detailed facts surrounding these differences.

Note

[1] For differences between teaching and nonteaching hospitals in general, see Frick, Martin, and Shwartz (1985), Sloan and Valvona (1986), Iezzoni et al. (1990), Association of American Medical Colleges (1985), and Goldfarb and Coffey (1987). For differences between faculty and non-faculty practitioners at Stanford, see Garber, Fuchs, and Silverman (1984).

Bibliography

Adams, E.K., Houchens, R., Wright, G.E., and Robbins, J. 1991. "Predicting Hospital Choice for Rural Medicare Beneficiaries: The Role of Severity of Illness." *Health Services Research* 26(5): 583–612.

Al-Haider, A.S., and Wan, T. 1991. "Modeling Organizational Determinants of Hospital Mortality." *Health Services Research* 26(3): 303–323.

Amemiya, T. 1985. *Advanced Econometrics.* Cambridge, MA: Harvard University Press; Oxford: Blackwell.

American College of Physicians. 1994. "Magnetic Resonance Imaging of the Brain and Spine: A Revised Statement." *Annals of Internal Medicine* 120(10): 872–875.

American Hospital Association. 1986. *AHA Hospital Statistics.* Chicago: American Hospital Association.

Anderson, O. 1991."Occupational Impacts on Mortality Declines in the Nordic Countries." In *Future Demographic Trends in Europe and North America,* ed. W. Lutz. New York: Academic Press/Harcourt-Brace-Jovanovich.

Aoki, K., and Urushi, H. 1994. "Data Envelopment Analysis and Technical Efficiency: An Application to Public and Private Hospitals in Japan." *Sophia Economic Review,* forthcoming.

Aoki, K., Bhattacharya, J., Vogt, W.B., Yoshikawa, A., and Nakahara, T. 1995. "Measuring Technical Efficiencies of Japanese General Hospitals: DEA Analysis of Public vs. Private Hospitals." *mimeo,* Stanford University.

Aoki, K., Bhattacharya, J., Vogt, W.B., Yoshikawa, A., and Nakahara, T. 1995. "The Relationship Between Functional Differentiation and Competition: Existence and Interpretations." *mimeo,* Stanford University.

Aoki, M. 1988. *Information, Incentives, and Bargaining in the Japanese Economy.* Cambridge, England: Cambridge University Press.

Aoki, M. 1979. *Bunpai no Riron (Theory of Distribution).* Tokyo: Chikuma Shobo.

Araki, K. 1993. "Understanding Japanese Health Care Expenditures." In *Japan's Health System: Efficiency and Effectiveness in Universal Care,* ed. D. Okimoto and A. Yoshikawa. New York: Faulkner & Gray.

Association of American Medical Colleges. 1985. *Medicare Prospective Payment and the American Health Care System.* Washington, DC: Association of American Medical Colleges.

Atkinson, S., and Halvorsen, R. 1984. "Parametric Efficiency Tests, Economies of Scale and Demand in U.S. Electric Power Generation." *International Economic Review* 25(3): 647–662.

307

Bautz, J.B., Schectman, J.M., Elinsky, E.G., and Pawlson, L.G. 1992. "Magnetic Resonance Imaging: Diffusion of Technology in an Ambulatory Setting." *International Journal of Technology Assessment in Health Care* 8(2): 301–308.

Becker, E., and Sloan, F. 1985. "Hospital Ownership and Performance." *Economic Inquiry* 23(1): 21–36.

Benham, L., Maurizi, A., and Reder, M.W. 1968. "Migration, Location and Remuneration of Medical Personnel: Physicians and Dentists." *Review of Economics and Statistics* 50(3): 332–347.

Benton, W. 1991. "Safety Stock and Service Levels in Periodic Review Inventory Systems." *Journal of the Operational Research Society* 42(4): 1087–1095.

Berndt, E.R., and Khalad, M.S. 1979. "Parametric Productivity Measurement and Choice Among Flexible Functional Forms." *Journal of Political Economy* 87(6): 1220–1245.

Berry, S.T. 1994. "Estimating Discrete-choice Models of Product Differentiation." *Rand Journal of Economics* 25(2): 242–262.

Bhattacharya, J., Vogt, W.B., Yoshikawa, A., and Nakahara, T. 1996. "Outpatient Medical Demand in Japan." *Journal of Human Resources* 31(2).

Bhattacharya, J., Vogt, W.B., Yoshikawa, A., Nakahara, T. 1995. "In-Hospital Mortality." *Mimeo*, Stanford University.

Bhattacharya, J., Kupor, S., Vogt, W., Woo, A., Slezak, L., Christ, D., Hopkins, D.S.P., Middleton, B., Nishimura, M.Y., Yoshikawa, A., Du, H., Ishikawa, K., Yamada, Y., Kaihara, S., Kobayashi, H., and Saito, H. 1996. "Surgical Volumes and Operating Room Efficiency in Stanford and Tokyo University Hospitals." *Occasional Paper Series*, Asia/Pacific Research Center, Stanford University.

Blumberg, M. 1986. "Comments on HCFA Hospital Death Rate Statistical Outliers." *Health Services Research* 21(6): 715–739.

Bombardier, C., Fuchs, V.R., Lillard, L.A., and Warner, K.E. 1977. "Socioeconomic Factors Affecting the Utilization of Surgical Operations." *New England Journal of Medicine* 297(29): 699–705.

Bonnano, G. 1987. "Location Choice, Product Proliferation and Entry Deterrence." *Review of Economic Studies* 54: 37–45.

Boutwell, R.C., and Mitchell, J.B. 1993. "Diffusion of New Technologies in the Treatment of the Medicare Population." *International Journal of Technology Assessment in Health Care* 9(1): 62–75.

Bridenbaugh, L.D. 1979. "Operating-room Utilization and the Care of the Surgical Patient." *Bulletin of the American College of Surgeons* 64: 11–14.

Bunker, J.P and Brown Jr., B.W. 1974. "The Physician-patient as an Informed Consumer of Surgical Services." *New England Journal of Medicine* 290(19): 1051–1055.

Burns, L.R., and Wholey, D.R. 1992. "The Impact of Physician Characteristics in Conditional Choice Models for Hospitals." *Journal of Health Economics* 11(1): 43–62.

Callthorp, J. 1989. "The Swedish Model Under Pressure—How to Maintain Equity and Develop Quality?" *Quality Assurance in Health Care* 1(1): 13–22.

Caves, D.W., Christensen, L.R., and Swanson, J.A. 1981. "Productive Growth, Scale Economies, and Capacity Utilization in U.S. Railroads, 1955–74." *American Economic Review* 71(5): 994–1002.

Charnetski, J.R. 1984. "Scheduling Operating Room Surgical Procedures with Early and Late Completion Penalty Costs." *Journal of Operations Management* 5: 91–102.

Cherkin, D., Grothaus, L., and Wagner, E.H. 1992. "Is Magnitude of Copayment

Effect Related to Income? Using Census Data for Health Services Research." *Social Science and Medicine* 34(1): 33-41.

Cherkin, D.C., Grothaus, L.G., and Wagner, E.H. 1990. "The Effect of Office Visit Copayments on Preventive Care Services in a Health Maintenance Organization." *Inquiry* 27(1): 24-38.

Cherkin, D.C., Grothaus, L.G., and Wagner, E.H. 1989. "The Effect of Office Visit Copayments on Utilization in a Health Maintenance Organization." *Medical Care* 27(7): 669-679.

Chiho Koeikigyo Keiei Kenkyukai, ed. 1994. *Chiho Koei Kigyo Nenkan (Annual Report of Regional Public Corporations)*. Tokyo: Chiho Zaimu Kyokai.

Chuo Shakai Hoken Iryo Kyogikai. 1991. *Iryo Keizai Jittai Chosa (Financial Status of Hospitals)*. Tokyo: Ministry of Health and Welfare.

Conrad, R.F., and Strauss, R.P. 1983. "A Multiple-Output Multiple-Input Model of the Hospital Industry in North Carolina." *Applied Economics* 15(3): 341-352.

Cowing, T., and Holtman, A. 1983. "Multiproduct Short-run Hospital Cost Functions: Empirical Evidence and Policy Implications from Cross-Section Data." *Southern Economic Journal* 49(3): 637-653.

Cravens, D.W. 1991. *Strategic Marketing*, 3rd ed. Homewood, IL: Richard D. Irwin.

Dayhoff, D.A., and Cromwell, J. 1993. "Measuring Differences and Similarities in Hospital Caseloads: A Conceptual and Empirical Analysis." *Health Service Research* 28(3): 293-312.

Deaton, A.S., and Muelbauer, J. 1980. *Economics and Consumer Behavior*. Cambridge, UK: Cambridge University Press.

Debreu, G. 1951. "The Coefficient of Resource Utilization." *Econometrica* 19(3): 273-292.

Diewert, W.E., and Wales, T.J. 1987. "Flexible Functional Forms and Global Curvature Conditions." *Econometrica* 55(1): 43-68.

Dionne, G., Langlois, A., and Lemire, N. 1987. "More on the Geographical Distribution of Physicians." *Journal of Health Economics* 6(4): 365-374.

Dixit, A.K., and Stiglitz, J.E. 1977. "Monopolistic Competition and Optimum Product Diversity." *American Economic Review* 67 (June): 297-308.

Donabedian, A.D. 1987. "Commentary on Some Studies of the Quality of Care." *Health Care Financing Review*, Annual Supplement: 75-85.

Doughty, A., Nash, S.I., and Gift, D.A. 1992. "Deployment and Utilization of MR Imaging in Michigan: Observations of a Statewide Data Base." *Radiology* 185(1): 53-61.

Dranove, D., Shanley, M., and Simon, C. 1992. "Is Hospital Competition Wasteful?" *RAND Journal of Economics* 23(2): 247-263.

Dranove, D., and Wehner, P. 1994. "Physician-Induced Demand for Childbirths." *Journal of Health Economics* 13(1): 61-73.

Dranove, D., and White, W.D. 1987. "Agency and the Organization of Health Care Delivery." *Inquiry* 24(4): 405-415.

Dranove, D., White, W., and Wu, L. 1993. "Segmentation in Local Hospital Markets." *Medical Care* 31(1): 52-64.

DuBois, R., Rogers, W., Moxley, J., III, Draper, D., and Brook, R. 1987. "Hospital Inpatient Mortality: Is It a Predictor of Quality?" *New England Journal of Medicine* 317(26): 1674-1680.

Duffy, S.Q. 1992. "Do Competitive Hospitals Really Adopt Technology Faster: An Analysis of the Influence of Alternative Relevant Market Definitions." *Eastern Economic Journal* 18(2): 187-208.

Dugum, C. 1990. "On the Relationship between Income Inequality Measures and Social Welfare Functions." *Journal of Econometrics* 43(1-2): 91–102.

Eakin, B.K., and Kniesner, T.J. 1988. "Estimating a Non-Minimum Cost Function for Hospitals." *Southern Economic Journal* 54(3): 583–597.

Economic Planning Agency. 1990. *Kenmin Keizai Keisan Nenpo (Calculation of Prefectural Economy)*. Tokyo: Economic Planning Agency.

Economides, N. 1986. "Minimal and Maximal Product Differentiation in Hoteling's Duopoly." *Economic Letters* 21(1): 67–71.

Efron, B. 1979. "Computers and the Theory of Statistics: Thinking the Unthinkable." *SIAM Review* 21: 460–480.

Eisenberg, R.L. 1988. *Diagnostic Imaging: An Algorithmic Approach*. Philadelphia: Lippincott.

Eisenberg, J.M., Schwartz, J.S., McCaslin, F.C., Kaufman, R., Glick, H., and Kroch, E. 1989. "Substituting Diagnostic Services: New Tests Only Partly Replace Older Ones." *JAMA* 262(9): 1196–1200.

Elzinga, K.G., and Hogarty, T.F. 1973. "The Problem of Geographic Market Delineation in Antimerger Suits." *Antitrust Bulletin* 18(1): 45–81.

Erikson, G.M., and Finkler, S.A. 1985. "Determinants of Market Share for a Hospital's Services." *Medical Care* 23: 1003–1018.

Escarce, J.J. 1993. "Would Eliminating Differences in Physician Practice Style Reduce Geographic Variation in Cataract Surgery Rates?" *Medical Care* 31(12): 1106–1118.

Evans, R.G., and Evans, R.G. Jr. 1991. "Analysis of Economics and Use of MR Imaging Units in the United States in 1990." *American Journal of Radiology* 157: 603–607.

Farley, D.E. 1989. "Measuring Case-mix Specialization and the Concentration of Diagnoses in Hospitals Using Information Theory." *Journal of Health Economics* 8(2): 185–207.

Farley, D.E., and Hogan, C. 1990. "Case-mix Specialization in the Market for Hospital Services." *Health Service Research* 25(5): 757–782.

Farrell, M.J. 1957. "The Measurement of Productive Efficiency." *Journal of the Royal Statistical Society*, Series A, General 120(3): 253–281.

Feigenbaum, E. 1985. *Magnetic Resonance Imaging*. National Center for Health Services Research and Health Care Technology Assessment Report 13.

Feldman, R. 1979. "A Model of Physician Location and Pricing Behavior." *Research in Health Economics* 1: 185–215.

Fink, A., Yano, E., and Brook, R. 1989. "The Condition of the Literature on Differences in Hospital Mortality." *Medical Care* 27(4): 315–336.

Fizel, J.L., and Nunnikhoven, T.S. 1992. "Technical Efficiency of For-profit and Non-profit Nursing Homes." *Managerial and Decision Economics* 13(5): 429–439.

Flanders, W.D., Shipp, C.C., FitzGerald, D.M., and Lin, L.S. 1994. "Analysis of Variations in Mortality Rates with Small Numbers." *Health Services Research* 29(4): 461–471.

Flood, A.B., Scott, W.R., and Ewy, W. 1984. "Does Practice Make Perfect? Part I and II." *Medical Care* 22(2): 98–114 and 115–124.

Folland, S.T. 1983. "Predicting Hospital Market Shares." *Inquiry* 20: 34–44.

Fournier, G.M., and Mitchell, J.M. 1992. "Hospital Costs and Competition for Services: A Multiproduct Analysis." *Review of Economics and Statistics* 74(4): 627–634.

Frank, R. 1985. "Pricing and Location of Physician Services in Mental Health." *Economic Inquiry* 23(1): 115–133.

Frick, A.P., Martin, S.G., and Shwartz, M. 1985. "Case-mix and Cost Differences Between Teaching and Nonteaching Hospitals." *Medical Care* 23: 283–295.

Fuchs, V.R. 1986. *The Health Economy*. Cambridge, MA: Harvard University Press.

Fuchs, V. 1978. "The Supply of Surgeons and the Demand for Operations." *Journal of Human Resources* 13(Suppl): 35–56.

Gabszewicz, J., and Thisse, J.F. 1979. "Price Competition, Quality and Income Disparities." *Journal of Economic Theory* 20(3): 340–359.

Garber, A.M., Fuchs, V.R., and Silverman, J.F. 1984. "Case-mix, Costs, and Outcomes: Differences Between Faculty and Community Services in a University Hospital." *New England Journal of Medicine* 310(19): 1231–1237.

Garber, A.M., and MacCurdy, T.E. 1993. "Nursing Home Discharges and Exhaustion of Medicare Benefits." *Journal of the American Statistical Association* 88(423): 727–736.

Garnick, D.W., Lichtenberg, E.L., Phibbs, C.S., Luft, H.S., Peltzman, D.J., and McPhee, S.J. 1989. "The Sensitivity of Conditional Choice Models for Hospital Care to Estimation Technique." *Journal of Health Economics* 8(4): 377–397.

Goldfarb, M.G., and Coffey, R.M. 1987. "Case-mix Differences Between Teaching and Nonteaching Hospitals." *Inquiry* 24: 68–84.

Granneman, T., Brown, R., and Pauly, M. 1986. "Estimating Hospital Costs: A Multiple-output Approach." *Journal of Health Economics* 5(2): 107–127.

Greene, W.H. 1993. *Econometric Analysis*. New York: Macmillan.

Grosskopf, S., Magaritis, D., and Valdmanis, V. 1990. "Nurse Productivity and Wages." *New Zealand Economic Papers* 24(1): 73–86.

Grosskopf, S., and Valdmanis, V. 1987. "Measuring Hospital Performance: A Nonparametric Approach." *Journal of Health Economics* 6(2): 89–107.

Halliday, M.L., and Leriche, W.H. 1987. "Regional Variation in Surgical Rates, Alberta, 1978, and the Relationship to Characteristics of Patients, Doctors Performing Surgeries, and Hospitals Where the Surgery Was Performed." *Canadian Journal of Public Health* 78(3): 193–200.

Hama, R. 1994. "Kokusai Yakka Hikaku no Igi to Nippon no Yakka no Mondaiten" (International Comparison of Pharmaceutical Price and Problems in Pharmaceutical Prices in Japan). *Osaka Hoken-i Zasshi* 22(12): 7–13.

Harris, J. 1977. "The Internal Organization of Hospitals: Some Economic Implications." *Bell Journal of Economics* 8(2): 467–482.

Hartz, A., Krakauer, H., Kuhn, E., Young, M., Jacobsen, S., Gay, G., Muenz, L., Katzoff, M., Bailey, R., and Rimm, A. 1989. "Hospital Characteristics and Mortality Rates." *New England Journal of Medicine* 321(25): 1720–1725.

Health and Welfare Statistics Association. 1991. *Hoken to Nenkin no Doko* (*Trends in Health Insurance and Pensions*). Tokyo: Health and Welfare Statistics Association.

Health Care Financing Administration (HCFA). 1989. *Medicare Hospital Mortality Information*. Washington, D.C.: U.S. Department of Health and Human Services.

Hejna, W.F., and Gutmann, C.M. 1984. *Management of Surgical Facilities*. Rockville, MD: Aspen Systems Corporation.

Hillman, B.J., Neu, C.R., Winkler, J.D., Aroesty, J., Rettig, R.A., Williams, A.P. 1987. "The Diffusion of Magnetic Resonance Imaging Scanners in a Changing U.S. Health Care Environment." *International Journal of Technology Assessment in Health Care* 3(4): 545–559.

Hisashige, A. 1994. "The Introduction and Evaluation of MRI in Japan." *International Journal of Technology Assessment in Health Care* 10(3): 392–405.

Holt, M. 1993. *Differences in the Cost of Surgery Between the U.S. and Japan: A Comparison of Patients Undergoing Laparoscopic Cholecystectomy at Stanford University Hospital and the University of Tokyo Hospital.* Master Thesis, Stanford University, Department of Health, Research, and Policy.

Holt, M., Ishikawa, K.B., Kaihara, S., Yoshikawa, A., Hopkins, D.S.P., Mason, M., and Shimizu, M. 1993. *Medical Ivory Towers and the High Cost of Health Care: A Comparison of Teaching Hospitals in the United States and Japan.* Stanford, CA: Asia/Pacific Research Center.

Hopkins, D.S.P., Gerson, A., Levin, P.J., and Merchant, R.S. 1982. "A Model for Optimizing the Number of Operating Rooms in a Hospital Surgical Suite." *Health Care Management Review* 7: 49–64.

Horn, S.D., and Schumacher, D.N. 1979. "An Analysis of Case-mix Complexity Using Information Theory and Diagnosis Related Groupings." *Medical Care* 17(4): 382–389.

Hughes, R.G., Hunt, S.S., and Luft, H.S. 1987. "Effects of Surgeon Volume and Hospital Volume on Quality of Care in Hospitals." *Medical Care* 25(6): 489–503.

Iezzoni, L., Herren, T., Foley, S., Daley, J., Hughes, J., and Coffman, G. 1994. "Chronic Conditions and Risk of In-Hospital Death." *Health Services Research* 29(4): 435–460.

Iezzoni, L.I., Shwartz, M., Moskowitz, M.A., Ash, A.S., Sawitz, E., and Burnside, S. 1990 "Illness Severity and Costs of Admissions at Teaching and Nonteaching Hospitals." *JAMA* 264: 1426–31.

Ikegami, N. 1991. "Japanese Health Care: Low Cost Through Regulated Fees." *Health Affairs* 10: 87–109.

Iglehart, J.K. 1988. "Health Policy Report: Japan's Medical Care System—Part Two." *New England Journal of Medicine* 319(17): 1166–1172.

Incalzi, R.A., Gemma, A., Capparella, O., Terranova, L., Porcedda, P., Tresalti, E., and Carbonin, P. 1992. "Predicting Mortality and Length of Stay of Geriatric Patients in an Acute Care General Hospital." *Journal of Gerontology: Medical Sciences* 47(2): M35–39.

Ireland, N.J. 1983. "Monopolistic Competition and a Firm's Product Range." *International Journal of Industrial Organization* 1(3): 239–252.

Ishikawa, K.B., Holt, M., Kaihara, S., Yoshikawa, A., Hopkins, D.S.P., and Mason, M. 1993. "Performance, Characteristics and Case Mix in Japanese and American Teaching Hospitals." *Medical Care* 31: 542–51.

Ishihara, K. 1995. "Entoropii ni yoru Shinryo Hoshu no Hukuzatsusei no Keiryoka ni tsuite" (On the Metric Method to Measure the Complexity of Reimbursement Schedule by Utilizing Entropy). *Shukan Shakai Hosho* 1824(49): 54–59.

Javitt, J.C., Kendix, M., Tielsch, J.M., Steinwachs, D.M., Schein, O.D., Kolb, M.M., and Steinberg, E.P. 1995. "Geographic Variation in Utilization of Cataract Surgery." *Medical Care* 33(1): 90–106.

Kaihara, S. 1991. "Japanese Health Care: A Physician's Perspective." Seminar at the Comparative Health Care Policy Research Project at the Northeast Asia-U.S. Forum on International Policy, Stanford University, Stanford, CA.

Kalbfleisch, J.D., and Prentice, R.L. 1980. *The Statistical Analysis of Failure Time Data.* New York: Wiley.

Keeler, E.B., Buchanan, J.L., Rolph, J.E., Hanley, J.M., and Reboussin, D.M. 1988. *The Demand for Episodes of Medical Treatment in the Health Insurance Experiment*, Report R-3454-HHS. Santa Monica, CA: RAND Corporation.

Kelly, J.V., and Hellinger, F.J. 1987. "Heart Disease and Hospital Deaths: An Empirical Study." *Health Service Research* 22(3): 369–95.

Kenko Hoken Kumiai Rengokai. 1990. *Kenko Hoken Kumiai Jigyo Nenpo (Annual Report)*. Tokyo: Kenko Hoken Kumiai Rengokai.

Kent, D.L., Haynor, D.R., Longstreth, W.T., and Larson, E.B. 1994. The Clinical Efficacy of Magnetic Resonance Imaging in Neuroimaging. *Annals of Internal Medicine* 120(10): 856–871.

Kikuchi, T. 1985. "Kokumin-Iryo-Hi no Furou to Sangyorenkan-Bunseki" (Flow of National Health Expenditures and Interindustry Analysis). *Byouin (Hospital)* 44(1): 28–31.

Kimura, B., Fukami, A., Yanagisawa, S., and Sato, K. 1993. "The Current State and Problems of Japan's Pharmaceutical Market." In *Japan's Health System: Efficiency and Effectiveness in Universal Care*, ed. D. Okimoto and A. Yoshikawa. New York: Faulkner & Gray.

Kind, P. 1990. "Outcome Measurement Using Hospital Activity Data: Deaths After Surgical Procedures." *British Journal of Surgery* 77(12): 1399–1402.

Knaus, W., Draper, E., Wagner, D., and Zimmerman, J. 1986. "An Evaluation of Outcome from Intensive Care in Major Medical Centers." *Annals of Internal Medicine* 104(3): 410–418.

Koopmans, T.C. 1951. "An Analysis of Production as an Efficient Combination of Activities." In *Activity Analysis of Production and Allocation*, ed. T.C. Koopmans. Cowles Commission for Research in Economics, monograph no. 13. New York: Wiley.

Kopit, W.G., and McCann, R.W. 1988. "Toward a Definitive Antitrust Standard for Nonprofit Hospital Mergers." *Journal of Health Politics, Policy and Law* 13(4): 635–662.

Kupor, S., Liu, Y., Lee, J., and Yoshikawa A. 1995. "The Effect of Copayments and Income on the Utilization of Medical Care by Subscribers to Japan's National Health Insurance System." *International Journal of Health Services* 25(2): 295–312.

Lau, L.J., and Yotopoulos, P.A. 1971. "A Test for Relative Efficiency and Application to Indian Agriculture." *American Economic Review* 61(1): 94–108.

Lee, H., and Cohen, M. 1985. "A Multinomial Logit Model for the Spatial Distribution of Hospital Utilization." *Journal of Business & Economic Statistics* 3(2): 159–168.

Lee, M.L. 1971. "A Conspicuous Production Theory of Hospital Behavior." *Southern Economic Journal* 38(1): 48–58.

Lee, R., and Waldman, D. 1985. "The Diffusion of Innovations in Hospitals: Some Econometric Considerations." *Journal of Health Economics* 4(4): 373–380.

Lewis, C.E. 1969. "Variations in the Incidence of Surgery." *New England Journal of Medicine* 281(16): 880–884.

Lovell, C.A.K. 1993. "Production Frontiers and Productive Efficiency." In *The Measurement of Productive Efficiency: Techniques and Applications*, ed. H.O. Fried, C.A.K. Lovell, and S.S. Schmidt. New York: Oxford University Press.

Luft, H.S., Garnick, D.W., Mark, D.H., Peltzman, D.J., Phibbs, C.S., Lichtenberg, E., and McPhee, S.J. 1990. "Does Quality Influence Choice of Hospital?" *JAMA* 263(2): 2889–2906.

Luft, H., and Hunt, S. 1986. "Evaluating Individual Hospital Quality Through Outcome Statistics." *JAMA* 255(20): 2780–2784.

Luft, H.S., Robinson, J.C., Garnick, D.W., Maerki, S.C., and McPhee, S.J. 1986. "The Role of Specialized Clinical Services in Competition among Hospitals." *Inquiry* 23(1): 83–94.

Luft, H.S., Hunt, S.S., and Maerki, S.C. 1987. "The Volume-Outcome Relationship: Practice-Makes-Perfect or Selective Referral Patterns?" *Health Service Research* 22(2): 157–82.

Maasoumi, E., and Zandvakili, S. 1990. "Generalized Entropy Measures of Mobility for Different Sexes and Income Levels." *Journal of Econometrics* 43(1–2): 121–33.

Management and Coordination Agency. 1985, 1990. *Kokusei Chosa Hokoku (Population Census of Japan)*. Tokyo: Statistical Bureau.

Manheim, L., Feinglass, J., Shortell, S., and Hughes, E. 1992. "Regional Variation in Medicare Hospital Mortality." *Inquiry* 29(1): 55–66.

Manning, W.G., Newhouse, J.P., Duan, N., Keeler, E.B., Leibowitz, A., and Marquis, M.S. 1987. "Health Insurance and the Demand for Medical Care: Evidence from a Randomized Experiment." *American Economic Review* 77(3): 251–277.

Manning, W.G., Newhouse, J.P., Duan, N., Keeler, E., Benjamin, B., Leibowitz, A., Marquis, M.S., and Zwanziger, J. 1988. *Health Insurance and the Demand for Medical Care: Evidence from a Randomized Experiment*. Santa Monica, CA: Rand Corporation Report R-3476-HHS.

McFadden, D. 1981. *Econometric Models of Probabilistic Choice in Structural Analysis of Discrete Data with Econometric Applications*, ed. C. Manski and D. McFadden. Cambridge, MA: MIT Press.

McFadden, D. 1973. "Conditional Logit Analysis of Qualitative Choice Behavior." In *Frontiers in Econometrics*, ed. P. Zarembka. New York: Academic Press.

McGuirk, M.A., and Porell, F.W. 1984. "Spatial Patterns of Hospital Utilization: The Impact of Distance and Time." *Inquiry* 21(1): 84–95.

McLauglin, C., Normolle, D., Wolfe, R., McMahon, L., Jr., and Griffith, J. 1989. "Small-area Variation in Hospital Discharge Rates: Do Socioeconomic Variables Matter?" *Medical Care* 27(5): 507–521.

McQuarrie, D.G. 1981. "Limits to Efficient Operating Room Scheduling: Lessons from Computer-Use Models." *Archives of Surgery* 116: 1065–1071.

Minami, S., and Gunji, A. 1994. "Iryokikan ni okeru koritsusei hyoka ni kansuru kenkyuu (Study of Efficiency of Medical Facilities)." *Byoin Kanri* 31(1): 33–40.

Ministry of Health and Welfare. 1955, 1965, 1975, 1984, 1990. *Kanja Chosa (Patient Survey)*. Tokyo: Statistical Bureau, Ministry of Health and Welfare.

Ministry of Health and Welfare. 1961–1989. *Kokumin Kenkohoken Jigyonenpo (Kokoho Annual Report)*. Tokyo: Ministry of Health and Welfare.

Ministry of Health and Welfare. 1986. *1985 National Health Survey*. Tokyo: Kosei Tokei Kyokai.

Ministry of Health and Welfare. 1989. *Kokumin Kenkohokin Gojunenshi (Kokoho in Fifty Years)*. Tokyo: Gyosei.

Ministry of Health and Welfare. 1990. *Iryo Shisetsu Chosa (Facility Survey)*. Tokyo: Statistical Bureau, Ministry of Health and Welfare.

Ministry of Health and Welfare. 1990. *Kokuho Handbook*. Tokyo: Shakai Hoken Shuppansha.

Ministry of Health and Welfare. 1990. *Kokumin Iryo-hi (National Medical Expenditure Estimates)*. Tokyo: Ministry of Health and Welfare.

Ministry of Health and Welfare, Health Policy Bureau, ed. 1990. *Nihon no Iryo* (*Medical Care in Japan*). Tokyo: Gyosei.

Ministry of Health and Welfare. 1990. *Shakai Iryo Shinryo Koibetsu Chosa Hokoku* (*Point Survey*). Tokyo: Ministry of Health and Welfare.

Ministry of Health and Welfare. 1990. *Shinryo Kijun Hayamihyo* (*Fee Schedule*). Tokyo: Igaku Tsushinsha.

Ministry of Health and Welfare. 1990, 1992. *Ishi, Shika-ishi, Yakuzaishi Chosa* (*Survey of Doctors, Dentists, and Pharmacists, Statistics & Information Department*). Tokyo: Statistical Bureau.

Ministry of Health and Welfare. 1990. 1992. *Jinko Dotai Tokei* (*Vital Statistics of Japan*). Tokyo: Statistics Bureau, Ministry of Health and Welfare.

Ministry of Health and Welfare Institute of Population Problems. 1992. *Nihon no Shorai Suikei Jinko* (*Estimation of Future Population*). Tokyo: Ministry of Health and Welfare.

Ministry of Health and Welfare. 1992. *Seimei Hyo* (*Life Table*). Tokyo: Ministry of Health and Welfare.

Ministry of Health and Welfare. 1994. *Kani Seimei Hyo* (*Life Table*). Tokyo: Ministry of Health and Welfare.

Ministry of Home Affairs. 1991. *Shichouson-zei Kazei Jyokyo-tou no Shirabe* (*A Report on the Status of Municipality Taxation*). Tokyo: Ministry of Home Affairs.

Ministry of Labor. 1990. *Chingin Sensasu* (*Wage Census*). Tokyo: Rodo Horei Kyokai.

Ministry of Local Government. 1990. *Koei Kigyo Nenkan* (*Annual Report on Public Enterprises*). Tokyo: Ministry of Local Government.

Morrisey, M.A., Kletke, P.R., and Marder, W.D. 1991. "The Role of Local Hospitals in Physician Rural Location Decisions." *Inquiry* 28(1): 7–18.

Morrison, C. 1988. "Quasi-Fixed Inputs in U.S. and Japanese Manufacturing: A Generalized Leontief Restricted Cost Function Approach." *Review of Economics and Statistics* 70(2): 275–287.

Muroff, L.R. 1992. "Economics." In *Magnetic Resonance Imaging, 2nd ed.*, ed. D.D. Stark and W.G. Bradley. St. Louis: Mosby.

Nakanishi, S., Bhattacharya, J., Vogt, W.B., Yoshikawa, A., and Nakahara, T. 1995. "Measuring Misallocation of Labor Inputs in Japanese Hospitals: Public vs. Private Hospitals." *mimeo*, Stanford University.

Nakanishi, S., Kupor, S., Yamada, T., and Yoshikawa, A. 1993a. "Explaining Japanese Health Expenditures." *Current Politics and Economics in Japan* 3(1): 17–28.

Nakanishi, S., Yamada, T., Kupor, S.A., and Yoshikawa, A. 1993b. "Medical Expenditures: Uncovering the Costs of Care," in *Japan's Health System: Efficiency and Effectiveness in Universal Care*, ed. D. Okimoto and A. Yoshikawa. New York: Faulkner & Gray.

Nakayama, N., Bhattacharya, J., Vogt, W.B., Yoshikawa, A., and Nakahara, T. 1995. "Equilibrium Wages of Hospital-based Doctors." *mimeo*, Stanford University.

Nattinger, A.B., Gottlieb, M.S., Veum, J., Yahnke, D., and Goodwin, J.S. 1992. "Geographic Variation in the Use of Breast-Conserving Treatment for Breast Cancer." *New England Journal of Medicine* 326(17): 1102–1107.

Newhouse, J.P. 1970. "Toward a Theory of Nonprofit Institutions: An Economic Model of a Hospital." *American Economic Review* 60(1): 64–74.

Newhouse, J.P., and Phelps, C.E. 1976. "New Estimates of Price and Income Elasticities of Medical Care Services." In *The Role of Health Insurance in the Health Services Sector*, ed. R. Rossett. New York: National Bureau of Economic Research.

Newhouse, J.P., Williams, A.P., Bennett, B.W., and Schwartz, W.B. 1982. "Does the Geographical Distribution of Physicians Reflect Market Failure?" *Bell Journal of Economics* 13(2): 493–505.

Niki, R. 1993. "How to Balance the Wide Diffusion of High-Technology Medicine and Cost Containment: A Case Study of Magnetic Resonance Imaging in Japan." Mimeo. (Seminar at Stanford University, Stanford, CA.)

Niki, R. 1993. "Why Japan Has Been a 'Winner' in a Cost Containment Race: The True Story of Recent Health Care Financing Policy in Japan." Presented to the Comparative Health Care Policy Research Project. Stanford, CA. Mimeo.

Niki, R. 1992. *Kyujunendai no Iryo to Shinryo Hoshu (Medicine and Fees in the 1990s).* Tokyo: Keiso Shobo.

Niki, R. 1990. *Gendai Nippon no Iryo no Jissho Bunseki (Empirical Studies of Japanese Medical Care).* Tokyo: Igakushoin.

Niki, R. 1985. "The Wide Diffusion of CT Scanners in Japan." *Social Science and Medicine* 21(10): 1131–1137.

Nishimura, S. 1987. *Iryo no Keizai Bunseki (Economic Analysis of Medical Care).* Tokyo: Toyo Keizai Shinposha.

Niskanen, W. 1971. *Bureaucracy and Representative Government.* New York: Aldine Atherton.

Ogura, S. 1990. "Iryo Zyuyou no Kakaku Danryokusei ni Kansura Yobiteki Dousatsu" (Preliminary Study on the Price Elasticity of Medical Care Demand). In *Koureika Shakai no Keizaigaku (Economics of Aging Society),* ed. H. Kanamori and H. Ibe. Tokyo: Tokyo University Press.

Okamoto, Y., Sasagawa, N., Ohta, R., Yoshioka, E., and Suzuki, S. 1993. "Shakai Shinryo Hoshu ni Yoru Kangoryo no Saisansei (Profitability of Nursing Fees under the Fee Schedule)." *Byoin Kanri* 30(3): 23–29.

Okimoto D., and Yoshikawa, A, eds. 1993. *Japan's Health System: Efficiency and Effectiveness in Universal Care.* New York: Faulkner & Gray.

Okorafor, H. 1983. "Hospital Characteristics Attractive to Physicians and the Consumers: Implications for Public General Hospitals." *Hospital & Health Services Administration* Mar/Apr: 50–65.

Organization of Economic Cooperation and Development. 1993. *OECD Health Systems: Facts and Trends, 1960–1991.* Paris: OECD.

Panzar, J.C., and Willig, R.D. 1981. "Economies of Scope." *American Economic Review* 71(2): 268–272.

Parks, R.W. 1971. "Price Responsiveness of Factor Utilization in Swedish Manufacturing, 1870–1950." *Review of Economics and Statistics* 53(2): 129–139.

Paul-Shaheen, P., Clerk, J.D., and Williams, D. 1987. "Small Area Analysis: A Review and Analysis of the North American Literature." *Journal of Health Politics, Policy and Law* 12(4): 741–809.

Pauly, M., and Redisch, M. 1973. "The Not-for-profit Hospital as a Physicians Cooperative." *American Economic Review* 63(1): 87–100.

Pearson, Whettle. 1986. "Long Term Care." In *Health Care Delivery in the U.S.,* ed. S. Jonas. New York: Springer.

Peddecord, K.M., Janon, E.A., and Robins, J.M. 1988. "Substitution of Magnetic Resonance Imaging for Computed Tomography." *International Journal of Technology Assessment in Health Care* 4(4): 573–591.

Phelps, C.E., and Sened, I. 1989. "Market Equilibria with Not-for-Profit Firms." Working paper, University of Rochester, Rochester, N.Y.

Phibbs, C.S., Mark, D.H., Luft, H.S., Peltzman-Rennie, D.J., Garnick, D.W., Lichtenberg, E., and McPhee, S.J. 1993. "Choice of Hospital for Delivery: A Comparison of High-Risk and Low-Risk Women." *Health Services Research* 28(2): 201–22.

Pope, G.C. 1989. "Hospital Nonprice Competition and Medicare Reimbursement Policy." *Journal of Health Economics* 8(2): 147–172.

Powell, M., and Anesaki, M. 1990. *Health Care in Japan*. London: Routledge.

Register, C.A., and Bruning, E.R. 1987. "Profit Incentives and Technical Efficiency in the Production of Hospital Care." *Southern Economic Journal* 53(4): 899–914.

Robinson, J. 1988, "Market Structure, Employment, and Skill Mix in the Hospital Industry." *Southern Economic Journal* 55: 315–325.

Robinson, J.C., and Luft, H.S. 1985. "The Impact of Hospital Market Structure on Patient Volume, Average Length of Stay, and the Cost of Care." *Journal of Health Economics* 4(4): 333–356.

Roos, N.P., and Roos, L.L. 1982. "Surgical Rate Variations: Do They Reflect the Health or Socioeconomic Characteristics of the Population?" *Medical Care* 20(9): 945–958.

Rubinstein, R.Y. 1981. *Simulation and the Monte Carlo Method*. New York: Wiley.

Russell, L.B. 1979. *Technology in Hospitals: Medical Advances and Their Diffusion*. Washington, DC: Brookings Institution.

Salop, S. 1979. "Monopolistic Competition with Outside Goods." *Bell Journal of Economics* 10: 141–156.

Schieber, G., Poullier, J., and Greenwald, L. 1993. "Data Watch: Health Spending, Delivery, and Outcomes in OECD Countries." *Health Affairs* 12(2): 120–129.

Schmalensee, R. 1977. "Comparative Static Properties of Regulated Airline Oligopolies" *Bell Journal of Economics* 8(2): 565–576.

Senoo, Y. 1985. "Iryo-hi Yokuseisaku no Keizaibunseki" (Economic Analysis of Health Expenditure Cost Containment Policy). In *Iryo Shisutemuron* (Medical System), ed. Shakai Hosho Kenkyujo (Social Development Research Center). Tokyo: University of Tokyo Press.

Shakai Hoken Kenkyujo (Social Development Research Center). 1993. "Byoin Keiei no Do Ko" (Trends in Hospital Management). *Shakai Hoken Junpo* no. 1791, p. 39.

Shakai Hoken Kenkyujo (Social Development Research Center). 1991. *Chiiki Iryohi Soran (Regional Health Care Costs)*. Tokyo: Shakai Hoken Junpo.

Shaked, A., and Sutton, J. 1990. "Multiproduct Firms and Market Structure." *RAND Journal of Economics* 21(1): 45–62.

Shaked, A., and Sutton, J. 1982. "Relaxing Price Competition Through Product Differentiation." *Review of Economic Studies* 49(1): 3–13.

Shannon, C.E. 1948. "A Mathematical Theory of Communication." *Bell System Technical Journal* 27: 379–423, 623–656.

Showstack, J.A., Rosenfeld, K.E., Garnick, D.W., Luft, H. S., Schaffarzick, R.W. and Fowles, J. 1987. "Association of Volume with Outcome of Coronary Artery Bypass Graft Surgery vs. Nonschedule Operations." *JAMA* 257(6): 785–89.

Showstack, J.A., Stone, M., and Schroeder, S.A. 1985. "The Role of Changing Practices in the Rising Cost of Hospital Care." *New England Journal of Medicine* 313: 1201–1207.

Shukan Shakai Hosho. 1994. "Ishi Kajo no Kanosei to Shoshisaku wo Shiteki" (Possibility of Excess Doctors and Policy Measures). No. 1814.

Shumaker, L. 1981. *Spline Functions: Basic Theory*. New York: Wiley.

Sloan, F.A. 1980. "The Internal Organization of Hospitals." *Health Services Research* 15(3): 203–230.

Sloan, F., and Bentkover, J. 1979. *Access to Ambulatory Care and the U.S. Economy*, Lexington, MA: Lexington Books.

Sloan, F.A., and Steinwald, B. 1980. *Insurance, Regulation, and Hospital Costs*. Lexington, MA: Lexington Books.

Sloan, F.A., and Valvona, J. 1986. "Uncovering the High Costs of Teaching Hospitals." *Health Affairs* 5: 68–83.

Sloan, F.A., Valvona, J., Perrin, J.M., and Adamache, K.W. 1986. "Diffusion of Surgical Technology: An Exploratory Analysis." *Journal of Health Economics* 5(1): 31–61.

Spence, M. 1976. "Product Selection, Fixed Costs, and Monopolistic Competition." *Review of Economic Studies* 43(2): 217–235.

Steen, P., Brewster, A., Bradbury, R., Estabrook, E., and Young, J. 1993. "Predicted Probabilities of Hospital Death as a Measure of Admission Severity of Illness." *Inquiry* 30(2): 128–141.

Sullivan, D. 1989. "Monopsony Power in the Market for Nurses." *Journal of Law and Economics* 32(Suppl.): 135–178.

Takimura, K., Narita, K., Ishii, Y., Imamura, T., Fukushima, Y., and Nakahara, T. 1994, "Shinryotokusei kara mita Byoin no Ruikeika ni kansuru Kenkyu" (The Classification Study of Hospitals Based on Case)" *Kousei no Shihyo* 41(3): 13–21.

Tanaka, S., and Nishimura, M. 1984. "Jinteki Shihon Riron ni Motozuku Iryo Zyuyou no Keizaibunseki" (Economic Analysis of Medical Care Demand: Human Capital Theory Approach). *Quarterly of Social Security Research* 20(1): 67–80.

Theil, H. 1971. *Principles of Econometrics*. New York: Wiley.

Theil, H. 1969. "A Multinomial Extension of the Linear Logit Model." *International Economic Review* 10(1): 251–259.

Thornton, J., and Eakin, B.K. 1992. "Virtual Prices and a General Theory of the Owner Operated Firm." *Southern Economic Journal* 58(4): 1015–1029.

Tobin, J. 1958. "Estimation of Relationships for Limited Dependent Variables." *Econometrica* 26(1): 24–36.

Toda, Y. 1976. "Estimation of a Cost Function when Cost Is Not Minimum: The Case of Soviet Manufacturing Industries, 1958–71." *Review of Economics and Statistics* 58(3): 259–268.

Trajtenberg, M., and Yitzhaki, S. 1989. "The Diffusion of Innovations: A Methodological Reappraisal." *Journal of Business & Economic Statistics* 7(1): 35–47.

Urushi, H. 1986. "Waga Kuni ni Okeru Ishi no Chiikiteki Bunpu ni Tsuite" (*Distribution of Doctors in Japan*). *Kikan Shakai Hosho Kenkyu* 22(1): 51–63.

Urushibara, K. 1985. "Gendai Iryo ni okeru Byoin no Kinobunka ni tsuite" (On the Functional Differentiation among Hospitals in Modern Health Care Systems). In *Iryo Shisutemuron* (*Health Care Systems*), ed. Shakai Hosho Kekyujo (Social Development Research Center). Tokyo: University of Tokyo Press.

Ushimaru, S. 1988. "Kokumin Iryohi no Josho, Kogaku Iryo-kiki no Zodai oyobi Iryo Saabisu no Kyokyu Shutai" (Rising Medical Expenditures, Increasing Use of High-Technology Medical Equipment, and Suppliers of Medical Services). In *Seijukuka Shakai no Kokumin Iryo Keizai Bunseki* (*A Health Economic Analysis of the Matured Society*), ed. S. Jinushi. Tokyo: Tokei Kenkyu-kai. (Institute of Statistical Research).

Utsunomiya, O., and Yoshikawa, A. 1993. "Health Status and Patients in Japan." In *Japan's Health System: Efficiency and Effectiveness in Universal Care*, ed. D. Okimoto and A. Yoshikawa. New York: Faulkner & Gray.

Valdmanis, V. 1992. "Sensitivity Analysis for DEA Models: An Empirical Example Using Public vs. NFP Hospitals." *Journal of Public Economics* 48: 185–205.

Valdmanis, V. 1990. "Ownership and Technical Efficiency of Hospitals." *Medical Care* 28(6): 552–561.

Vayda, E., Mindell, W.R., and Rutkow, I.M. 1982. "A Decade of Surgery in Canada, England and Wales and the United States." *Archives of Surgery* 117(6): 846–853.

Vita, M.G. 1990. "Exploring Hospital Production Relationships with Flexible Function Forms." *Journal of Health Economics* 9(1): 1–21.

Vogt, W.B., Bhattacharya, J., Kupor, S., Yoshikawa, A., and Nakahara, T. 1996. "Technology and Staffing in Japanese University Hospitals: Government vs. Private." *International Journal of Technology Assessment in Health Care* 12(1).

Vogt, W.B., Bhattacharya, J., Yoshikawa, A., and Nakahara, T. 1995. "Hospital Choice in Japan." *Occasional Paper Series*. Asia/Pacific Research Center, Stanford University.

Vogt, W.B., Bhattacharya, J., Kupor, S., Yoshikawa, A., and Nakahara, T. 1995. "The Role of Diagnostic Technology in Competition among Japanese Hospitals." *International Journal of Technology Management Series on Management of Technology in Health Care*, No. 1.

Vogt, W.B., Bhattacharya, J., Yoshikawa, A., and Nakahara, T. 1995. "Substitution of MRI for CT." *mimeo*, Stanford University.

Vogt, W.B., Bhattacharya, J., Yoshikawa, A., and Nanbu, T. 1995. "Hospital Utilization Among the Elderly." *mimeo*, Stanford University.

Weiss, E.N. 1990. "Models for Determining Estimated Start Times and Case Orderings in Hospital Operating Rooms." *IIE Transactions* 22: 143–50.

Wennberg, J.E. 1987. "Population Illness Rates Do Not Explain Population Hospitalization Rates." *Medical Care* 25(4): 354–359.

Wennberg, J. E. 1985. "On Patient Need, Equity, Supplier-induced Demand, and the Need to Assess the Outcome of Common Medical Practices." *Medical Care* 23(5): 512–520.

Wilkinson, R.G. 1986. "Socioeconomic Differences in Mortality: Interpreting the Data of Their Size and Trends." In *Class and Health: Research and Longitudinal Data*, ed. R. Wilkinson. London: Tavistock.

Wilkinson, R.G. 1992. "Income Distribution and Life Expectancy." *British Medical Journal* 304 (6820): 165–168.

Woodland, A.D. 1975. "Substitution of Structures, Equipment and Labor in Canadian Production." *International Economic Review* 16(1): 171–187.

Working, E. 1926. "What Do Statistical Demand Curves Show?" *Quarterly Journal of Economics* 41: 212–235.

Yett, D.E. 1970. "The Chronic 'Shortage' of Nurses: A Public Policy Dilemma." In *Empirical Studies in Health Economics*, ed. H. Klarman. Baltimore, MD: Johns Hopkins University Press.

Yoshikawa, A., Vogt, W.B., Hahn, J., and Bhattacharya, J. 1994. "Towards the Establishment and Promotion of Health Economics Research in Japan." *Japanese Journal of Health Economics and Policy* 1: 29–45.

Yoshikawa, A. 1993. "Doctors and Hospitals in Japan." In *Japan's Health System: Efficiency and Effectiveness in Universal Care*, ed. D. Okimoto and A. Yoshikawa. New York: Faulkner & Gray.

Yoshikawa, A., Holt, M., Ishikawa, K., and Kasumi, W. 1993. "High Tech Fad: Medical Equipment Use in Japan." In *Japan's Health System: Efficiency and*

Effectiveness in Universal Care, ed. D. Okimoto and A. Yoshikawa. New York: Faulkner & Gray.

Yoshikawa, A., and Utsunomiya, O. 1993. "Japan's Health Insurance System: From Cradle to Grave." In *Japan's Health System: Efficiency and Effectiveness in Universal Care*, ed. D. Okimoto and A. Yoshikawa. New York: Faulkner & Gray.

Yoshikawa, A., Shirouzu, N., and Holt, M. 1991. "How Does Japan Do It? Doctors and Hospitals in a Universal Health Care System." *Stanford Law and Policy Review* 3 (Fall): 111–137.

Yoshimoto, K. 1990. *21 Seiki Heno Iryou To Igyou Keiei* (*Medical Care and Hospital Management Toward the 21st Century*). Tokyo: Asahi Shinbun-Sha.

Young, S.W. 1988. *Magnetic Resonance Imaging: Basic Principles*, 2nd ed. New York: Raven Press.

Index